A GRATEFUL
MENNONITE

a memoir

by Harold A. Voshage

Top: Harold with (L) Vel Teichroew on Fairy and (R) Vernette
Teichroew on Mae on the Voshage farm. Bottom: Harold in Papua New
Guinea Highlands with native in front of house built by volunteers.

Produced by:

FriesenPress
Suite 300 – 852 Fort Street
Victoria, BC, Canada V8W 1H8

www.friesenpress.com

Distributed to the trade by The Ingram Book Company

Cover design by Steven Ollenburger

Table of Contents

Introduction

THIS BOOK TELLS THE STORY OF TWO PERSONS, THEIR FAMILIES, THEIR COMMU-
nities and their interaction with the larger world. It is thus in a way unique and fascinating, but in other ways reflects so many experiences and events that can so easily
be generalized, that it can be considered a contribution to *Mennonitica Americana*.

The book includes a very detailed history of two genealogies, the Voshages, (non-
Mennonite) and the Teichroews and will serve the two families as a good source.

Second, it is also a remarkably specific and careful description of the Mountain
Lake community culture as the Voshages were growing up. The same applies to the
localities to which they moved later. It also provides specific information and analysis
and even some source materials on Mountain Lake's history, religion and economy.

The book includes an important story of the Civilian Public Service Camp in
Montana at Terry, apparently the only extensive history of the camp available. The
way the camp reached out into the larger community is instructive. The strengths
and weaknesses of CPS experiences come through.

The travels the couple took literally encompass the globe and provide engaging
detailed elements of the culture and geography. Many concrete allusions to reli-
gious/ethnic groups they visited indicates serious encounter with the people there.

Their Christian faith, especially the Mennonite version, is reflected by their
open, honest and positive understanding, free of great doubts and disappointments
in their lives, though there were some. This reviewer resonated very positively to the
emphases on Christian service, which both Carol and Harold expressed through
many years of meaningful service in many countries.

This is also a personal diary of both Harold and Carol revealing their devoted
married life, their health problems, and the challenges and experiments in making a
living. This openness is rare, and hence commendable. Thus it is very accessible to
readers who can easily identify with their own gaps between the ideal and the real.
The positive and thankful attitude the book exudes chides those of us who may be
more cynical and demand a more jaundiced view of life.

I think the dedication both Carol and Harold showed in this contribution to
Mennonitica Americana will be well received.

Calvin W. Redekop

To Carol my supportive partner, patient critic, loving and devoted wife.

Also to Lisa Anne our beloved daughter; a discerning critic and amazing woman.

Harold A. Voshage

Harold A. Voshage
hcvoshage@ sbcglobal.net

Chapter 1
Prologue

On April 2, 1927 I was born to Katherine (Kate) Teichroew Voshage and Christian H. Voshage in Mountain Lake, Minnesota. My mother was the daughter of Abram and Katherina Teichroew. Mother's parents came to Minnesota in the first migration of the Ukrainian Russian Mennonites from the Molotschna settlement in 1874.

My parents were members of the First Mennonite Church of Mountain Lake and I was baptized there upon confession of faith in Jesus Christ in the fall of 1941. I was married in First Mennonite Church in 1951 and was a member until 1952, when we moved to California and joined Clark Street Mennonite Brethren Church in San Jose, California.

I have enjoyed speaking the Mennonite Low German at home and all over the world when visiting other Mennonite communities (South, Central and North America; Europe; and Ukraine, Siberia of Russia).

How fortunate I have been to travel extensively as I volunteered overseas and at home; and I also took many Mennonite History Tours to experience more Mennonite culture.

I write this book with much gratitude to my Mennonite heritage fostered by my family, the community of Mountain Lake, Minnesota and First Mennonite Church and the other Mountain Lake area Mennonite churches. An overarching event in my life was having been born and raised in Mountain Lake, a village of nearly 2,000 in southwestern Minnesota. It was largely a Mennonite community populated in 1874 by a group of Mennonites who had left the colonies of Chortitza and Molotschna in the Ukraine area of Russia, seeking more personal freedom. They settled in Minnesota, Nebraska, Kansas, South Dakota and the prairie provinces of Canada: Alberta, Saskatchewan and Manitoba.

The Mennonite faith is based on the teachings of Menno Simons, a former priest of Pingjum, Holland, who became converted through his study of Holy Scriptures.

His bedrock theme was I Corinthians 3:11: "For no one can lay any foundation other than the one already laid, which is Jesus Christ."

In the 1600's when Menno Simons lived, his followers were severely persecuted and often killed for their faith. Some of the reasons for this persecution were the belief in baptism for adult believers, rejection of infant baptism, repentance and conversion, discipleship, separation of church and state, non-resistance, and a personal faith in Jesus Christ. Also, Simons was troubled by the Roman Catholic doctrine of the physical presence of the flesh and blood of Christ in the bread and wine of the Mass.

Further Menno Simons said, "True evangelical faith cannot lie dormant; it clothes the naked, it feeds the hungry, it comforts the sorrowful, it shelters the destitute, it serves those that harm it, it binds up that which is wounded, it has become all things to all men."

Virtually all Mennonite believers moved: first from Holland to Poland where they farmed and others were craftsmen. They drained the below-sea-level Vistula River Delta and were excellent farmers. In 1780 Catherine the Great of Russia invited them (among many German farmers) to move to the underdeveloped Ukraine, where they were promised religious freedoms. Many of them later even became wealthy.

Thus began the Mennonite history in Poland and the Ukraine. An interesting bit of history concerning the Mennonite persecution in Holland, Switzerland and later Russia is that Poland is perhaps the only country in Europe that did not kill people for their faith.

Later the Mennonites in Ukraine realized that the promises and privileges of Catherine were now in jeopardy. This brought about the migration to America in order to retain their religious freedom. History has shown how wise their decision proved to be.

Menno Simon's teachings of Anabaptism or rebaptism in adulthood and "believer" baptism upon confession of faith as an adult, committing one's life to Christ, service to others and mission endeavors, as well as a "peace position" of "non-resistance" in time of warfare and strife had an effect on my life, leading to volunteerism, good work ethic, deeper spiritual values and an attempt to make a difference in this world.

The common language of Mennonites was "Plautdietsch" or Low German. At one time, all of the business of Northern Europe's Hanseatic League was performed in this language. It is still spoken in many Mennonite communities all over the world; on my travels to Ukraine, Siberia, Northern Germany, Paraguay, Canada and Mexico, I have freely conversed with Mennonites living there in Low German.

I will always cherish my growing up and maturing and getting married in The First Mennonite Church. Singing under Johnny Janzen in the choir provided many happy memories.

So it is with deep gratitude to my Mennonite heritage of Mountain Lake that I celebrate the special aspects of the Mennonite influence; it is unique. Hence the title given: "A Grateful Mennonite".

Chapter 2
Teichroew Family

My mother's parents, Abram and Katherina Goossen Teichroew, were born in Ukraine, South Russia.

The Teichroew name may have originated in the Netherlands. It means "Dike preserver". In the Handbook for the Low German genealogist using "Brother's Keeper", which lists all of the Mennonite family names, the name "Teichroew" has twenty-six spelling variations, more than any other name in the book. It is now thought to have over 50 different spellings.

Grandfather Abram Teichroew was born in Fuerstenau, north Molotschna Colony, South Russia, on September 10, 1872. He was the son of Peter and Anna Neufeld Teichroew. His family emigrated to North America in 1878 and settled on a farm six miles northeast of Mountain Lake, Minnesota. He was baptized, upon confession of faith, in 1894 by Elder Gerhard Neufeld in the First Mennonite Church.

My grandmother Katherina Goossen Teichroew was born to Heinrich Goossen and Katharina Andres Goossen in South Russia on September 21, 1874. Her family emigrated to North America in 1875.

My grandparents each grew up on their respective parents' farms near Mountain Lake, Minnesota and married on July 8, 1894. They lived on a substantial farm a few miles north of town. A continually flowing creek running through a portion of the farm provided a good natural pasture for their dairy herd. The Teichroews were a God-fearing family, loving and close-knit. The aunts, uncles and cousins visited often, sharing many Sunday afternoon "faspas" (lunches) of freshly baked zwieback, jams, butter, cold meat, cheese and hot beverages. Wow!

In my Teichroew clan, my mother was Kate Teichroew and her parents were Abram and Katherina Goossen Teichroew. They had six children: three sons, Henry, Abram and Peter and three daughters, Anna, Kate (my mother) and Susie. They all married with the exception of Susie.

Teichroew family: front: Abram, Pete, Katherina.
Back: Susie, Anna, Henry, Kate & Abe.

We congregated every late fall for the annual hog butchering – what an event that was. There was probably no single event in the life of a close-knit Russian Mennonite family that solidified their cohesiveness as much as the annual late fall hog butchering; it was a virtual festival.

This entire clan butchered several 350 – 400 lb. hogs in late October or early November. To call this a celebration would be an understatement. We gathered at a Teichroew relative's farm that had good equipment and space to conveniently perform all of the required operations. This story will be described in a later chapter.

I will never forget one time when my family was visiting at the farm, when Grandpa took me on a ride to perform an errand at a hilly field in a Model T Ford. He decided to back up the hill and return to the yard. I later learned that the Model T Ford had a gravity-flow carburetor, not a fuel pump, so backing up the hill assured my grandfather of a successful run.

My Teichroew grandparents farmed their estate until 1937, when they moved to Mountain Lake, where they purchased a substantial Victorian style two-story home that is still very impressive and desirable.

Grandfather served on township and school boards. He enjoyed singing very much. He and his wife were blessed to celebrate their fiftieth wedding anniversary in 1944.

The Teichroew family has always impressed me very much. I reread the obituary of my great-grandmother Mrs. Heinrich Goossen, who died at 87 in 1937. I shall always remember attending the funeral. I was ten years old. The hymn they sang has a warm place in my heart. A casual English translation would be that "my home is on high".

This is the amazing obituary that Rev. J.J. Balzer wrote in her presence a few months prior to her passing. This obituary of my great-grandmother's choosing is very close to my heart; it is precious. "A long life lies behind me, a life, which has extended over the biblical borders about which Moses said in the 90th Psalm. 'The days of our life are three score years and ten, and if by reason of strength they be fourscore years, yet it is their strength, labor and sorrow.' That was my experience and in the knowledge of this truth I have always been satisfied. I am now living in the expectation that the end of my earthly life's trail is not far away and that in the resurrection I will have a permanent home of glory. Now I have reached life's evening and my physical strength is giving way to old age. The dear Lord, however, has given me much grace and joy to make my long life's journey happy, and I have been fortunate to see His wonderful workings daily and I praise Him in the words of the Apostle Paul, 'My grace shall be sufficient unto thee.' And Jesus says 'And lo, I am with you always even unto the end of the world.' This shall be my comfort until he calls me. Two weeks before my end, however, sickness was knocking at my door and severe headaches and weakness made me feel that my end was near. However I had the promise of everlasting life and the Lord's help, this together with the best of care, were my comfort to the end."

Mountain Lake, Minnesota, the community where I was born and reared, was largely a Mennonite village populated in 1874 – 1880 by a group of Mennonites who had left the Ukraine. At one time there were eight thriving Mennonite churches in the greater Mountain Lake area.

An interesting facet of Mennonite life is that many Mennonites worldwide *still* speak the Low-German "Plautdietsch", so interaction with them on trips is very easy.

The extended Teichroew family has sent out missionaries to Nigeria and ministered to North American natives in northwestern Montana. One of my cousins was active in Child Evangelism fellowship. Another cousin and her husband ministered at several Mennonite churches. A number of my cousins have four-year college degrees, some have advanced degrees and one has a PhD. I have much respect and love for every one of my numerous Teichroew cousins and families. Many of my cousins have very important employment positions.

An interesting aspect of my family is that my Dad's sister, Susie Voshage, married my Mom's brother, Abe Teichroew, and so I have "double cousins": Velma, Vernette and Elaine. We have always been especially close and Vel and I almost look like twins.

Double cousins: Vernette (Regier), Elaine (Unruh),
Uncle Abe and Velma Teichroew.

Another result of genes: even though both of my parents had very thin hair in older years, I have inherited the thick, dark-brown hair of my grandfather, Abram Teichroew, my uncle Abe Teichroew and another uncle Peter Teichroew. Of course at this writing my hair is thick *white*!

I also inherited the famous (or infamous) "Teichroew sneezes" from my mother and Uncle Pete. These can occur in a series of anywhere from four to almost twenty! And they are extremely loud!

Having had the privilege to participate in several Mennonite Heritage Tours to Ukraine and Crimea, those experiences have truly cemented my gratefulness to God for the Mennonite faith. Out of this faith grows spiritual values, a work ethic as well as mission and volunteer endeavors. I have had many blessings as I attempt to carry out these Christian mandates. I have always been grateful for the heritage of my Teichroew clan. A trait that both my grandfather and grandmother exhibited: they were very even- tempered and gentle in their demeanor. I would have to say they were grandparents of virtue and quality. I was grown when they passed away and I always remember them with much fondness. All of their six children exhibited this same trait in their respective personalities.

In talking to Harlan Teichroew, my cousin in Yankton, South Dakota, we would reminisce on our memories of our Grandfather Abram Teichroew. I mentioned to Harlan one time that I clearly remember as a lad, when I would overhear my elders discuss the Mountain Lake community "goings on", I would hear men talk of Abram Teichroew, and it was always with a certain awe and respect. I have a picture of the

Teichroew family on a file cabinet in my small office. My Grandfather was probably in his late fifties or early sixties. And was he handsome, with a groomed mustache and a full head of hair!

One vignette I recall well is that my Uncle Abe Teichroew was a pioneer in initiating combine threshing. In Minnesota grain doesn't ripen evenly so it must be swathed in winrows to allow for drying, and then the winrow is picked up with a special attachment on the combine.

Uncle Abe was one of the first farmers to purchase a small six-foot header capacity pull-type combine. If my memory serves me correctly it was powered by power-take-off from the pulling tractor. Soon he purchased a new combine with a "Wisconsin" self-contained power unit. I remember my father contracted Uncle Abe to combine some of our grain in the early 1940's. It was a very satisfactory arrangement.

Another reason I'm grateful to be of the Teichroew clan, a year or so ago my cousin Melroy Penner, a successful bachelor farmer, passed away and I was able to attend his large auction in November of that year. He had quite a large estate and in his will he bequeathed a significant portion to MCC.

The extensive home place has a creek flowing through a portion of it. The Penners, who purchased the property, are establishing a ministry to young people through a horse-riding program affiliated with YFC (Youth for Christ). They have constructed riding trails along the extensive creek and they hope to open this ministry to youth this summer of 2014.

Many of the Teichroew relatives displayed an impish sense of humor in their daily life. I remember Uncle Pete Penner and his wife, Aunt Anna (my mother's sister) would be doing dishes together after a meal, and would suddenly start chasing each other around the kitchen while snapping sopping wet dishrags at each other! This sense of teasing and playfulness brought much laughter into their homes, and lightened the seriousness of life and duties. I consider this an admirable trait in my Teichroew heritage.

Chapter 3
Voshage Family

MY GRANDFATHER, HENRY VOSHAGE, WAS BORN IN VAHLBRUCH, GERMANY JUST south of Hameln and Bad Pyrmont on December 5, 1865, the son of Christian Heinrich Friedrich Voshage and Justine Wilhelmine Meyer Voshage. He came to America in his late teens. He and a friend traveled to London, England, and during this time he contacted a cousin, Ferdinand Henze, in Grundy Center, Iowa, for a pass to America. The other fellow received a pass from another source and they travelled together. His friend stayed in Illinois and Grandfather Henry went to Iowa.

Grandfather worked for people in Iowa for a number of years for twenty dollars a month, and then, when his pass was paid for, he worked for people by the name of Franken. After working several years as a hired man, he went west a few hundred miles from Grundy Center, Iowa, to meet people from George, Iowa, who were relatives.

Grandmother Stintje Schipper was born on January 23, 1869 in the province of Groningen in the village of Westerlee in northern Holland. Her parents were Hendrik and Antje (Kramer) Schipper. She was one of five children. She came to Little Rock, Iowa in her early twenties; a stepsister lived there.

Grandmother was brought up in the Dutch Reformed faith. When young, she was allowed to attend an Evangelical church, and here she learned many of the gospel songs she loved to sing. In the Reform church only Psalms were sung and they had no Sunday school. The only time a child attended church would be for baptism.

Henry Voshage and Stintje Schipper met in the George, Iowa area where they both had relatives, and they married on November 30, 1891. They began house-keeping on a small farm near George, in the northwest corner of Iowa. Here their first child, Minnie, was born. They moved to a rented farm near Little Rock, Iowa a few miles away. Here were born Anna, and later their only son, Christian (July 14, 1896).

3.Grandma and Grandpa Voshage. Minnie, Christ and Anna. About 1899.

Henry & Stintje Schipper Voshage with Minnie, Christ and Anna (1899).

When the family had lived on the rented farm a few years, Grandpa bought 160 acres of raw prairie land near Little Rock. Buildings were erected and a well and windmill installed. The windmill would drive a small feed grinder and occasionally they would grind corn into fine corn meal which grandmother made into corn bread. A family orchard was planted, also shade trees for a windbreak. The school at Little Rock was two miles from home. While the family still lived here, the twins, Tina and Bertha were born. Then Grandpa Voshage decided to sell this farm, because he wanted to locate a farm that was closer to a grade school in the country. Grandpa sold this farm for $35.00 an acre and bought a 200-acre farm at Mountain Lake, Minnesota, three miles from town. The farm had improvements and was only one mile from District #33 local country school. At this farm the three girls, Ella, Susie and Henrietta were born.

We believe that Grandpa Voshage might have been a Lutheran in Vahlbruch, Germany. Our somewhat sketchy information indicates that in Mountain Lake, Minnesota the family attended the First Mennonite Church. Since the students in the country school District #33, where the Voshage children attended, were nearly all Mennonites, most of them attended First Mennonite Church; I feel this explains how my father and five of his sisters got acquainted with and married their future spouses.

To me, an interesting example of an amalgamation of parents from adjacent countries, Holland and Germany, that spoke similar but different languages, is that the Voshages spoke Grandma's Dutch language and also a low Holland-Dutch dialect. I distinctly remember at numerous family gatherings Dad's sisters were speaking this Holland-Dutch dialect. Grandpa, of course, spoke fluent High German, his mother tongue, and his children also spoke Low German fluently, which I am certain they learned in country school from their peers and from neighbors and others. And of course they needed to speak English as well; what a multi-lingual family!

When I reminisce on the years of childhood to adulthood, I have many, many happy memories of the times the Voshage family would meet to socialize. The gatherings would usually be held at Aunt Anna Wall's home. Her husband Henry D. Wall had developed a fine home on their farm. Anna was the second oldest of Dad's seven sisters. Father's siblings were very fortunate to have married excellent Christian spouses. All of the sisters were superb mothers and great cooks and housekeepers. Their Christian example has been a model to me. I have nothing but the best of memories of my parents and *all* my uncles and aunts. The heritage they provided is very gratifying. When we would all join in a great gathering there might have been over twenty cousins present.

Voshage siblings and spouses: Abe & Susie Teichroew, Hank & Bertha Bartel, Christ & Kate Voshage, Emil & Henrietta Zirul, George & Tina Rempel, Henry & Anna Wall, Leonard & Ella Bartel, Leo & Minnie Behrends.

My father, Christian H. Voshage was married to Katherine (Kate) Teichroew on June 19, 1924. This wedding took place at the home of her parents, Abram and Katherina Teichroew, where my mother grew up.

In March of 1997 I visited the birthplace of my Grandfather Henry Voshage. I knew he had been born and raised in Vahlbruch in northern Germany. When I arrived in Frankfurt and rented a car, I looked up church planter Paul and Ina Warkentin in Bad Reichenhall near Salzburg, Austria. While there I asked Paul to print the names of Voshages in Germany and lo and behold he produced three papers and they were ninety-five percent in northern Germany.

Since I knew where Grandpa was raised I was rather excited when I consulted an extensive German roadmap book; when I arrived at Vahlbruch, near Hameln, south of Hanover, I decided to stop and ask for local information. This first farm was the home of Lilly Voshage. She lived on one side of a spacious two-story duplex and her daughter Ingeborg and husband, Werner Oerke on the other side. Ingeborg is therefore also related to me.

While Lilly prepared lunch, I visited the very well-kept cemetery where husband August was buried. Her next-door neighbor was gardening so I introduced myself and mentioned my interest in Vahlbruch. His name was Burkhard Seebaum and he was a high school teacher at a nearby Bad Pyrmont facility. He also mentioned he might help me with my genealogical search since he was the record keeper of all of the records of Vahlbruch since 1585. He invited me to his office.

Later he showed me his extensive archives of the 300- person village and suggested upon returning to California that I provide some data that I had in my home. He also said he was in the process of compiling a book called "Hausercronik von Vahlbruch". It was a compilation of every household's picture and history of residents since 1585. He said the Voshages migrated to northern Germany in 1630 from Sweden at the end of the thirty years war.

The book Burkhard Seebaum completed in 1998 encompasses the history of Vahlbruch from 1585 through 1997. It has pictures and the history of 106 residences. I obtained a number of copies and have provided copies to my interested cousins. It is a fascinating historical genealogical compilation. A number of households have Voshage names in their history. House No. 22, where Lilly Voshage lives, is especially interesting to me because Lilly's husband August was a distant relative of the U.S. Voshages. Her daughter Ingeborg and husband take care of the land and dairy. I remember her as being rather reserved, a fine lady. She passed away in 2004.

In 1997 I also visited Heinz and Sophie Voshage, a retired couple living in an apartment in Bremen. They graciously put me up for several days and showed me the sights of Bremen. They invited their son, Detlev, to meet me. He lives in Dersenow and is self-employed as an insurance agent.

I also heard of Margarthe Voshage Haake who lived with her husband in Heber, a country town. They were in the process of selling a large restaurant called Kutcher II. They could seat several hundred patrons. They lived next door to their restaurant in a fine home, with a BMW and motorhome. She showed me the Voshage coat of arms displayed on a well-crafted 3'x4' wooden panel that a professional cabinet-maker had designed and constructed for her. Before I left she put me in touch with her son Axel Voshage, who lived in Hameln on Schlachthof Strasse. He met me Saturday after his work; he was the manager of a large electronics store in Hameln. He was very cordial; he spoke no English and my German is marginal, however, I got along reasonably well. He complimented me on my good German. It was an ill-deserved compliment.

The last time I visited Vahlbruch was in April of 2012. Lilly Voshage is still in her home on the family farm and 94 years of age, still hale and hearty. Burkhard Seebaum, the author of the genealogical book "Hausercronik von Vahlbruch" was also home. He still teaches nearby at Bad Pyrmont. It is always a pleasure to visit these dear folks.

Chapter 4
My Childhood

ON APRIL 2, 1927, I WAS BORN TO CHRISTIAN H. AND KATE TEICHROEW Voshage at Mountain Lake, Minnesota and lived on the Voshage home place (estate) until 1938.

Kate, Harold and Christ Voshage.

My father had seven sisters; he was the only son, so he could rent his father's 200 acres when Grandfather Voshage retired to town in 1920. Grandpa had improved the farmstead well, with a good house and outbuildings. There was a long tree-lined driveway and the yard with buildings was impressive. Prior to my Dad's marriage, sometimes an unmarried sister would keep house for him.

I shall always remember a few months before I was to start first grade in District #33, my parents realized that I couldn't speak English! I was six years old and spoke only Low German, "Plautdietsch", the language most Mennonites spoke at home. When they realized that I needed to learn English, because the school classes would be in English, they decided to speak *only* English at home. Did I ever have a time! But since they totally immersed me in English, it wasn't long until I could "get along" in the English language.

Those years, the school day was opened with scripture reading and prayer. School was dismissed in the same way. At this time, the schoolhouse was a center where they would have literacy programs and later Farmers' Club meetings. Sunday school and church services were also conducted there for a number of years.

In the thirties, when I was eight or nine, my parents sent me to the Mountain Lake German Bible School. Mr. Cornelius Wall was the leader of this program. All of the classes were in High German. We began by studying an elementary German grammar text called the Fibel. I will always cherish those weeks learning German and German scripture. The services at First Mennonite church were largely in High German: both the sermon and hymns were in German prior to World War II.

I shall always recall the year my father heard about a Shetland pony that was for sale. She was black and in foal. He purchased her and in due time she produced a beautiful female colt. The mare was named "Fairy" and we named the colt "Mae". The little colt was very lively; she would run virtually full-speed to a fence and then put all four little hoofs ahead of her to slide to a stop. She was very gentle and a joy to play with and eventually halter broken. Mae was a real treasure. When she was almost mature, we got a bridle for her and I could ride her. I never used a saddle; I rode her to country school bareback. I had several enjoyable years training her and riding her to school and on errands. I was probably eight or nine years old when I trained her. A few years later, my father sold her mother, Fairy. School District #33 was a mile east of our farm. I rode to school on my pony "Mae". Sometimes I would meet Harvey and Edgar Stoesz, brothers from an adjoining farm, on their ponies at the section corner one-half mile from school. The school was in the neighborhood of Walls, Klassens, Franzes, Schultzes and Nordbys.

Harold at Voshage farm with his ponies: (L) Velma
Teichroew on Fairy, (R) Vernette Teichroew on Mae.

The three ponies that Harvey, Edgar and I rode to school were tied up in a small barn and fed a little hay and water. During recess and lunch, two of the oldest boys in school agitated the ponies. At a program in the Mountain Lake High School auditorium, my father and a neighbor, whose two ponies were also in the barn, talked about how teasing of the ponies was not acceptable and that the teacher should be apprised of this.

The next day the teacher instructed the perpetrators to desist from teasing the ponies. Later one afternoon as I was approaching my home driveway on my other pony, Fairy, the boys had been hiding behind the mailbox and knocked me off and beat me up. The pony ran home and when the boys let me go, I ran home crying. Since it was a long driveway, the fellows left for home long before I arrived at our place.

When my parents realized what had happened, they cleaned me up and later decided to confront one of the fellows who lived a half-mile beyond our driveway. The next day, after school was out, when that fellow walked by our driveway, my father confronted him and warned him that if he didn't cease teasing the ponies and the beating, my father would report to his father what had happened. My father knew his behavior would have displeased that father. This confrontation settled the issue.

All of my teachers were excellent. Susan Schroeder was a gifted teacher in all subjects. Henry S. Ewert taught several years and was proficient in all subjects also. I still remember his instructions in rudimentary woodworking: making a footstool and other items. He was very gifted in teaching some of the girls to do charcoal drawings. Two of my cousins, twins Laura and Lillian, did excellent artwork.

My father was known for his excellent draft horses. He had several sorrel mares and he had them bred to a purebred Arabian stallion. They foaled gorgeous colts, that when mature, resembled the large Clydesdale breed. The horses were impressive and were amazingly sturdy draft horses. I learned to ride one of these huge horses without a saddle and never fell off. The horses were Percherons, these are a breed of powerful, rugged draft horses from the Perche region of France. These horses had a brownish orange to a light brown color. They were very handsome and could pull very well.

One winter that I will never forget was the 1936 blizzard and snowstorm. It was one of the coldest winters. There was a lot of snow and hard-blowing winds, creating a memorable series of blizzards in southern Minnesota. There are pictures in an historical pictorial of Mountain Lake that show men on top of snow drifts who were able to touch the telephone wires with outstretched arms. To top it off, a family with a number of students in my school brought scarlet fever to the classroom. Many of the kids contracted it, including my family and yours truly. I also came down with a painful earache that caused the eardrum to break and drain, then the pain subsided. We had no indoor plumbing or running water, although the house was comfortable. Dad took the "honey bucket" out to the outhouse several times a day, but soon the outhouse was completely covered with hard-packed snow, so he had to chop a hole in the hard snow and just empty the bucket. My parents also had a slight case of scarlet fever, but my condition was the worst. When we could finally get to town to see our physician, he discovered that I had a heart murmur. He advised my parents to go easy with heavy farm chores when I got a little older, and that I should not participate in the school physical education program. He thought that I would outgrow the heart issue as I matured, and he was right.

Blizzard of 1936.

Mountain Lake in blizzard of 1936.

In those early thirties it was challenging to live off the land. Often rainfall was below normal, so some year's crop yields were also below normal.

We also survived the terrible "dust bowl" years when red clouds of dust blew to southwestern Minnesota from Texas, Oklahoma and Kansas. Some days the red dust obliterated the sun.

Between the Voshage farm property line that was shared with Dietrich D. Stoesz property was a woven wire fence with four or six inch square wire weave, designed to keep sheep and cattle out. When the blowing dust finally subsided, it was possible to walk over the fence in several locations. It acted similar to a "snow fence", designed to keep snow from building up drifts on roads and intersections. The reason that the red soil was so noticeable was that the Minnesota soil is black.

My parents were educated through grade eight. My father took some business classes in Mankato. He did mention several times that he could have attended high school in town when he completed eighth grade with his father's stipulation that in fall and spring he would be required to assist his father in field work, and each morning and evening, before and after school classes, he must help with chores. My father made a decision that I believe he regretted years later, not to sacrifice his time so that he could realize his wish for a high school education.

Nevertheless, I shall always remember my father's sincere interest in studying the Bible, and he wrote about some of his impressions of God's word. He also read a lot. He had excellent handwriting. He grew up knowing parts of four languages, and he could read and write the old German script. I will always marvel at his language skills and his immaculate handwriting. In those days the "Palmer method" was taught and promoted, and he became very proficient with this method.

There were occasions when I feel my father was an "unfulfilled intellectual". I am certain he realized that choices have consequences. When we would see Dr. Harvey R. Basinger at his Mountain Lake clinic, he would mention to Dad how he had sacrificed in order to get an education and become a medical doctor and finally a fellow in the American College of Surgeons. He and his brother and brother-in-law came to Windom and Mountain Lake from Pandora, Ohio to set up a medical practice with a surgeon, obstetrician and pharmacist.

Voshage Cousins Nov. 1939 at the Henry Wall farm before the Behrends' family move to Oregon.
Ft row: Harry Wall, Harold Voshage, Virgil Bartel, Leonard Bartel, Vernon Behrends, Marvin Bartel
Seated: Elaine and Vernette Tiechroew, Elfrieda Rempel, Marcella Bartel, Marion Behrends, Dorothy Bartel
3rd row: Lillian Wall, Lauretta and Myrtle Behrends, Verna Rempel, Velma Tiechroew, Laura Wall, Kenneth Behrends
Back: Eleanor and Esther Wall, Uncle Emil holding Ronald Zirul, Leonard and Donald Behrends

Voshage cousins in November 1939.

Chapter 5
Farm Life

IN 1937 WE WERE STILL LIVING ON THE VOSHAGE FARM AND THIS WAS A MOMEN-
tous year for me because my Dad purchased a new WC Allis Chalmers rubber-tired
row-crop (narrow front) tractor.

Lo and behold, a ten-year-old farm kid could now cultivate corn, pull a four-
section drag and, after a little more practice and experience, even pull a disc. I could
do almost all tractor work except plowing. Don't think I didn't "walk tall in the
saddle". Many times I think back to how my Dad taught me to drive tractor and later
our 1941 four-door Chevy. I really believe his encouragement and teaching me to
drive the tractor and car has stood me in good stead. Later driving professionally,
RV's, and rental cars in Germany numerous times, God has protected me so that I
never had an accident; my earthly father and of course my heavenly father deserve
all of the credit.

*John Deere G.T. Tractor pulling 2 loads of hay up
to hay mow at Voshage farm barn.*

Probably my earliest paid job was detasseling hybrid corn for a neighbor when we lived on the Voshage place. I am not absolutely certain of the date, but I believe it was probably 1938 when I was eleven. A very progressive neighbor, Sam Franz, who lived across the road from us, was experimenting with his own strains of hybrid seed corn. To help accomplish this, alternate rows of tassels had to be removed. He taught us youngsters how to pull the tassels off and discard them. On one row we removed all the tassels and on the next row they remained, in other words, every other row was detasseled.

Moving six miles northwest of Mountain Lake to the 160 acre farm my father purchased from Mrs. Art Dickman meant adjusting to a new neighborhood and school district, #67, for me. The farm was well improved, except the house was very modest.

Memory tells me that the house on the farm my parents purchased in 1938 was poorly constructed and drafty and cold in the winter. For some years it had probably sufficed in a manner of speaking for renters. The owner had invested resources and improvements to facilities and tiling (draining off excess water) the land that would probably bring an additional income. The house had very little improvement. There was no running water or other indoor plumbing and no insulation with rickety doors and storm windows for the winter.

The farm did have a flowing well and a year after we moved a Rural Electrification line was installed past our driveway and that gave rural living a huge boost. We had electric lights, a yard light, a refrigerator, electric motors replacing gas engines; it was a tremendous improvement for farm families. It made life a lot easier for housewives in particular. What a blessing!

Attending District #67 was a fairly straightforward transition. The instructor was Carl Goossen from Mountain Lake and he was a good teacher. He developed a band and he taught me to play the cornet. Another fine teacher was Mrs. Wendelyn Neufeld from Mountain Lake. She was an excellent teacher and she could keep order. I attended District #67 for three years, grades five, six and seven. My parents enrolled me in grade eight at the Mountain Lake City Public School District #9. A bus picked me up and delivered me home with all of the rural pupils that lived in our area that were in District #9. Attending the Mountain Lake School was a broadening experience and I enjoyed the challenges. It was different! However thankfully, there were no "initiations" or mean or bullying kids and the transition developed smoothly and uneventfully. The instructors were excellent; playing in the band and singing in chorus was very enjoyable.

Returning to the transition of moving to our new neighborhood, all of the neighbors were most gracious and we were welcomed. Several farmers had threshing machines and they presented their service to my father and he needed to make a choice. The decision wasn't easy as both neighbors were, he felt, equally competent. Finally he decided to accept John Klassen's proposal and his service proved to be more than adequate.

In those days, prior to the combine era, a group of neighboring farmers would contract with an operator of a threshing machine and large tractor to move it and to power the machine on each farm. Generally there were from six to eight farms that a threshing machine operator would serve.

In our neighborhood lived three sets of Klassen brothers and families. John, who also operated the threshing rig, his brothers Henry and Jacob; Ernest Hieberts, Gerhard Peters family, Herman G. Fast family, the Ben Meyers family and the Voshage family.

The threshing machine that Mr. Klassen operated had a large conveyer at one end of the machine that received the bundles that the bundle rack drivers would toss into the conveyor on both sides. The straw was blown out the opposite end of the machine through a long large metal pipe. The grain was gathered in wagons and when they were full they were unloaded onto an elevator into a granary or the large city elevator.

In the mid to late 1940's, small six-foot header pull- type combines appeared. My uncle Abram Teichroew, a very progressive farmer, was one of the first to take advantage of that technology. The grain was "swathed", and the cut grain was winrowed onto the stubble field. Then, after properly drying, it was placed into a pull-type combine with a pick up attachment and threshed. This equipment superseded the threshing machines and "rings".

In the years prior to combines, even before my time, grain was cut with a binder. This machine was earlier pulled by a team of horses and later by a tractor. The grain was cut, gathered and tied into bundles and accumulated in a bundle carrier. When the carrier was full, the bundles were ejected. The bundles were then placed in shocks of 6-12 bundles upright to dry. In Minnesota this method was used because grain doesn't uniformly dry. Then these bundles would be hauled to the area where the threshing machine would later be set up and placed in a large stack, maybe twenty-five feet in diameter and twenty feet high. Usually two stacks were placed eight to ten feet apart and the threshing machine operator would place the large conveyor about six-eight feet above the ground between two stacks and the bundle pitchers would feed the conveyor that moved the bundles to be threshed.

Later, all of the farmers picked up shocks and unloaded them into the machine. After World War II, small six-foot pull-type combines became popular. A farmer in the 1940's, A.P. Balzer, invented a swather attachment for Ford-Ferguson tractors that were rear-mounted and the tractor was modified to travel in reverse to cut grain. Mr. Balzer has since passed away and the manufacturing company that he pioneered is a large prosperous factory to this day in Mountain Lake.

The highlights of the harvesting and threshing season were the sumptuous "faspas" and noon-meals the women provided to the hungry men. Three or more neighbor women helped the host lady to prepare meals and they were the most original gourmet meals that I've ever eaten! They were banquet-like feasts. I will always consider this as the original gourmet cooking.

When we were threshing at our farm, my mother ran out of butter; Mrs. Hiebert, who was one of several women graciously assisting my mother, volunteered her supply and my mother wanted me to drive there to get it. Mrs. Hiebert insisted that her son drive their car and away Eldon and I went. When we were returning we had already talked about how fast I had driven our '41 Chevy and he wanted to equal or exceed my record. About a fourth of a mile short of our place he lost control and the right front wheel hit the side of the ditch and the car fell on its' side, perpendicular to the road bed. Thank God we were not injured, only slightly shaken up (no seat belts in those days). There was hardly any damage to the car. The farmers came running and righted the car, we delivered the butter and the threshing resumed.

Prior to enrolling in my freshman year, grade nine, in the fall of 1941, Mr. Tschetter, the newly hired agriculture class instructor visited all incoming farm boys in order to sign them up for this class. This was a new program at Mountain Lake High School and Mr. Tschetter was hired with outstanding credentials. He visited me on our farm numerous times and I always demurred. I enjoyed living on the farm, however an agriculture pursuit never seemed to interest me. He was disappointed that I wouldn't enroll in his class. I believe there was only one other classmate who also didn't enroll and he also completed his high school education without being in the FFA (Future Farmers of America) organization. However he did go into farming and he did quite well. So I guess I was sort of unique.

An advantage my parents had while on the Voshage estate of 200 acres and the eighty acres east across the road that my father owned with a brother-in-law, was that Dad farmed 280 acres, which was a good-sized acreage to work with horses. Later rudimentary tractors came in vogue; the first tractor he bought was a steel wheeled Fordson. So even though my parents paid shares of their crop proceeds of the 200 acres to his sisters, my parents managed well and could purchase a 1935 two-door Chevrolet. Commodity crop prices were very low but Dad had learned how to successfully farm and manage resources from his father and mother. Kate Teichroew was *also* reared by an astute farmer and manager, her father Abram.

The years on our own farm were good years. Prices had improved and Dad purchased a new 1941 four-door Chevrolet and we traveled to Oregon and California during Christmas vacation in 1940-1941. My father's oldest sister, Minnie, and her husband Leo had moved to Oregon prior to World War II. We had a good visit with them and other relatives and friends in Oregon and Washington. We also visited friends in Reedley and Fresno and Pasadena, California. It was a memorable trip, with a sand storm between Barstow and Las Vegas. We had to get a new windshield and later the car needed to be repainted and the front bumper re-chromed.

In recent years, when I have driven past that farm, I've noticed that the present owners have leveled the entire yard, including a beautiful red brick silo. There is only a small clump of broken concrete and rocks.

When I look back at the time my parents moved from the Voshage farm, I feel that I benefitted from this. I was not really interested in becoming a farmer and consequently I moved to California where I found my best career. The Voshage family estate was wisely run by my Uncle Henry Bartel, later by his son Virgil and now Virgil's son Neal, who has made it a showplace, both as a farm and a beautiful home.

I am grateful that this historical home of the Voshage family has been owned and occupied by them over 100 years and continues to remain in the family. Neal has done an extensively superb complete makeover of the house and it is impressive. He has constructed a large "leg" which is a pit- type elevator system where trucks unload grain and feed and it is elevated on special conveyors fifty to a hundred feet high, shunted into various grain-holding bins.

Neal Bartel has removed the red barn, granary, machine shed and small garage and replaced these with several impressive buildings for a successful pickup and car customizing business the Bartels conduct. Neal has also developed a large successful pig farrowing operation.

Chapter 6
Hog Butchering

Teichroew family hog butchering,
remembered by Esther Penner Fast.

As I was growing up I experienced many pleasant times with my extended family. How I enjoyed playing with my cousins at Grandpa and Grandma Teichroew's home, while my aunts and uncles helped them with butchering, threshing and silo-filling. All of the family working together made hard work seem so much easier.

How we also enjoyed the meals we ate that Grandma prepared for these occasions. I remember eating zwieback, homemade bread, schnetke, perishki (fruit pockets), cakes, pies and cookies. Of course the homemade dill pickles were always great. Her grape jelly or ground cherry jelly that we spread on our zwieback was so good! There was always much good food.

Since I'm going to record my remembrance of butchering at grandparents' and my parents' homes, I remember that the task began very early in the morning – at least by 7:00 o'clock all who were coming to help were there. So that meant that a lunch at mid-morning, a big meal at noon and an afternoon faspa had to be planned for and the ladies had to serve it. So much planning and baking was done in advance. Chicken or ducks were butchered.

Many preparations were made in advance. A pig was selected for butchering and put in a pen by itself so it could be given extra food allowing it to gain lots of weight.

A fat pig would provide extra lard and the meat would be more tender. But about a day or so before butchering, the pig was not fed or given water to drink because its intestines and bladder needed to be empty. Every part of the hog was used for food, so it was important that none of the meat was contaminated with waste products, should an unwanted cut happen.

Some other things done to get ready for butchering were that the "butcher knives" were sharpened. These knives were stored and used only for butchering. The blade on the meat saw also needed to be checked and the scrapers gotten out. The wood to be used to build a fire under the cauldron needed to be chopped. Dad took care of the above while Mom did lots of baking zwieback, breads, cakes or pies and cookies, etc. Then there were lots of things that needed to be cleaned and washed. The "paddle" that was used to stir the fat when making lard would need to be washed as well as many crock-jars and bowls, which would be used to store lard, cracklings and brined meat. Large dishpans, which would be used to hold ground meat or fats, or to wash blood from meat or organs, needed to be cleaned. The butcher table was scrubbed and set up on sawhorses in the basement. The sausage stuffer and meat grinder had to be cleaned. She also laid out the big apron and sleeves, which the men used to protect their jackets. The sleeves had elastic at the bottom and were pinned on top of the arm.

To begin the day, the men had to wrestle the pig down so Dad could cut its jugular vein. If it was well done, the pig bled to death quickly and didn't thrash around too much. I remember how awful it was to hear the pig squeal when it was being killed. The next step was to transfer the pig to the barn where it was hung from the rafters in such a way that it could be lowered and raised. Hot boiling water was brought and poured into a barrel and the pig was lowered into it so that it would be easier to remove the hog's bristles by scraping. When this was done, the pig was washed and then its belly was cut open so the intestines could be removed. The intestines were put into a large pan and carried into the house so the women could remove the fat and tissues to separate them to make it like a long rope. They were then turned inside out. Grandma taught my mother how this was done, and my mother taught me how by using this special pitcher, which had its pouring spout bent to aid in pouring small amounts of water into the turned-up open end so that the intestines would continue to slide down until it was completely turned inside out. Then they were scraped with the dull side of a knife or spoon and the clean casings were ready to use. To see if you'd done a good job, you'd blow into one end and check. Later, this time-consuming task was eliminated because we could buy casings uptown.

Pig hanging after slaughter.

The men worked at removing the organs and cutting the carcass in half. The pig was lowered and the head was cut off and put in a pan and carried into the basement so it could be skinned. The tongue was removed, the meat from the "cheeks" cut out, which would be used to make head cheese. The men carried the half of the carcasses into the house on their shoulders and put them on the butchering table to be cut up after they had eaten lunch.

All parts of the pig were used – even the tail part of it was used for soup meat, but the tip of the tail was pinned to one of the unsuspecting workers during butchering.

The first thing that was done was to trim the layer of fat – being sure to leave some around the hams and shoulder. Lard and cracklings were made from the fat. It was coarsely ground up and cooked in the cauldron until the cracklings were golden brown. Once the fat became liquid, the spare ribs were also placed in the cauldron and cooked until done. To test if done, you twist one of the bones and if you could easily remove it, it was time to take the ribs out. They then were lightly sprinkled with salt. How we looked forward to tasting them at breakfast the next morning. One of the women would be continually stirring the fat with the wooden paddle so nothing would stick to the bottom of the cauldron. Also the fire under the cauldron needed to be watched and kept burning – not too hot and not too cold. If the fat became too hot, the cracklings would be too crisp and dark so the lard would not be as white as we liked. When the cracklings were golden brown they were removed from the lard with a strainer and placed in a bowl. The lard was cooked until the liquid was clear but not brown and then it was poured into large pans to cool. When cool, it was poured into crock jars. The brown particles on the bottom of the pan were kept separate. This lard (Graeva Schmult) was used for baking piecrusts or schnetke and sometimes if butter was not available it was used to "butter" your bread.

Stirring cracklings at **Schmeckfest** *in Montana.*

The hams were nicely trimmed and this meat and other scraps of meat as well as some fat was ground up to use to make sausage. Salt and pepper was added and kneaded until it was well blended. Then it was packed into the sausage stuffer. The casings were slipped on to the pipe at the bottom of the stuffer. One person would turn the crank so the meat would be pushed into the pipe and into the casing while another person would regulate when it was time to move the casing ahead so that the casing would be firmly filled yet not so much that the casing would burst. It was an art! When the sausage was as long as you like, you left a space of empty casing, cut it and pulled out some casing to start again.

Making German sausage in our garage in Saratoga.

The stuffed sausages were then pulled through a bowl filled with liquid smoke first one side and then the other side. A broomstick was hung by wire from the ceiling. Sausages were hung up to dry and newspapers were placed on the floor underneath to catch the drips of liquid smoke. A day or so later, the sausages were coiled up and stored in the coldest part of the basement. To serve, we fried them. After removing the casing we placed it in a frying pan with a small amount of water and fried until browned on both sides. They were so good with potatoes and the gravy made using the fat, so tasty too. I like to serve these with verenika.

Liverwurst was one of the meats that we enjoyed eating at breakfast. I liked it with dark bread spread with jelly.

The liver was used in this way. Grind one part liver, three parts of meat and some fat in the grinder. Repeat it then add salt and pepper and mix well. Stuff the mixture in casings of the narrow large intestine each about 10-inch lengths. Tie both ends with strong string and tie strings together. Prick each ring with darning needles. Place in boiling water and cook until done (don't overcook). The liverwurst is done if juice is clean when ring is poked.

Because there was no refrigeration available, there were several different methods of preservation used.

Some of the meats were packed in jars and canned. Others were cooked and then covered with a salt-brine (sometimes enough salt in boiling water so an egg would float). It was important that there was enough fat to completely cover the top of the meat. Then this meat was prepared. It was first soaked in water to reduce the salt. Soup bones were done this way also.

Some of the meats were pickled. The heart, tongue, feet and hoofs were fixed this way. The meat was cooked in salted water until done. The pickling solution is two parts water and one-part vinegar. In a few days the meat is ready to eat. We serve it with bread, raw onions and vinegar.

Head Cheese was also pickled.

To make head cheese, use the meat on the "cheeks" of the pig's head, some rind, neck bone, other bones with little meat, ears, feet and any meat not used for other things. Cover with water and cook until very tender. Remove and cool until you can handle the meat and remove the bones and gristle. Chop or grind coarsely. Strain broth and boil about 15 minutes. Combine meats and salt and pepper, then pat into a shallow pan and cover with hot broth. Cut into squares when cooled.

We would often serve this meat with vinegar and raw onions.

Even the stomach was cleaned and fried for a meal. To prepare the stomach, we first had to cut it open, take it out of doors and turn it inside out and rub in snow until it was clean. Then, scrape, trim and rub with dry salt. After a thorough washing it was cooked and pickled with the same syrup used to pickle the feet, heart, etc. – after some days. To serve, cut into serving-size pieces and fry until lightly brown.

I think there is another part of the pig that was sometimes used – the brain. It was soaked in water to remove the blood. To serve, fry with fried potatoes.

At the end of a long butchering day, we were tired, but there was still one more task to finish. We needed to check if any of the utensils and equipment that we used needed to be washed. How difficult they would be to clean if left dirty overnight! It was good to finish the chore. As we thought of all the work and visiting we did, we were so glad that it had been a good day!

Esther Penner Fast

Chapter 7
Town Life

WHEN MY FATHER SOLD THE 160-ACRE FARM AND WE MOVED TO MOUNTAIN Lake in 1943, this was a major change in my life. Though father was only 47 years of age, he decided to sell his farm. He wanted to be a retired farmer. A land agent approached him. I don't remember how my father and the agent met; I remember seeing them negotiate the particulars of the transaction a few times.

When the transaction was consummated, I remember my father telling other farmers that the price he received, $100.00 an acre, would never be exceeded and possibly not even equaled – how wrong he was. I am not certain why he was so anxious to sell. He had toiled on the land since his young years and he might have rationalized that the timing was opportune.

My parents bought an older modest two-story house in Mountain Lake, located in an established fine neighborhood within easy walking distance to the school and downtown.

Voshage house in town / Alton Penner, cousin.

Completing my high school classes was fulfilling. I enjoyed singing in the choir, playing cornet in the band and especially enjoyed playing in the pep band, a small group of mostly brass and percussion. The improvisation was enjoyable.

Erling O. Johnson, the superintendent, taught first and second year Latin classes as there were a number of students who elected to take Latin; I took it for two years. It was a great aid in helping me understand English grammar. It took only a month or two to sort out my issues with grammar.

I enjoyed my history, English and current event subjects, but I had difficulty with geometry and algebra. I elected to enroll in a "farm shop" course under instructor Emil Ludtke. He was a master craftsman and instructor. He taught mechanical drawing, woodwork, metal work and nearly any discipline requiring industrial arts. My wife and I still sleep on the black walnut double bed I made. I also made an upholstered chair of black walnut and numerous other items we still use.

I look fondly at my Mountain Lake schooling experiences. We had excellent facilities, boards, administration, instructors and support staff. I will always remember December 7, 1941 when President Franklin Delano Roosevelt declared war on Japan. The class of 1945 was the first class to graduate from the newly constructed facility that was completed in 1944. Each room had an intercom communications system so that we could hear President Roosevelt's war declaration as he delivered it from the oval office in Washington D.C.

I will always remember some of the other great instructors at Mountain Lake High School. Mrs. Tweet was an excellent instructor as was Miss Baker. Mr. Chermak could get a lot out of us budding musicians in choir and band. Burt Munson was an outstanding athletic coach and instructor. J.H. Tschetter had a tremendous reputation in the Agriculture Department. Music groups, sports teams and FFA agriculture departments garnered their share of statewide recognition.

One of the first episodes that helped determine how much of a country bumpkin I was, happened late afternoon near dusk. Pete Unruh organized an attempt to take me on a "snipe hunt". He provided a gunnysack and a flashlight and we started walking to where I could find a snipe. Admittedly I was a green kid, but as we walked past the cemetery toward the lake, I finally felt I'd been "had" and the hunt was called off. Pete and the boys were a little downcast, but I think we all saved face and continued jabbering, laughing and walking to the restaurant to recap the evening's event.

So here we were, small town dwellers after we had all grown up on farms. It was quite a transition, particularly for my mother who initially didn't enjoy the close proximity of our neighbors. Fortunately all of our neighbors were very cordial and welcomed us. They allowed us our privacy. We could not have asked for better neighbors. There were the Will Klassens, Anna Schroeder, Fred Steinhausers, the senior Schultz family, the Fred Behrends family and the John F. Stoesz family.

Town garden – Kate & Christ.

My parents had another full lot next door where they did intensive gardening, which resulted in prodigious canning for winter use. My own family later carried on this tradition over the years in our gardening. Our first home had walnuts, peaches, and a *huge* vegetable garden bordered with strawberries. At our last home in Saratoga, we usually made a vegetable garden as well as having a mini-orchard with oranges, lemons, tangelos, peaches, apples, apricots, cherries, grapes and berries. This bounty we usually enjoyed fresh, but we also canned and froze large quanti-ties of fruit sauces, jams, juices, relishes, chow-chow and pies. Of course we always loved fresh corn-on-the-cob, but one of our daughter's sorrows was not being able to eat that while she had braces on her teeth!

We enjoyed making some of the traditional Mennonite foods, but we also developed our own specialties: my special buttermilk pancake recipe (with raisin faces for Lisa), Carol's fluffy waffles (with the Mennonite white sauce on top, mixed and stirred by me) and Lisa's delicate cottage cheese crepes.

To this day, when I eat waffles with my white sauce on top, I feel as though I have died and gone to heaven!

How did I adjust to this urban environment? Needless to say, the young fellows who were my peers soon figured out ways to assimilate this country lad into an accepted small town city slicker. One advantage I had over some of the boys was that I had access to my Dad's 1941 four-door Chevy. Having been raised on the farm, I had successfully learned to drive virtually everything that had wheels and an engine. Pete Unruh, now senior pastor of a large retirement community in the foothills of San Jose, told me recently that I gave the fellows a ride over the Butterfield overcrossing at 85 miles per hour. I had forgotten all about that ride.

Another time, two Quiring brothers my age or nearly so challenged me to climb the water tower service ladder. Now these two brothers' father was a builder of large masonry structures and these fellows were used to daredevil climbing. Of course I thought my experience on the farm, climbing windmills and silos, would be adequate experience to climb the water tower ladder. I agreed to follow the fellows up the ladder. When we reached the top, they didn't just turn around and climb down the way they had gone up, oh no! They slid down the diagonal support rods of which there were three levels. I wasn't to be shown up for my inexperience, so I proceeded to come down the rods the way they did. The rods were at 45 degree to the tower legs and they intersected in an X. As soon as I grabbed the rod to slide down, I rotated upside down. I hung on for dear life. At the intersection of the X I had to maneuver to the 90-degree leg back to the ladder. How I managed this I'll never know. Needless to say, I only managed this feat on one of the three levels and managed to maneuver back to the ladder. I was one happy camper when I reached the ground.

Saturdays were busy for my mother, especially if we were going to have company for meals on Sunday. Until the 1950s she baked and cooked on a large wood-burning range, which superbly produced perfect baked goods.

Her usual output would be several loaves of bread, as well as a richer dough for rolls.

She pinched off dough for zwieback ("twebach"), with the larger bun on the bottom and a smaller bun on top, pressed together; also she made a much larger bun pressed flatter, dipped in milk, and then dipped into a mixture of sugar and cinnamon ("succa-twebach") to be served for Sunday breakfast. She often made pans of cinnamon rolls. And there were also pies and cakes to bake. Our kitchen had heavenly aromas each Saturday!

Sunday was a special day of fellowship and family. First we would join our Sunday School classes and afterward participate in the church service, enriched with four-part hymn-singing by the congregation. The mixed choir and the pipe organ added to the music as we awaited the morning sermon.

After church we would rush home to have dinner ready to serve to our guests. Often a beef roast would be fork tender, with potatoes, carrots, and onions simmering in the gravy. Homemade bread and zwieback, jam, jelly, pickles, and pie or cake with coffee would complete the repast.

After a restful time of visiting, at about 5:00 p.m., my mother would prepare the faspa. Often other guests would join us then. First we gave thanks to God for the food, and then enjoyed the zwieback, jam, butter, pickles, jello or potato salad, cold meats, slices of cheese, coffee and a finale of desserts. This time of fellowship was very delightful for all, and my mother was happy to provide such delicious foods to her guests.

One more custom: after a quiet evening during the week (reading or listening to radio music in the living room), my Dad would cut an apple into wedges with his pocket knife, and pass these around on the tip of his knife to the family for a bedtime snack.

In early 1951, my Dad bought a new state-of-the-art electric stove for our kitchen. In the summer this stove made it possible to keep the house much cooler (no need to fire up the wood-burning range) and was easier to clean. My mother was very pleased with this stove, but she always claimed that *nothing* could bake bread as perfectly as the old wood-burning range!

Carol baked zwieback in Mom's electric range.

On hot summer days we would look forward to a very special treat: watermelon and crullers! We would sit outside under the trees on someone's farm or yard where it was cool. The women would make a pastry that was rolled out and cut into strips and fried in deep fat until it puffed up and became a golden color. These crullers were served with cold watermelon slices. What a terrific treat! In later years this was often served at family reunions.

When all of my cousins would get together, we were a group of over 30 young people. This was very pleasing to this "only child".

Chapter 8
Civilian Public Service

GRADUATING FROM MOUNTAIN LAKE HIGH SCHOOL IN 1945, I WAS INVITED BY Henry Wiebe to take part in a wheat harvesting crew based in Henderson, Nebraska that had contracted to cut wheat for growers in Meade, Kansas, Garden City, Kansas and Paxton, Nebraska, near Ogallala.

Nearing the completion of this assignment, I received word that I was to report to Fort Snelling, Minnesota for my Selective Service physical examination. I had hoped to enter the U.S. Air Force, as I wanted to learn to fly, but my parents convinced me to register as a conscientious objector (CO). I passed the physical and was instructed to report to Civilian Public Service Camp No. 64 in Terry, Montana.

After a scenic uneventful trip to the camp in Montana, I was introduced to my dorm mates and I settled in to a very new experience. As an eighteen year old it never dawned on me that this association with Mennonite men ranging from very conservative men to liberal would be, I believe, a defining period of my life. It has been my privilege to have become lifelong friends with a number of these dear brothers.

This camp was operated by the Farm Security administration. As a base camp, it had formerly housed Civilian Conservation Camp men. This CPS camp No. 64 was operated by Mennonite Central Committee, opened in January 1943 and closed in

July 1946. The men worked on irrigation systems, built farm buildings and fences, and drilled wells.

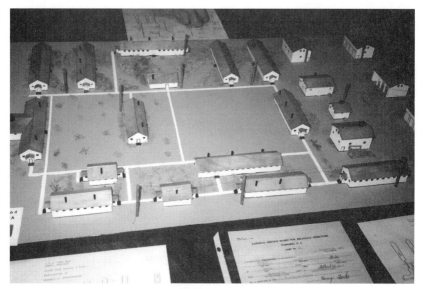

Model of CPS Camp at Terry, Montana.

Terry, the county seat of Prairie County in southeastern Montana, was located on the Milwaukie Railroad line. The former CCC camp was built a half-mile east of the town and the Yellowstone River ran adjacent to the township.

The COs worked on the Buffalo Rapids, a large irrigation project under construction to improve the Yellowstone River Valley. Varying in width from one to five miles, the project extended from Shirley, twenty miles west of Terry, to Glendive, forty miles east of the camp.

Work on the project began in November 1937. WPA, works project administration men, constructed the Glendive pumping station with some help from CCC men. At the same time they created a thirty-five mile canal to carry the water pumped up from the Yellowstone River. The war called these men away to serve in World War II.

The camp staff consisted of directors Ralph Beechy, Henry Guhr and Clarence Schrag. The dieticians were Gladys Neufeld and Mrs. Clarence Schrag. Nurse-matrons were Mildred Basinger, Mary E. Hosteller and Ruth Wedel.

By early 1946, two hundred and eighty-nine different men from twenty-two states had worked for varying periods of service at the camp. The majority of the men declared affiliation with Mennonite groups when entering CPS. Many were married. In general, we found the work at Terry to be interesting and varied.

Two agencies cooperated on the Buffalo Rapids irrigation project. While primarily under the Farm Security Administration, where sixty-five percent of the men were assigned, the remaining thirty-five percent of the camp men worked with the Bureau of Reclamation, which laid the foundation of the irrigation system. In the final stage, the Buffalo Rapids Farm Association built farm buildings, fences, drilled wells and other work necessary to provide habitable farm units.

The purpose of this project was to provide pumped water from the Yellowstone River to the adjacent arable land, and to eventually build farms that would be offered to veterans returning from the war. These farms are *still* being irrigated by these systems.

Main upper irrigation canal.

Control wheel of irrigation project.

CPS men surveyed and leveled land with Caterpillar tractors, built concrete forms, poured and finished concrete. They helped to complete farmsteads in the Buffalo Rapids Farm Association as they built a house, a barn and poultry house on each unit of eighty or one hundred sixty acres. Through cooperatives, farmers were able to replace land lost during the drought of the 1930s.

CPS men worked on the water pumping plant, cut native prairie grass, constructed fencing and built root cellars. They planted and maintained a twenty-acre garden plot in 1944 near the Shirley Pumping Plant, which made irrigation possible. It yielded large amounts of produce.

Camp Life

Before the camp opened, organizers invited community and church leaders to a meeting to learn the nature of a CPS camp community of conscientious objectors.

When the men arrived they were welcomed into local churches and community members' homes. The CPS men not only participated in religious services at the camp, but also gave programs in neighboring churches and in the two Mennonite Churches in Bloomfield.

During a teacher shortage, a CPS man, Glenn Graber, a graduate of Bluffton College, taught science at Terry High School in the spring of 1943.

The community also welcomed the wives of married assignees. They found employment in the hotel, café, dental office, dry goods store, hospital and the school, where one woman taught. Some wives performed housework. The women contributed to both the community and the camp. As one example, they sewed curtains for the social room and gave a Sunday evening program on "Christian living as CO girls".

In 1946, twenty-seven CPS wives began circulating a round robin letter as a testament to the community they developed while renting rooms or sharing houses near the camp. One of the wives made a list of all the CPS women who lived in Terry, wrote a letter, tucked it into an envelope with an address list and mailed it to the women whose name appeared next on the list.

After Carol and I married in 1951, we attended numerous reunions. She was privileged to meet my camper friends and their wives and was asked to join in the round robin letter. It continued until just a few years ago. Since Marvin Miller, Paul Bender and myself were the youngest campers (eighteen years old), many campers and their spouses have passed away. It seems as though the round robin letter just gently discontinued as a result of natural attrition.

It should be noted that the men did *not* receive any pay from the government in the CPS Camps.

The government supplied only the buildings of the abandoned CCC Camp, the work project, materials and equipment needed for the project, and supervision. Heating and cooking was done with lignite coal, which was plentiful in supply in the Montana area.

The Mennonite Central Committee (MCC) provided the food for the men, and paid each man $5.00 monthly to use as "spending money". Our usual lunch was "choke sandwiches", which consisted of Karo syrup and peanut butter (with maybe a little jelly) on bread.

The men of Terry developed numerous avocations, hobbies, and sports that made the days spent at camp interesting. The fellows fished and hunted, and ice-skated on the pond between camp buildings. One camper devised an ingenious sled to hold a barrel of hot water that dripped onto a pipe and wool pad that smoothed the ice for great skating.

CPS Camp ice rink and barracks.

And the men also made hooked rugs and purses, billfolds, and belts from leather; they also enjoyed woodworking. I made leather items and coat hangers for gifts. They also collected agates along the banks of the Yellowstone River, selling many to local jewelry stores for seventy-five cents per pound. Some men learned to cut, polish and make brooches, rings and other articles of jewelry. Dwight Jacobs was one example of a camper whose agate jewelry was outstanding. He located rocks along the Yellowstone, devised a diamond wheel saw, and cut and polished a lot of very fine examples of Montana moss agate jewelry.

During the winter of 1944-1945, the camp hosted a Farm and Community school. The educational program brought educators and church leaders to the camp for study of agriculture, applied courses in shop work and the rural community. The leader, Dan Neufeld, viewed this program as an alternative to college for those who planned to farm and desired to contribute to community life. In one component, men had the opportunity to develop personal philosophy of Christian community living.

In the summer of 1944, John Thut had conducted a ten-day music institute at the camp.

In 1944 the men produced an illustrated book, much like a college yearbook, called "This is Our Story". They also published a monthly camp paper, "Yellowstone Builder" from April 1943 to May/June 1946.

My first assignment was to top sugar beets on projects and later in early winter to work in the laundry area with Andy Raber. He taught me how to iron shirts; this was new to me. He could iron very fast; he could iron a shirt in less than a minute! (Andy was an Amish man from Shipshewana, Indiana.) My wife Carol and I visited him and his wife years later in their fine new home. He was a blacksmith and he shoed horses.

Later I had an opportunity to learn how to ink over penciled coordinates the surveyors had measured and that the experienced college-trained men had transferred to vellum, a plastic-like cloth document. Inking made this a permanent copy and duplicates could be obtained on the ozalid machine that utilized an ammonia-smelling solution for duplication. I have a copy of one of the farm units I inked.

In 1946, when the camp was scheduled to close and many men were discharged, those that weren't discharged were assigned to Camp Belton in Glacier National Park, one of the most beautiful of all of the CPS camps. I was one of twelve men chosen to close the Terry camp. It was a joy to work with the eleven men to prepare the camp for moving some items and the men to Belton and shutting down Camp No. 64 at Terry.

Looking back, I didn't know how to pace myself and I worked nearly day and night. This was my first very responsible position and I overdid it by knocking myself out. I stayed awake nearly all the time and worked. I took the responsibility inordinately seriously and I didn't get normal rest. To make a long story short, my parents were called to take me home to Mountain Lake, Minnesota. I don't remember the details but I was sedated and didn't come to until we arrived home. I soon recovered and was given a medical discharge from camp. This was a huge disappointment in my life. In a later chapter on disappointments I describe issues that were finally permanently resolved in 1961, mainly by proper treatment and very much by the support, love and continuing encouragement of my beloved wife, Carol. After sixty-two years of marvelous and very rewarding marriage, I must thank God every day for my beloved Carol, the love of my life!

The CPS experience mentioned was a defining moment of my life at age eighteen. I can't stress adequately how grateful I am to the Mennonite history; and when I look back at all the men I met, from very conservative to quite liberal persuasion, I find it difficult to verbalize how very thankful and grateful I am to God for this amazing privilege that I didn't choose, yet it forever changed my life.

The fine qualified camp directors, nurses, dieticians and other directors ran one of the best camps in the CPS program, in my opinion. An advantage the camp had was that it had a very meaningful and interesting project, also location. These attributes, I feel, all contributed to the cohesiveness of the men and the variety of jobs that made this camp No. 64 unique.

Camp Terry No. 64 men organized at least seventeen reunions. Carol and I attended nine. At one reunion, I believe in Indiana, Dwight Weldy, a former camper who had been professor of music at Goshen College, put together a quartet to sing at the program. Four of us picked up the songbooks and the piano accompanied us. After we had sung less than half of a stanza, the four of us realized something was remiss. Dwight stopped the singing and we discovered we were singing in different books and it didn't sound musical. We looked at each other and discovered the problem and had a good laugh. We made certain we were singing from the same books and it sounded much better.

The Christian friendships that developed as a result of CPS are priceless. Marvin Miller of Parnell, Iowa and I were the youngest and I believe the last men to be drafted in the fall of 1945. We are still good friends. I will always remember Bishop

Elmer G. Swartzendruber serving the camp in church service and meetings. He was an outstanding minister in (at that time) the conservative Amish denomination. His son, Ellis, was also a camper. At several all-unit Mennonite Disaster Service meetings, I have met Ellis's son, Loren, the president of Eastern Mennonite University at Harrisonburg, Virginia. At another meeting I happened to join Loren and his son when we ate dinner. It is gratifying that I have met four generations of this amazing family. Ellis and I visit by telephone occasionally.

Chapter 9
Carol, the Love of My Life

MEETING CAROL IN SEPTEMBER OF 1950 WAS, NEXT TO MY INTRODUCTION TO Jesus Christ my Savior (in fall 1941), the most momentous day of my life; it forever changed the direction my life has taken.

We met at Uncle Abe and Aunt Susie Teichroew's farm after church services for a delicious noon meal. The two first- year teachers at Mountain Lake High School that Aunt Susie had invited, asked if they could ride to town with my father and me. They mentioned that a young male first-year teacher would be joining them and if I was interested in meeting him, we could make it a "foursome." I agreed and we met outside the girls' rooming house and read the Sunday paper on the lawn.

The Abe Teichroew farm where we met.

As we didn't have lawn chairs, we sat on the grass and I relaxed a bit and stretched out. I noticed Carol had placed the part of the paper she was reading on my chest. When I noticed this, I thought to myself, that's interesting! I have always remembered that!

That evening we four ate at Harry Paskey's café. We two couples began double dating and eventually both couples married. Carol's friend, Maxine Crozier, married the other young teacher, Eugene Jacobsen, and they lived in Oklahoma City where he was a college professor. He passed away several years ago.

When Carol and I moved to California in 1952, we discovered her father's sister, Dora, had letters written in German from Poland to her great-grandfather, Henry Siebert, by his mother and sisters. My father and friends from Germany translated these letters. Carol's great-grandfather migrated to America from Pastwa, Poland and settled in New Ulm, Minnesota, a short distance north of Mountain Lake. His passport even stated that he was a Mennonite! We were surprised but grateful that she has Mennonite stock. Carol's genealogy is 25% Mennonite and my genealogy is 50% Mennonite.

After sixty-two great years of marriage, I often reminisce on the pleasant fall day in 1950 that I met my beloved Carol. This is a day I highly cherish. Carol's support and enthusiastic Godly encouragement has been legendary. Her desire to serve God influenced her to guide me into volunteer projects I felt were a little beyond my comfort zone. In 1991 when I was invited to spend two weeks at Echo Ranch Bible Camp, north of Juneau, Alaska, helping construct a two-story personnel building, I really thought the idea was a "stretch" for me. She looked at me and said, "Why don't we do it!" We drove to Washington, dropped our car off at friends and boarded the Alaska Ferry "MV Columbia" at Bellingham, Washington a few days later.

In 1992 when Carol and I visited Alaska in our motorhome we visited Harry and Adeline Reimer at Fairbanks. Before we departed for the lower forty-eight, Harry presented a project he and Adeline were responsible for in Papua New Guinea. He was in charge of organizing a twenty person staff to construct four buildings for married student housing on the campus of the Nazarene Bible School in Mt. Hagen, Papua, New Guinea.

When he found I had construction experience, he asked me to consider joining his team. When I talked to Carol, again this really appeared to be a big stretch for me. I had never traveled overseas and I didn't even have a passport! Believe it or not, this was beyond my comfort zone.

Carol talked me into agreeing to seriously consider helping with this project. This experience opened vistas in my life I am not certain would have developed had it not been for Carol.

Numerous times when I was making plans for volunteer projects where she wouldn't travel with me, not once did I hear a word of disappointment from her. She has always been supportive of these plans.

In another chapter it needs to be told what a great mother and friend she has been to our lovely daughter Lisa. It has been immeasurably gratifying to observe how close she is to our daughter.

Carol played piano at the El Camino Bible Church in Santa Clara in the late 1950's. She later organized a Mary Martha fellowship; she directed the choir, organized a triple trio, played organ and taught Sunday school.

She is the personification of Proverbs 31:10-29. I could go on and on in documenting her Godly attributes. I still marvel at how we met. It had to be due to God's leading in our lives.

The project of writing this book would not have been possible without Carol's support. Her counsel and editing have been absolutely invaluable.

This book project had been percolating for several years with previously little progress. I started writing a chapter about the Teichroew family and a chapter about the Voshage family several years ago. A number of times I got sidetracked because of a trip or working on a sales venture; it might be a month or more until I returned to attempting to complete the family chapters.

I decided to get serious, and when I couldn't make much sense of my erstwhile attempts at the family chapters, Carol decided to give me assistance. My problem was that I had virtually duplicated the chapters three or four times and to say I was confused would have been an understatement.

Carol gathered all these early family compilation attempts and, you guessed it,... she made sense of the confusion in short order.

As my writing finally got organized and she kept editing my work, I took renewed interest in the project and now a few months later I'm hoping to deliver the thirty-six chapters to the publisher for editing.

Carol is the key, the catalyst to actually completing this book. I am immensely grateful to her for her encouragement, her professionalism and prodding and critiquing of the work.

A page or two needs to be included that expresses Carol's unequivocal support for me during numerous illnesses; of course she had been very loving and supportive in normal times! Twice I was hospitalized with severe nervous breakdown issues for periods of six months. Not once did she give even a hint of rejecting me.

Her devotion and love for me has cemented and welded and kept our marriage stable and so loving that I have always cherished her devotion and love for me.

It has been very clear to me many, many times that she was God's choice for my life-companion and wife. She is always supportive and loving and when I need to go slow on a venture, trip or a purchase, her counsel and input has been legendary. When we had the business and I felt we needed to purchase an expensive computer-controlled machine, she never stood in my way; but she did convince me that I needed to justify the financial output.

Carol and I lived in our last home in Saratoga for forty years and this is where we raised our daughter, Lisa. We sold the house in 2007 and moved to a 645 sq. ft. cottage/duplex at Lincoln Glen Manor in San Jose, adjacent to our church (Lincoln Glen Church – Mennonite Brethren Conference). We are very comfortable and contented here. Our daughter lives five minutes away in San Jose.

Our Saratoga, CA home of 40 years.

It really is a pleasure to think of all the good times Carol and I have had. I thank God that, in our eighties, we can still drive, travel, explore, as well as serve and praise God for His blessings, which are manifold!

Observing my wife enjoying her fellowship and excursions with our daughter Lisa makes me doubly grateful for Carol! What a precious gift from God to me!

Chapter 10
We Were Guided
to Each Other

By Carol Siebert Voshage

MY BACKGROUND WAS VERY HUMBLE. I WAS A CHILD OF THE GREAT DEPRESSION years, when my parents also faced unexpected ill health and impoverishing circumstances. But my Mom and Dad were born-again Christians, very active in their church, and it was a home filled with music and love.

Mina and Herman Siebert holding 1 year old Carol in 1930.

I accepted Jesus as my personal Savior during college, gladly asking Him to guide me in my life-choices. My first teaching offer was in Mountain Lake, Minnesota.

My father was very concerned, because we learned that this was a largely Mennonite community, and he was worried that this might be a weird "sect". My mother asked a teaching relative to ask around, and found that Mountain Lake was considered to be a delightful community with wonderful families who supported their teachers and were also very musical. My father was reassured. This was also the home of my college chum Vel Teichroew. Her family farm was my base as I applied for and obtained my first position as an English and music teacher in junior and senior high school there.

The first weekend of staff meetings, I was invited by Vel's parents to attend church with them (First Mennonite) and to have dinner with another new teacher at the farm. There I met a relative, Harold Voshage, and his father. Later we returned to town with them and arranged an afternoon "foursome" with another new teacher. This led to "double-dating" and eventual marriage for both couples.

But *our* wedding was rather hasty, as my parents had decided to move permanently to California, giving us only two weeks notice. So we held our wedding in First Mennonite Church in Mountain Lake nine days later, after two crippling blizzards in one week! One hundred-fifty guests were invited but only sixteen could make it.

As a side effect of our rushed wedding, the school board wrongly assumed that our reason for haste was a pregnancy, so they did *not* renew my contract. Since I didn't know how to drive, I became jobless, which forced us to move to Mankato, where we worked at three jobs and still were going into debt.

After hearing of the good jobs and wages in California and the cheaper living costs at that time, we moved to California one year after our wedding.

God's guidance in our lives became very apparent several years later, when my father's sister brought out old family papers that were unknown to us, and asked my husband's parents to help translate them from the German language. As they did so, they realized that these were family letters to my great-grandfather Henry Siebert, who had immigrated to America in the 1800's. They recognized many family names mentioned as being common Mennonite names. Then my aunt produced his passport, which stated that he was a Mennonite from Poland!

He had settled in a German town in Minnesota, but had no more connection with the Mennonite Church and no one in my Dad's family had been aware of this origin. In fact, none of us had ever even *heard* of Mennonites before! So, as I look back over my early life, I realize that God had guided me in many ways into this marriage!

One indication had been my place of college instruction. I had wished to attend Berea College in Kentucky, which had a "Work-Study Program". But my Dad wished me to be nearer to home, so I attended a Minnesota teachers' college instead.

Also, my closest friend during my senior year there was Vel Teichroew, who was a "double-cousin" (her mother was a Voshage) to my future husband, who I met at her home farm.

Carol Siebert and Vel Teichroew at the Teichroew farm in 1950.

Another factor was my musical background. I played piano and bassoon, as well as being a vocal soloist and choral director. Harold had always wanted to marry a girl who was musical and who played piano.

But the main attraction leading to our marriage was the fact that we were both "born-again Christians" who loved the Lord and grew up in Christian homes.

Carol's Perspective regarding "Mennonites":

I was brought up in a variety of protestant Christian churches (Christian, Presbyterian and Methodist-Episcopal) due to frequent moves. When I started teaching in Mountain Lake, Minnesota, I felt right at home at the First Mennonite Church. However, there were some "rules" that I soon noticed. Women did not wear earrings; alcohol drinking, card games, dancing and movies were frowned upon. These rules were strange to me. But I decided that these were unimportant as opposed to joining my life with Harold. And these minor "rules" were later eased – they were not really basic Christian doctrine, just peripheral issues. They were not important to me anyway.

Actually, Mennonite home life was very much like my own upbringing; regular church attendance, a personal relationship with Jesus Christ, close family ties, frugal finances, hard work, music and helping others were some of the most common guidelines of our families.

However, one strong issue for Mennonites was that of "non-resistance". Harold had served in "Alternate Service, Civilian Public Service" when he was drafted.

But it just happened that no one in my family had ever been drafted in time of war. All were too young or too old! So I did not have any strong feelings for or against this view.

The "fun" differences were the ethnic Mennonite foods and the lovely Low German dialect.

I soon learned to cook and bake many of the foods: German chicken borscht (cabbage soup – no beets), pluma mos (cold fruit soup), zwieback (rolls), portzilke (fritters) and crullers (fried pastries).

But I never mastered the Low German, even though my Siebert grandparents spoke almost the exact same dialect. They and Harold understood each other perfectly. *I* was left out! I *have* learned to recognize many words and their meaning, but I am not able to converse (I only get the "gist").

As Harold and I dated, he shared fully with me regarding his history of mental illness. This did not scare me, because when I was 12 years old, my Dad had suffered a nervous breakdown and had been hospitalized for months. Mom and I gathered our support around him. Mom took a job in a department store for six days and one evening a week. I took on all of the housework, cleaning, washing, shopping and some cooking. Our neighbors and church friends helped us to get through this difficult time and we all loved Dad so much that he knew we would help him get well.

Harold Voshage and Carol Siebert dating.

Dad recovered and we, as a family, made the necessary adjustments in our own lives. We all came through successfully and rebuilt our life to be happy and satisfying. So I had faith that Harold and I could survive illness as well.

Carol Siebert Voshage

Chapter 11
Our Wedding

We became engaged in February and planned to be married the following June.

But when we visited Carol's parents in early March, upon their return from a California trip, we were stunned to learn that they planned to move permanently to California in *two weeks* – Herman had a job being held for him there! So I decided that we would get married in 9 days (March 19th) in the Mountain Lake church where we both attended. I called our pastor and my Dad to start arrangements.

Our troubles started that same weekend as we tried to return to Mountain Lake (150 miles away) in a blizzard. It took us three days to make that trip. On the way we shopped in Mankato, where I bought my wedding suit and Carol bought her wedding gown and borrowed the veil from a friend.

Luckily we found that Carol's employer, Mountain Lake High School, had been forced to call a "snow vacation" all week, so we got busy; we applied for the wedding license, hand-wrote 150 invitations and mailed them out, ordered a cake and flowers, and chose attendants.

But Minnesota weather had another surprise for us. On Saturday, March 17th, a second blizzard hit! Carol's parents decided to leave *early* for Mountain Lake; they had to leave their car halfway and continue the trip by train the rest of the way, as all roads were closing. They arrived on Sunday morning on the last train able to get through, and we met them just before all the town streets were closed by the storm.

Downtown Mt. Lake clearing snow on our wedding day.

The rest of the day that they arrived (Sunday), all of Minnesota was snowbound. No roads or streets were open. Our two families spent the day together at my parent's home with diminishing hopes, and finally decided that the wedding must be cancelled! Carol clambered back to her rooming house in tears – what would we do?

But Monday, March 19th, dawned clear, cold and sunny. We cancelled the cancellation and got substitutes for all of the wedding party who were stranded elsewhere: organist, singer, best man, maid of honor, and ushers.

We almost forgot to pick up our marriage license at the county seat, but Carol's father and I drove behind the first snowplow that opened the highway.

So we became Mr. and Mrs. Harold Voshage, with our parents, our pastor, and 16 plucky guests present who walked through the snowdrifts. After a group picture was taken outside in the church parking lot, blown clear by strong winds, we were all frozen - especially our bouquets!

Our wedding in First Mennonite Church, Mt. Lake.

After a small reception, we were ready to drive off on our honeymoon as soon as the plows went through. But Carol's parents needed to get home for their auction sale, so we took them along to Mankato, where they would be able to continue to their car the next day by bus! Luckily they were able to stay overnight with friends; *we* had the last hotel reservation!

Wedding reception at Mt. Lake Hotel: Herman & Mina Siebert,
Carol & Harold Voshage, Kate & Christ Voshage.

We two continued on to our honeymoon of three days, and then on Friday attended Carol's parents' auction in Plainview – held outside on top of the snowdrifts.

After we said our goodbyes to her folks and returned to Mountain Lake, the next day the Sieberts drove off to his job and their new life in California.

On the same day, the Saturday following our wedding, we held a reception at the church for all of our intended guests (both present and absent-though-invited), where we again wore our wedding finery.

As of this writing, we have celebrated 62 years of happy marriage. God has truly blessed us!

Chapter 12
Moving to California

CAROL AND I MET IN 1950 AFTER THE BUSINESS I HAD OPERATED IN THE SUMMER of 1950 was not viable. I had hauled refrigerated loads of eggs to New Jersey from St. Paul. I discontinued the business in September and after meeting and marrying Carol in March of 1951, we later moved to Mankato in November. I had several jobs there and Carol also worked. My final job in Mankato prior to our deciding to move to California was at Kato Engineering. This was my first exposure to operating a metal-cutting lathe. It was a new experience and I enjoyed it. The pay wasn't very good and rent was high because Mankato was a college town. One evening Carol and I looked at each other and we agreed we should call her parents and ask them if they thought it might be advantageous to relocate to the San Jose area in California. Her father was certain we could make a viable living.

Carol and I prayed about this possibility and discussed how we could make the move and soon we agreed we needed to pull stakes and plan our transition to the San Francisco California Bay Area. We obtained a used red "98" 4-door Oldsmobile and had a hitch and wiring installed to attach a 2-wheel trailer. We packed all of our worldly goods at Mankato in the car and trailer, placed a tarp on the trailer and left Mankato on March 29th to complete loose ends in Mountain Lake, and on April 1st we left there for our California trek.

We had planned on driving the southern route, but when we arrived in Omaha we were informed that the northern route highway #30 was open. In Utah the highway proliferated with one frost boil after another. To navigate each boil (and they seemed to be endless) we had to come to a complete stop before driving through it. It took a long time to negotiate these frost heaves. Late at night we finally arrived at Salt Lake City and located an adequate motel.

The next day when we left Salt Lake City for our next leg west, thankfully there were no more frost heaves. From here to Donner Pass the trip was uneventful. Over Donner Summit the snow cuts on both sides of the highway were twenty feet high!

Carol and I decided not to stay overnight in Reno as we were anxious to get to Sunnyvale, California. We arrived at the apartment where Carol's parents lived in the morning of April 4th at about 2:30 a.m. Carol's father was working the night shift at Hewlett Packard Company and so had just returned home and gave us a very warm welcome!

Our loaded car and trailer, April 4, 1952 in front of
Herman & Mina Siebert's house in Sunnyvale, CA.

Carol and I were fortunate to locate an upstairs apartment on the Louis and Kate Pavlina fruit ranch on El Camino Real in Mt. View. This fine Slovenian couple's children had left home and they had converted the upstairs of their ranch house to a furnished apartment. We were the first tenants. We will always remember the first night we stayed there. The bed collapsed on the floor so we had to set up our own bed frame that we had brought with us from Minnesota. By the way, we still sleep in the black walnut double bed I made in grade nine in Mountain Lake High School. The instructor Emil Ludtke made certain it was a securely designed bed frame; even the side rails are solid black walnut and needless to say it will "last forever".

The Pavlinas raised Bing cherries and Blenheim apricots. Their detached double garage faced the street and when the Bing cherries became ripe, the women packers would place the top layers of cherries in symmetrical rows with the stems down. These premium-packaged boxes were air-freighted to the eastern cities for top prices. They also sold fruit directly to the public here. We were allowed to pick cherries and apricots for eating. For canning purposes we paid nominal costs. When we decided to pit cherries for canning, Carol's cousin Nora Blalock loaned us a cherry pitter and we had cherry juice all over the kitchen, floor, walls, counters, ourselves and just everywhere! But that pitted cherry sauce was scrumptious!

Earning a Living

My first job in California was at a company the founders of Hewlett Packard created for eight of their key employees, called Palo Alto Engineering. They manufactured small transformers for HP instruments. Carol's father, Herman Siebert, introduced me to an HP manager and I was hired to help manufacture the transformers. I was the first man hired besides the manager. It turned out the manager and I didn't get along particularly well, so I left.

Almost immediately after terminating my employment at PAECO, I was hired at Western Gear Works in Belmont, California, fifteen miles north of Mountain View. In the early fifties Highway 101 (Bayshore Highway) was three lanes. The center lane was a passing lane and there were some signal lights. This was the main drag between San Francisco and San Jose. When I commuted to Belmont, sometimes there were accidents at intersections and I would look at the far right shoulder and just give the area a wide berth on the shoulder and this avoidance saved me time.

My two and a half years at Western Gear Works was very rewarding. This company manufactured large planetary transmissions for government personnel carriers. I learned a lot about machining and its various facets. I have happily been hooked by becoming involved in the many aspects of machining.

While I worked at Western Gear Works as a production specialist, similar to an apprentice machinist, I attended night school when I worked days and a daytime trade school when I worked nights. I enjoyed this job tremendously.

In 1955 we moved to Reedley, California for health reasons and after recovering, I obtain a job at Salwasser Manufacturing. This company founded by Fred Salwasser and his son Melvin manufactured automatic package-casing machinery. They employed six men and it was a thriving business. They needed my machinist skills and it turned out to be a very good fit for me. A lifelong benefit was meeting Wally Loewen, their engineer. Wally and his wife Esther and their five children are close friends to this day.

In 1957 we decided to return to Sunnyvale and I obtained a job operating a horizontal boring mill on the night shift at Westinghouse Electric. It was a great opportunity to learn how to operate a Gidding and Lewis machine. I remained there over a year.

In 1959 Varian Associates in Palo Alto hired me. Varian was founded primarily by Russ and Sigurd Varian, brothers who had been key engineering inventors of Klystron tubes used for navigation guidance in World War II. After the war the brothers and several of their close associates created this company and it was almost immediately successful.

My first job was in the radiation division. This division manufactured and marketed linear accelerators that universities used in their labs. The devices were so difficult to manufacture that for years the division was unprofitable. Today they use the linear accelerator to be the heart of a cancer treatment medical device and it is the most successful device to radiate cancer cells and the best seller.

A few months after being hired in the radiation division I transferred to the Super Power Klystron division. This was a most satisfying relationship.

In 1966 I had an opportunity to transfer to the shop in the Central Research Labs. These were very interesting years. After working in the Central Research support shop I was asked if I wanted to join a lab that was developing several interesting and challenging devices. I agreed and the final years of my career at Varian were very gratifying.

The first project I was assigned to was assisting several scientists with PhDs and engineers to build an electron microscope. After a little more than a year we worked on Auger Spectroscopy, performing surface studies on semi-conductor materials. These experiments were performed inside a stainless steel chamber under an ultra-high vacuum atmosphere and as pure as possible. Since Varian had invented ultra-high vacuum technology, with no moving parts and no contamination from oil, this made it possible to perform these sophisticated experiments.

Several years that I worked at the Central Research lab I attended San Jose City College taking evening classes in Vacuum Technology. I will always remember these rewarding classes. They were fascinating and related well to my responsibilities at Varian.

In 1972 I terminated my employment at Varian Associates and decided to take my part-time contract machine shop to a full-time basis. I had begun the shop in 1966 in my Sunnyvale garage with a lathe and a milling machine and several drill presses and ancillary tools. All indications were that it could be an opportune time to "go for it".

As an old man of eighty-six, I am still enamored with the many, many facets of machining and manufacturing. To this day I am sometimes involved in various sales activities that support machine manufacturing. The technological advances that have occurred in the last fifty years are mind-boggling. Occasionally I attend various technology shows and at one they demonstrated 3-D manufacturing. The machine was approximately a six foot cube and a program was activated that allowed this machine to produce a six-inch plastic adjustable (crescent type) wrench. When the wrench was ejected from the machine it was complete, assembled and ready to use. This is one of the most amazing technological advances I have seen. Recently I read that this is just the early stage of this technology and aluminum and possibly other metal components will be produced this way. Sometimes I have a difficult time believing my eyes. At other times I am again grateful to live in Silicon Valley!

Chapter 13
Early Work
Experiences

I LOOK BACK AT THE VARIED VOCATIONS THAT HAVE GIVEN ME MANY INTEREST-
ing memories. Most of them have been beneficial to my physical and emotional
development and maturity.

My father's first tractor was a Fordson, purchased in the late 1920's. It was a
steel-wheeled wide-front tractor. Since this tractor had several shortcomings, the
operator had to be very careful when hitching to an implement so that the front
end would not dangerously raise up when underway, and sometimes seriously or
even fatally injure the operator when the tractor came end-over-end toward the
towed implement.

Fortunately my father replaced the Fordson with a John Deere GP (general
purpose) two cylinder engine two plow wide front axle steel-wheeled tractor. It was
a great improvement over the Fordson. I was too small to operate the John Deere.

In 1937 Dad purchased a new Allis-Chalmers WC model rubber-tired narrow
front axle capable of cultivating corn. It was a great improvement over the previous
two tractors, especially having rubber-tired wheels. As a ten year old, Dad taught
me how to cultivate corn and soybeans and drag and disc. It really was a lot of
benefit to Dad that I could cultivate row crops. Farmers that used Farmall and John
Deere tractors had to drive these tractors themselves for cultivating or their sons
needed to be nearly mature. Dad's tractor was the only row crop that I remember

that utilized a power lift pedal-actuated mechanism to raise and lower the cultivator. The other tractors used long hand-operated levers to raise and lower the cultivator. These required considerable muscle to manipulate. Dad's tractor only required the tap of a pedal that a drum controlled.

Consequently, as a youngster, I could easily manage to control the cultivator's mechanism. I soon learned to raise the cultivator approximately fifteen feet from the end of the row and, as I was turning, I tapped the pedal that controlled the cultivator again and it would lower it in a timely manner. It didn't take me long to figure out the timing of this procedure; it was a little tricky because the mechanism had a time-lag that needed to be considered.

When I operated a four-section drag machine I would often drive in fourth gear, which was the fastest gear. When I got to the end of the field I would shift down to third gear and when I turned around to return to the other direction I would shift into fourth gear again, the fastest gear. However, I made certain Dad wasn't around because he wanted me to drag in third gear.

In addition to learning to drive a tractor at ten years old, I learned how to milk cows, clean the barn and chicken house (not fun!) and hog barn, also take care of and feed my ponies and help with the care of our draft horses. I shocked grain bundles and during threshing season, helped unload wagons of grain into an elevator and filled a granary.

I picked up rocks in the plowed fields and loaded them on a "stone boat". It seemed as though every spring more rocks came to the surface and needed to be removed.

"Walking" soybean fields and pulling cockleburr weeds was another rewarding (if boring) job for young folks.

After moving to town in 1943, I would sometimes help my Uncle Abe Teichroew on his farm.

My first city job was clerking and roasting sunflower seeds ("knack" seeds) for the Neufeld variety store in town. I was paid twenty cents an hour, with one cent deducted for social security, leaving a net of nineteen cents an hour take-home pay.

My Uncle George Rempel constructed large masonry buildings. He hired me to mix and supply mortar and also to supply 12-inch cement blocks to the block layers. This was exhausting work!

In the summer of 1943, my cousin Leonard Bartel and I (both 16 years old) were hired by Swift and Company in South St. Paul to operate bacon slicers. We placed smoke-cured sides of bacon on conveyors that fed the bacon into large-diameter slicers that would slice a side in seconds. Occasionally scrap pieces of bacon would get on one of the many chain sprockets and the chain would come off. There were hooks provided to pick up the chain and place it on the sprocket. We thought we didn't always need the hook, so one night I again picked up the unprotected chain with my left hand to place it on the sprocket. Probably being a little drowsy, I wasn't careful enough. Instead my left hand ring finger was moving around the sprocket shaft and it was stuck! I immediately jerked to free my hand and almost half of the nail joint was nearly torn off, barely hanging. I told my supervisor and they took me to the night nurse. She bandaged the finger and said that the next morning the doctor would repair the finger. He sutured the torn finger and after four sutures I told him I couldn't stand the pain (he gave me *no* pain killers or Novocain) so he completed the procedure.

Since I was laid up and couldn't work, my best friend, John Tieszen, invited me to attend a Bible camp with him at Medicine Lake near Minneapolis for a week. We had a great time in Bible studies and recreation. John arranged to rent a rowboat and he invited two girls to accompany us.

Harold's high school pal Johnny Tieszen and
wife – retired missionaries in Ecuador.

John taught me how to relate to girls. Yes, I liked girls, but I had not dated as yet. So this was a new experience for me!

In the fall John and I resumed our schooling at Mountain Lake High School and completed our junior year in 1944. We graduated from high school in 1945.

John was my best buddy in high school. We spent a few holidays in Minneapolis and enjoyed the sights and taking the elevator to the top of the Foshay Tower, the tallest building in the Twin Cities. We had a lot of good times together.

In 1945 Henry Wiebe, another classmate, invited me to accompany him to work on a combine crew from Henderson, Nebraska to help harvest wheat in Meade and Garden City, Kansas and Ogallala, Nebraska. It was a great experience. At times I drove the large Case tractor pulling the combine and also drove a truck to remove the wheat from the combine and deliver it to a commercial elevator.

Before I completed this job, I was called to report to Fort Snelling to take my draft physical and was assigned to work in a CPS camp (Civilian Public Service).

In the spring of 1946, after being discharged from CPS camp #64 in Terry, Montana, I was hired by Kenneth Porath to help prepare his 400-acre farm for planting and seeding. He was a great man as an employer. He had good machinery and a well-maintained F30 Farmall 3-plow tractor that I ran for four weeks. We took only Sundays off, except for chores. His wife, Noreen, cooked superb meals. They had five children. In the morning before breakfast Mr. Porath and I milked the cows and then we ate. These four weeks are probably the most memorable farm employment experience that I had. Many fond memories of the Poraths remain in my memory bank.

In the summers of 1946-1949 I was employed at Green Giant canning factory in Le Seur, Minnesota. The first summer I worked on a pea vinery in the field where vines were harvested. My job was shoveling wet heavy pea vines into a machine that removed the peas from the vines and pods. It was back breaking work since the vines were green and heavy and soggy! I soon learned that there were more skilled jobs available in the retort cooking department of the cannery itself.

After applying for a retort operator position, I was accepted and this was my assignment for several summers. We operated overhead traveling cranes carrying large baskets of sealed cans ready for cooking. The work was hot and humid, but it paid better and it was an enjoyable and challenging job to place and later remove the large baskets into and out of the retorts.

After this assignment was completed, I was employed a short time at Butterfield Produce, a poultry processing plant. I only lasted several weeks as it was very wet and cold and I couldn't handle it. My Aunt Susie Teichroew spent years employed there – I don't know how she could do it!

Then the Peter J. Sweitzer Co. of Windom hired me to haul bales from large stacks to their processing plant. I enjoyed this work and remained until all of the stacks of bales had been delivered to the plant.

In 1947-1949 while attending Augsburg College in Minneapolis, I was in charge of the janitorial and custodial responsibility of their music building. It was an old church building near the college that they had purchased and converted to a music hall. Another part-time weekend job I had was at the Toddle House, a ten-stool restaurant, which I enjoyed a lot.

After college, in the spring of 1949, I was hired by Reuben Wiens, who owned several "for-hire" trucks (one was a 26' semi-trailer and tractor). He taught me how to handle the rig. A major portion of his business was picking up cattle from farmers who consigned their animals to the South St. Paul Stockyards for slaughtering and packing.

When we had enough cattle picked up by a smaller truck and penned in a building on his property on the edge of town to fill the same trailer, I would load the trailer and head to South St. Paul. After unloading the cattle, I bedded down in a bunk provided by the stockyard companies. In the morning I would pick up previously ordered freight from wholesale houses on University Avenue between the Twin Cities for delivery to Mountain Lake businesses.

After off-loading this freight in Mountain Lake, the next day we would haul most anything that needed transporting in southwestern Minnesota, including flat bed loads. My pay was only $25.00 a week and this truck line had the poorest equipment of the three trucking companies in Mountain Lake, yet we provided a very adequate service. This job was quite a letdown, because I had higher aspirations, hoping college would help prepare me for a respected occupation. Needless to say, I was humiliated and I could tell that I had lost the respect of some of my peers and relatives, although they were all too tactful to express their disappointment in me. I worked at this job during summer, fall and winter of 1949 to 1950.

In 1950 I also worked for a former high school classmate. Whitney Frost had a successful cabinet manufacturing company in Windom, Minnesota and I worked for him for several months.

Caldwell Packing Plant of Windom hired me to deliver beef quarters to grocery stores in the area. I stayed there less than a month. It was backbreaking work!

Chapter 14
Disappointments

FROM 1941 THROUGH 1961 MY LIFE TOOK VARIOUS SIDETRACKS ON THE ROAD to the satisfying, stable life that commenced in the summer of 1961.

In the fall of 1941 at the beginning of my freshman year at Mountain Lake, Minnesota high school, I became very depressed. My grades were poor and I couldn't laugh; I was in trouble. A local medic tried various pills and I wound up having my appendix removed. After I recovered several weeks later in winter my depression left me. My grades improved and I was okay again. This depression returned each fall as I entered High School and then when I recovered several months later I felt like a new person.

In August of 1945 I was drafted to a Civilian Public Service Camp in Terry, Montana. The camp was closing in late summer of 1946 and we would be transferred to Belton, Montana. A group of twelve people were chosen to close the camp and I was one of them. Unfortunately I took the responsibility too seriously and worked very long days, not getting enough rest. I withdrew and my parents were called to take me home to Mountain Lake, Minnesota by automobile. I had always hoped to be assigned to Belton before being assigned to Terry and now I wasn't able to finish my CPS days at Belton, a beautiful Glacier Park area camp.

At home I soon recovered. I found odd jobs in the Mountain Lake area, I was living with my parents; I didn't have a car.

When I was at Terry my father rode my Harley Davidson motorcycle to Montana in late fall 1945. The roads became icy and he drove into a ditch several times and decided to sell the motorcycle on the way, which he could do. He got what I had paid for it, but my "wheels" were gone and of course I wasn't happy.

After I had been home several months I bought a Model A Ford from a friend and my father made me rescind the deal. Needless to say I nearly lost a friend. But my life stabilized, I obtained odd jobs and kept busy and my social life was satisfactory. Later in 1946, prior to late fall, I took the Norfolk and Western train to Newport News, Virginia to apply for a Coast Guard Seaman's card and prepared to join a crew that tended cattle to be transported to Europe on a Victory ship. Several men of Mountain Lake had served as cattlemen on a Victory or Liberty Ship freighter and their stories intrigued me.

After I arrived in Newport News, I was issued a Coast Guard Seaman's card and all the documents necessary for the voyage. While I was awaiting the loading of the cattle on the ship, the ugly feeling of depression again appeared and I knew I must cancel this responsibility and not become incapacitated and ill on the way to Europe on the North Sea. It became evident that I needed to travel home. Needless to say I have always regretted missing out on this opportunity, but looking back, it was the correct decision.

The years of 1947 – 1949 I attended Augsburg College in Minneapolis. Graduating from Mountain Lake High School, I was given a small scholarship, paying second semester tuition the freshman year.

Highlights for me at Augsburg were working out with the wrestling team, trying out for freshman football team as a guard, and singing in the Choral Club. However, I wanted to play in the band but had no instrument. My Dad had purchased a used high-quality cornet for my high school band years, but sold it after my graduation and pocketed the money. So when I entered Augsburg I had to learn to play French horn on a school instrument.

Also, I felt pressured by my parents to start off with a "Pre-Med course", so I took math and science classes. But in high school I had *not* taken these classes, making me unprepared for the college level classes. I did *not* do well, and I could not grasp how *any* of these subjects would help me make a living. The only classes I liked were zoology, college algebra and German.

After my sophomore year I dropped out. I don't think anyone was more disappointed than my parents, although they didn't verbalize it. Emotionally I was never a happy person at Augsburg College.

In the summer of 1949 I started driving a semi-truck for Reuben Wiens in Mountain Lake, hauling freight. A primary business was picking up cattle to be trucked to the Southern St. Paul stockyards. Sometimes we would remove the rack on the trailer and haul flat bed loads, culverts, large fuel tanks, etc.

In early spring of 1950 I heard that a truck brokerage, Adent Brothers of Benton Harbor Michigan and St. Paul, MN contracted with truck tractor owners and they hauled refrigerated vanloads of equipment to Jersey City and Bayonne, New Jersey.

I decided to buy a truck tractor and they agreed to provide refrigerated vans loaded with eggs for transfer to ship transport to Europe via Jersey City, New Jersey.

After making four round trips from St. Paul to Jersey City and even though dry freight back hauls helped pay expenses to Minnesota, at nineteen cents a mile it was not a viable enterprise. Arriving in St. Paul I drove the truck to the dealer that had sold it to me, handed him the keys and took the streetcar to the broker's office. The broker relayed a message from my father that my mother was seriously ill in a Mountain Lake hospital recovering from a gall bladder operation. I hopped on another streetcar to Fort Snelling and walked to highway #169 that leads to Mankato and stuck out my thumb for a ride. A lady semi-truck driver from Sioux Falls stopped. She asked where I was headed and when replying Mountain Lake, she said to hop in. She was going through Mountain Lake to Sioux Falls, So. Dakota. My mother was making a good recovery at the hospital and she was released a few days later.

In April of 1952 Carol and I moved to Sunnyvale, California. It turned out to be an excellent destination, weather-wise, good earning opportunities, very good geographic location, forty-five minutes from the Pacific Ocean, one hour from San Francisco and four hours away from our beloved Yosemite Park.

In the summer of 1953 I suffered the first of numerous kidney stone attacks. Urologists at the Palo Alto Medical Clinic hospitalized me in the Stanford Hospital. I was overweight and lost 65 pounds in eight days of excruciating pain. A ureteral catheter was inserted and the pain subsided.

In 1954, this stone that had caused the initial attack was removed and after seven days, the catheter was taken out and I went home. Carol was employed at Westinghouse Electric, within walking distance of our home (she didn't drive). It was soon apparent that the procedure had not been completely successful. I wasn't recovering, I was in bed most of the time, and the urine was soaking the surgical bandage and the bed. Carol would walk home on her noon hour, change the bandages and the bedding, and return to work! I was getting more ill each day. Carol called my parents in Dallas, Oregon and they came to help. Dad took me to the urologist and before we returned, the doctor called Carol and said to admit me to the Stanford Hospital for a second surgery.

The next day the surgeons extended the wound and inserted the urinary catheter from the right kidney into the bladder and after this they discharged me to home and the catheter remained for 37 days. I drove to the barbershop with catheter and two glass bottles. When the catheter was removed, I had to deal with chronic prostatitis for three years and the only relief was sitting in a warm tub of water.

Back in 1955, when we were living in our Sunnyvale house, I decided to quit my machinist job after two and a half years at Western Gear Works and embarked on making redwood slats for a fellow who marketed redwood baskets and tubs. I had purchased a complete Delta woodworking equipment shop previously. After a month or so of this venture, it was apparent that I couldn't make a living wage at this enterprise, so I sold the machinery. But I had a difficult time accepting this reality.

Reedley

In the fall of 1955 I had a severe bout of depression and was sent to Kings View in Reedley operated by the Mennonite Central Committee. I was there six months. I was given one electric shock treatment, drug therapy and counseling. The counseling Mr. Drudge gave my wife Carol, she attributes to be of great benefit.

As I look back over the years spent at home with my parents, I now see that a pattern was emerging. They began to assume that I would always be plagued by this recurring mental illness, and thus would never be a well, independent man living my own life separately from them. They seemed to be taken completely by surprise when I married Carol. Rather, they had expected to provide a home for me for the rest of my life. They did not want me to have my own "wheels" because I could use their car. So when I bought a cheap Chevy Coupe a few months after our marriage, my mother cried due to the shock!

Of course, some of this reaction to my illness was to be expected, because in those days mental problems were still kept rather "hush-hush".

While I was under treatment at Kings View, my Dad wrote me a letter blaming my illness on my marriage to Carol, and attempted to drive a wedge between my wife and me! We immediately turned that letter over to the hospital for their consideration.

Their response was swift: they directed my parents to delay any visits to me until I could regain my equilibrium. There were to be no more "secret" letters to upset me or to be divisive to my marriage.

It then became clear that Carol and I, as a married couple, needed to forge our independence from my parents' need to "dominate", and yet somehow keep our relationship with them healthy and loving. I thank God that we were given wise counsel through the Holy Scriptures, pastoral guidance, discerning medical social workers, warm Christian fellowship, and answers to our fervent prayers from God.

We came to realize that my parents were locked into an old time frame reaction to my illness, and therefore made many mistakes in their response, while we also were unwittingly taking wrong steps as well. Here my Mennonite/Christian heritage helped me to accept God's healing and to lead me to a better, healthier relationship with my parents in their remaining years.

When I was ready for discharge, my doctor insisted I obtain a job. We didn't know many people in Reedley. We did know several Boldt families that had grown up with my father in Mountain Lake. We also were good friends of the H.S. Ewert family. He had been my instructor at District 33 rural school in Mountain Lake in the early 1930's.

Carol had learned to drive in Reedley, so she could take me to various places to seek employment. We knew there was a concern that manufactured fiber-cooling pads for evaporative coolers. We visited them and they didn't need help. On one of my weekends away from the hospital, I had noticed a company with the name Salwasser Mfg. on the front of the building near Buttonwillow on Manning Ave. We stopped in and I applied for a job, and was hired. This company produced automatic package-casing machines. These machines would package most anything sold in supermarkets, such as soaps, candy bars, cereal, etc. I was the 8th or 9th man hired as a machinist.

The following week the co-owner, Mr. Fred Salwasser, died. I had met Wally Loewen and he said that he and Esther, his wife, could take us to Fresno for the memorial service.

My employment at Salwasser Manufacturing lasted nearly two years. After that we determined to return to Sunnyvale where we still had a home. Carol and I both feel that the experiences we had in Reedley, even though perhaps somewhat humiliating, were meant by God for good. I learned many lessons from these years and a number of highlights emerged. Wally Loewen and I became lifelong friends. His wife Esther was a jewel and we love their five children and extended families. Wally is an experienced glider and powered-ship pilot. We had many fascinating rides. Wally and I drove to Adelanto, near George Air Force Base in the Mojave Desert for a glider meet. We left in the early morning darkness and all of a sudden the entire Sierra Range was visible in an orange-yellow silhouette due to a nuclear bomb test in Nevada. It was eerie. While one of Wally's gliders was being towed, I talked the Stearman pilot to take me along – my first ride in an open cockpit airplane. Normally this wasn't allowed because of the extra passenger weight in the tow plane. The Stearman was a powerful radial biplane and the tow went up very well.

The Loewens, Carol and I are lifelong friends. One time Wally and Esther asked their five children who they would want to live with if something happened to them. With virtually one voice they said they wanted to live with Harold and Carol. We have always remembered that affectionately.

Their son Paul and I had a special relationship. I had purchased a used 59 Harley Davidson Sportster after we returned to Sunnyvale in 1957 and later Paul purchased one too. He was an excellent rider.

We also met Jack and Vi Boldt, who lived on a fruit ranch. Jack had an old Harley Davidson, 1934 74 cu. in. motorcycle in his barn covered in dust. We looked at it and he decided to sell it to me after I thought I could have some fun with it. Jack and I made a deal and I had a motorcycle. This was now my second Harley-Davidson! It gave me much relaxation.

Wally and Esther invited us to worship at the Dinuba Bible Chapel in a migrant worker camp a short distance west of Dinuba. This was a very enriching and growing Christian experience. Wes Neufeld was the pastor. We became friends of the Neufelds also. Wes has gone home to be with his maker.

As I mentioned earlier, those years in Reedley profoundly impacted my life. The relationships that developed as a result of these traumatic six months are still precious to me. My wife learned principles from the Kings View social worker that she still remembers. The actual side benefits, aside from my recovery, have really been life- changing, naturally for the better. I can today thank God for this time and I am firmly convinced that God meant it for our good.

Regarding this chapter in our lives I am reminded of the places we lived in Reedley. After I was hospitalized, Carol needed to learn to drive our '55 Chevy four-door Bel Air, since she hadn't learned to drive when I married her. The hospital arranged for a Mrs. Jost to teach her how to drive our Chevy and Carol received her California license. Carol located a very small studio apartment that Joe and Bertha Becker, a dear couple, were renting and she moved in. Down the alley was a young mother with two small boys, Ethel Kleinsasser, whose husband, Willis, coached at the academy. We became good friends and Ethel taught Carol many recipes to save money and stretch out provisions. She also let Carol babysit her boys and then fed her, as our budget was "zero".

We continued our relationship with Willis and Ethel when they lived in Glendora where Willis was teaching. When our daughter attended Azuza Pacific University, we visited them several times. A few years ago they moved to Reno and we have visited them there.

Later, in Reedley, we rented a house on Washington Avenue. A few days later a Sheriff's deputy came to the door with his gun drawn and asked us what we were doing in this house. We had paid the first and last months rent. It seemed that the house belonged to a veteran and his loan agreement specified he could not rent the house out. We contacted a lawyer, Myrtle Burgess, and we could legally remain for two months since we had paid the first and last months.

Then we located an older but well maintained house from a Mrs. Jost on 1405 F Street. This was a comfortable place. We remained there until 1957 when we moved back to Sunnyvale into a duplex since our house was still under lease.

Before we decided to return to Sunnyvale, I had another kidney stone attack and was hospitalized at St. Agnes Hospital in Fresno. The urologist inserted a catheter and just let me lay in the bed of a four-bed ward, seeming not to care to treat me! I got impatient and my mates in this ward and I decided my doctor really wasn't proactive, so I called my urologist at the Palo Alto Clinic and they accepted my case. They told me to bring the latest x-ray with me and they would treat me. I dismissed my St. Agnes urologist, he removed the catheter and we drove to Palo Alto. The Palo Alto Clinic urologists examined me and hospitalized me in the Stanford Hospital and decided to remove the kidney stone. This time everything went well. They exited the catheter just below the navel and when I was discharged, my three-year bout with chronic prostatitis was also cured with medication, praise God! I had several more attacks but thankfully I could always pass the stones.

In 1971 I had a surgical repair for a hydrocele and the only related issues today are pain in the right kidney and the minor prostate issues old men deal with. I had a TURP Prostate procedure in December of 2011 and it was successful. At age eighty-six I hadn't had a kidney stone attack for thirty years or more. However, a month ago I developed severe back pain, and a scan has shown kidney stones in *both* kidneys, so I am now awaiting laser surgery.

My first job returning to the Bay Area was with Westinghouse Electric in Sunnyvale as a horizontal boring mill machinist on the swing shift for a year.

In 1959 Varian Associates in Palo Alto hired me and I was employed there for thirteen years. It was a fascinating time for me. The only fly in the ointment, so to speak, was in 1961.

To finally conclude this chapter of some of the vicissitudes of our world, in 1961 when I had been employed at Varian Associates in Palo Alto as an experimental machinist, I decided to take evening classes at San Jose City College to study Klystron tube technology. Successfully completing this course would lead to advancement to senior tube technician and perhaps even to master tube technician with a much better salary. After a few weeks of school, I realized some of the technical subjects were a stretch for me so I reluctantly dropped out. This disappointment was almost more than I could accept. Instead of maturely moving on without any trauma, it got the best of me and I completely withdrew.

I had to be admitted to San Jose Agnew State Hospital in the fall of 1961. I had no knowledge of my surroundings. Soon electric shock treatments were prescribed and I had a series of thirty or more treatments and thank God I slowly recovered. The turning point that shall always be remembered was when the staff psychiatrist would invite twenty-five or thirty of us recovering patients to be seated in a large circle. He sat among us and did his best to draw us out in order that we would verbalize our feelings.

One session I will never forget, he elicited a response from me and he carefully responded and continued his discussion. After some time he mentioned to the group my name and how I had responded to his discussion. This recognition of my response seemed to make me feel that I did have self-worth. I have never forgotten the recognition I got from him. We all need recognition and my parents simply couldn't, or didn't, feel comfortable complimenting me for good grades or good job performances on the farm.

I worked for a while in the treatment recovery room but this was not agreeable because some fellows had convulsions when they recovered. I asked to be transferred to work in the diet kitchen, transferring meals to designated patients. I enjoyed this work and it was good therapy.

During this time my recovery was taking place and soon the staff suggested I could be discharged, particularly if I could resume my employment at Varian Associates in Palo Alto.

My company insurance coverage paid a maximum of $50 a day benefit for at least six months. The Agnew Hospital, being a state hospital, charged $8 a day. So my stay for the entire six months was covered in full; also, I received $25.00 state disability insurance coverage a week, which my wife put into a savings account for me.

Upon my discharge, Varian gladly gave me my job back and I resumed a satisfying relationship. When I left the hospital, I remember making up my mind that I would endeavor to do everything possible to keep from ever having another nervous breakdown issue. I was told to see a psychiatrist at the Palo Alto Clinic where our doctors were and I saw him on no more than six or eight visits. I needed no medications.

In retrospect, as I returned to a normal home, work and social life, one thought has never left me and it began to really help me evaluate those traumatic six months. Carol's belief in me and her love and amazing complete support, the love of God and His word, and support of our El Camino Mennonite Brethren Church people in Santa Clara and our families helped me formulate a determination that this would be the last time I would succumb to the above illness. History has proven in

---

over 40 years that God is faithful. My wife has wholeheartedly and lovingly upheld me. Thank God I have been healed of mental illness! Carol says that the advice she received from the social workers at both Kings View and Agnew State Hospital was "*I need to take one day at a time!*" This advice has served me well and I still endeavor to practice it.

While I was laid up, Carol was employed in an office at FMC Corp, personnel records section and finally in charge of people (one half of the alphabet) for insurance coverage. By 1963 we had saved enough cash to pay off my parents and Carol's parents who had loaned us money in 1955 to pay the expenses at Kings View in Reedley. When I was there I had very little insurance, it soon ran out and we continued to get deeper and deeper in debt. Now, eight years later, we could pay off our parents in full with interest. This was a great relief to both of us and I know it also contributed to my complete recovery.

In 1971 I was operated on at the Stanford Hospital in Palo Alto for a repair procedure that was necessitated by repeated kidney stone surgeries. As I was recovering, one evening Carol visited me and I could immediately discern she was stressed. She said Alton had died. He was a very favorite male cousin, four days younger than I was; he and I were very close. He farmed with his wife and they had four lovely children. He suffered a cranial aneurism and passed away in days. I couldn't attend his memorial service.

December of 2009 I suffered a heart attack and three stents were inserted at Kaiser Hospital in Santa Clara. My recovery has been uneventful.

December 2011, because of an inability to urinate, a TURP prostate procedure was required, and like all men who have experienced this procedure have told me, "it's no fun". My patience wore a little thin, but five or six weeks later my recovery was virtually complete and I thank God for a complete and satisfactory recovery.

It has taken me years to say "thank you God, my Father, for these tough times." As a willful person there were many lessons I needed to learn and when I reminisce, I don't know if God would have obtained my attention if these traumatic issues hadn't occurred. Formerly I thought that I received more than my share of being laid up because of illnesses. Now years later I believe I am on safe ground when I strongly believe not one person in God's creation has not had serious health issues and/or other life changing adversities. I believe everyone has had as bad or worse issues as I had.

In retrospect, these difficult experiences have made me, I believe, a better, more well-rounded individual. Even though at times it seems a stretch, I truly believe my life has truly been blessed, particularly because of the numerous dear friends we befriended and the many contacts we made.

Today I really believe I am a better person for having to experience the tough times and that we have made amazingly loving friendships. The scripture verse that often comes to mind is that God meant it for good (Genesis 50:20).

Having read a number of Aleksandr I. Solzhenitsyn's books I shall always remember that he said "a people needs defeat just as an individual needs suffering and misfortune; they compel the deepening of the inner life and generate a spiritual upsurge."

Chapter 15
Business Ventures

MENNONITE HERITAGE EVOKES A LIFE OF WORK; TOILING TO PROVIDE AN ADE-
quate living for one's family, whether it be on a farm or in the city. Idleness or lazi-
ness is not considered virtuous – rather a hard-working ethic is promoted. Over the
years I changed jobs often, seeking a career where I felt fulfilled, but I seldom spent
more than one day between jobs!

The first full-time business venture that I embarked on was an opportunity that
I heard advertised when I was working for a Mountain Lake Trucking Company.
Adent Brothers, a truck brokerage business in St. Paul, Minneapolis had a contract
to supply truck loads of eggs to be delivered to Bayonne, New Jersey and shipped
via ocean-going freighters to Europe. In 1950, only a few years after the war's devastation in Europe, this commodity was still required in the mainland of Europe,
particularly Germany.

I purchased a used Federal gasoline engine powered truck for a down payment
of $1,700 and contracted with Adent Brothers of St. Paul, MN and Benton Harbor,
Michigan. The brokers provided 32 foot refrigerated vans and the owner operators
backed and connected their tractors onto fully loaded trailers with manifest in hand
and headed for Highway 30, all two lanes, except for only 140 miles of toll road
between Irwin and Carlisle in PA. After delivering the payload I would pick up
freight for the Twin Cities from either Boston or Atlanta.

All of my trips were uneventful except one. On a run through the Kentucky blue-
grass country, I was traveling nearly sixty miles an hour with a 30,000 pound load
down a hill and lo and behold, a farmer in a pickup truck, without looking, came

onto the two lane road traveling the same direction I was. This was scary. My mind immediately alerted me to three alternatives (there was an approaching vehicle I must avoid): I could drive in the ditch, rear-end the slow moving farmer's pickup, or try to accelerate and pass the pickup truck. Thank God, He heard my prayer; I decided to attempt to pass the pickup and just barely avoided the oncoming vehicle. Whew! Thank God for His protection!

Twice returning to St. Paul with a load of freight the rig's engine ran erratically, both times at Fort Wayne, Indiana. At a truck stop I heard that a truck repair concern located in an alley could take care of my truck. Their name was Sipes. They allowed me to do the simple "wrench work" and they finished the skilled technical repair. On my last of four round trips, again I broke down, believe it or not at Fort Wayne! I only had sufficient money to get me to St. Paul. If I paid the mechanic in full I wouldn't have cash to get to my home base.

They asked if I had collateral. Well, I had a very nice Gruen Curvex wrist watch my parents had given me for my high school graduation. I also carried a nearly new dress sports jacket and slacks. They accepted these items as collateral and I was on my way again. These items are still in Fort Wayne.

As mentioned in a previous chapter, I had already decided that this fourth trip was my final trip to New Jersey. The brokers paid me nineteen cents a mile and it was difficult to make a living at that rate. I delivered the truck to the dealer where I had purchased it, gave him the keys and located a streetcar and traveled to the Broker. He said my father had called and wanted me to come home because my mother was in the hospital recovering from surgery. Then I rode the streetcar to Fort Snelling and stuck out my thumb to hitchhike to Mountain Lake. I don't think it was long before a semi truck and trailer stopped, the driver asked where I wished to go, and I replied Mountain Lake, 140 miles southwest. The driver was a well-dressed matronly lady who said she was headed to Sioux Falls, So. Dakota. She owned the rig and a fleet of trucks. She was a very good driver, as good as the best! She took me all the way to Mountain Lake within a block of my parents' house.

So this venture, hopefully my first business venture, left me with a negative cash flow of $1,700. Nevertheless as time went on this was the first of three attempts at getting ahead by venturing into entrepreneurship, and this first venture had lessons to teach me.

My second opportunity to develop my own business occurred in 1955 in Sunnyvale, California. I had completed two and a half years as a machinist at Western Gear Works in Belmont when I discovered an opportunity to subcontract with a producer of redwood products. These were mostly used in gardens, some homes, etc. The baskets, tubs and containers were constructed of various sizes of redwood slats.

A short time before I had seen an ad in the San Jose daily paper where a fellow wanted to sell a complete shop of woodworking machinery. He had retired from his shop and was moving to Italy. He wanted $400 for all of his equipment. I didn't want all of it, but he insisted on selling all. I purchased all of it and began my business making redwood slats in our one-car garage in the house we had purchased in 1953 in Sunnyvale.

It soon became apparent it would not be easy to make a living, even if I worked long hours, six days a week; and the whole house seemed to smell of redwood saw dust and the dust seeped everywhere, especially the garage. After a few weeks I gave up on this endeavor.

My third and final business venture began as part time in 1966. We had purchased a new tract house in a nice subdivision in 1963. In becoming acquainted with our neighbors, one fellow had a responsible job at Litton Industries, Electron division in San Carlos. When he learned that I was a machinist and interested in having my own contract shop business, he suggested he could possibly help me get a contract salvaging "cooker tubes" for microwave ovens manufactured by Litton.

This appeared to be an opportunity I should consider. I proceeded to purchase a used Bridgeport vertical manual Milling machine in good condition. Carol's father sold me his Logan 12 inch manual lathe with a turret that he had purchased new. I had already located two Delta drill presses and a pedestal grinder and soon I located a vertical band saw.

My neighbor made the necessary connections with his company and we were very pleased with the first account for our fledging business. We were immediately profitable.

Beginning in 1966, Carol and I called our new company "Voshage Machining". There were several reasons we established our own business. For me the overriding desire was that I was my own boss and I could call the "shots". This desire had percolated since high school years.

We moved to Saratoga in 1967 after a fellow at Varian Associates, my employer in Palo Alto, described the home he wanted to sell in Saratoga. I inspected the place and announced to my wife that I had found a place with a four and a half car garage of over 1,000 sq. ft. After she saw it she was horrified. (Our new home was freshly landscaped and comfortably set up the way we wanted it).

When I showed Carol the place in Saratoga she could not imagine moving there. The wife of the owner was going blind, he smoked and they had a dog. The one-third-acre yard was vastly overgrown and the house needed work, particularly the interior. It had two fireplaces, the newest one with a large brick hearth, very well built in a remodeled double garage turned into a family room. The only saving grace reason to even think of relocating was the large garage for my growing business. Our daughter, Lisa, was a crawling baby and the house necessitated serious cleaning, repainting, new carpeting and fumigating! It needed a lot of TLC. When the carpets were removed, fleas were jumping everywhere.

We did make an offer and it was accepted. We purchased the house directly from the owner. He dealt with an attorney and I talked to several experienced real estate brokers for advice. When the deal closed there were no surprises.

It soon became apparent after we moved that the large garage was a distinct advantage to grow my business. The large lot was also of benefit, it was large enough to contain several 32' motorhomes, and we had one for a few years. Since the lots in this location were large, we had plenty of privacy, which we enjoyed. We also had good neighbors.

From 1967 to 1972 I operated the contract machining business part-time as I was still employed at Varian Associates in Palo Alto. In Central Research a photo-lithographic facility had been installed and another senior technician and I were in charge. The PhD scientist I reported to had me develop silicon circuits on a small wafer. It was a very fascinating discipline and I shall always cherish learning how semi-conductors are manufactured.

Harvey Byrd, co-worker at Varian Associates and
an employee in our backyard shop.

I almost hated to terminate this interesting phase of my employed life. In order to fully utilize the potential of my business, I resigned the Varian position in 1972.

Thus began eighteen years, probably the most challenging and "mind boggling". Frankly, until I had been in business a few years, particularly after we moved and became "legitimate" in a rented facility in 1980, I had never really faced issues and vicissitudes of the business world: such as paying rent for a building space, paying all necessary benefits of full-time employees, dealing with government regulations, fire department's rules, etc., and last but not least, the need to develop more customers and accounts and dealing with customer's purchasing agents and personnel. I had a lot to learn and occasionally had to deal with surprises.

We remained in this 3,300 sq. ft. space for ten years. Regardless of the stress and demands, I would do it again in a heartbeat! My DNA expects me to be independent.

In retrospect, what I remember the most are my outstanding employees and excellent customers and buyers.

In the mid 1980's Charlie Mitchell, a mechanical engineer, visited us and asked if I would be interested in being introduced to a purchasing agent at Quantum, a successful disc drive manufacturer. I thought it over and we developed a satisfying relationship with the buyer at Quantum. Charlie Mitchell's father had been the personal physician to the David Packard family. David Packard was a partner of the Hewlett Packard Company. One day Charlie asked me if we could make several metric parts for David Woodley Packard, the son of the co-founder of Hewlett Packard. Charlie had grown up with the Packard children and knew them well. David Woodley Packard was a PhD classical Greek, Hebrew and Latin language scholar and had created a computer dealing with these languages. He needed some parts for his computer and we accommodated him when he came by and introduced himself.

The goal of my business of course was to make a decent living. My wife, Carol, managed the business office, payroll, payables, receivables, and drove to pick up materials as well as delivered finished parts to customers, so I had no surprises there. I performed sales, marketing, purchasing and selling of equipment and hiring of personnel. The maximum number of employees we had was twelve. We had some good years, some down years, but always managed to "make" payroll, pay taxes, living expenses and remain viable. For one down year we lived off our savings, didn't even contribute to social security. At one time interest rates on business loans were 23 percent. Our low house payment was a primary factor in surviving this downdraft.

Hardinge high-precision toolroom lathe.

Before we moved to a rented facility we had filled our large garage with equipment. In the late 1970's we purchased a new Hardinge computer-controlled lathe with automatic stock bar feed. I could run errands and the machine would make parts while I was away. Since the garage was full of machines, we needed to move in order to expand the operation. In 1980 we rented and moved to a 3,300 sq. ft. facility and purchased another Hardinge computer-controlled lathe and hired full-time employees. Needless to say, our overhead escalated and our profit margin decreased. These ten years were an eye opening learning experience for me.

Slowly we learned how to deal with the reality of our position and again we became profitable, after one tough year. We added to our customer base when we acquired a medical imaging manufacturer. Another time an engineer walked in and asked us to bid on a part for the Apple "Lisa" computer. These parts, which we successfully made, were shipped to Carrolton, Texas. We had a good relationship with the engineer and Apple.

In early 1981, I worked alone late until 1:00 or 2:00 a.m. and the next morning at 6:00 a.m. I got a phone call from our employee who opened the shop. We had been robbed! They had broken a window and ransacked the place, stealing measuring tools and rifling an employee's precision tool chest. It was devastating! Fortunately we had good insurance, even covering employee's tools. We documented the stolen inventory (over $35,000) and it was promptly paid. We bought new tools and were back in business (without our measuring equipment we had to shut down for 2 days).

Bridgeport milling machines: employees (L) Chris
Archuleta and (R) Carmine Buonaiuto.

At one time in 1986 a neighbor wanted to buy me out. He operated the business 24 hours, five days a week and Carol was paid to manage the office. He didn't come up with a down payment; he only paid us as if we were his employees. After a month or so he informed me that he couldn't "make" payroll. I saw things weren't progressing too well, so I hired a locksmith and we changed the locks. Now *I* was in control of business, building and machines.

One of the ways I handled the stress of our business was to get outdoors: 1. I would ride my 15-speed bicycle up the Santa Cruz Mountains to the Saratoga Gap at Skyline without a rest stop, 2. I took long hikes in Saratoga alongside the railroad tracks, and 3. I would go camping alone over a weekend in our truck/camper at Big Sur and hike on the steep trails. I was at my leanest and these activities really helped me deal with the stress of operating a full-time business.

After ten years at this location, I was no longer as enthusiastic as I had been earlier. I was now sixty-three years old and had been in business twenty-four years and that seemed to be adequate. I had achieved my dream of so-called independence, but the financial rewards seemed to exact a price. In observations of how shop owners and other business owners have dealt with the pursuit of success, I have come up with a little saying, "The pursuit of money can be expensive; it is seldom cheap." Numerous times I have seen families split up because I think they are too narrowly focused in the pursuit of financial success. Carol and I never considered paying that high a price for success.

In May of 1990 Carol and I had meetings with Lloyd Ashman, an auctioneer and industrial equipment appraiser. I had noticed that the business climate was showing signs of fatigue and since our equipment and house were paid for and also Lisa, our daughter, had graduated from Azusa Pacific University in May, Carol and I decided that this could be a good time to move from our business world. Even though we were debt free we weren't quite ready for retirement.

We nevertheless held the auction on June 27, 1990. It was well attended and we were very satisfied with the results; and we have never looked back. A computer-controlled milling machine I purchased new in 1985 for $70,000 sold for $60,000 after five years of use. A Bridgeport vertical manual milling machine, with all accessories, I purchased new in 1984 for $10,000 sold for $10,000! We were very grateful the sale went well, and it was well attended. As an aside, I attended the auction and had a very good time. It simply was the right time to "move on to better things". Carol also attended the auction and she also enjoyed herself. She really poured as much of herself as I had of myself into our venture and I think we had many similar emotions on the day of the sale. Both of us were ready for new opportunities and challenges and we were open to God's leading.

When we auctioned our business, Voshage Machine, Inc. in June of 1990, I was left with lots of free time that I didn't quite know how to handle. It wasn't long until I learned a number of contract shops similar to the one we had operated were willing to hire me on a temporary basis. After working for five companies, a few months here and a month there, Ken Friesen, a general contractor friend from Lincoln Glen Church, and I were visiting. He was completing a 4,000 sq. ft. house and his journeyman carpenter had quit. The house was unfinished, only a shell. He decided to hire me to help him finish the house, so I worked for him three months. This was a very satisfying experience for me.

Harold working at a lathe after retirement for a personal project.

Through this training experience I learned some finishing skills, how to install premium double-paned windows, etc. When Carol and I had the opportunity to help at Echo Ranch Bible Camp, north of Juneau, Alaska, this skill came in handy and with the assistance of two men we installed all of the Anderson windows on two floors of a large personnel and office building. The numerous other volunteer ventures I took part in are the subject of another chapter. Ken Friesen also hired me for remodel jobs and assorted construction work. He was an outstanding Christian brother and an excellent employer.

Sometime in 1996 and 1997 a successful machine tool dealer and I developed a good working relationship. I represented him to shop owners that needed equipment. Carol and I traveled to Alaska in a motorhome and we paid for the entire four-month trip with commissions I received.

This company, Performance Machine Tools, and I still have a good working relationship, both with the owner and his son. They have an excellent business and since I am not on the payroll, they only pay me when I sell a machine. This arrangement works very well for all of us. My retirement income is modest so I am motivated to enhance our income whenever possible. So far our budgeting had paid the bills.

In September of 2011 a very successful fifty-man shop owner mentioned to me that he would like to sell his machine shop. He was over seventy years old and he really was ready to move on. He had signed on with a professional business broker and in nearly two years he had not been able to put together a deal.

Well, I put on my M+A hat (mergers and acquisitions) and, yes, I had an interesting challenge. It seemed to be that the network I had established could pay off.

The first prospect I contacted was very interested. He had a 100+ man shop. He was very successful (he had worked for me in our backyard part-time in the late 1970's when he was in high school). We performed due diligence and everyone thought the deal would be a slam-dunk. The reason the seller's business was very desirable to a number of successful shops was that he had a very desirable medical device company account and these are not easy to form initially.

We worked on all of the due diligence, non-disclosure agreements ad infinitum, and after five months the seller walked away, so back to base one. I located another fellow I knew who had a 500-man company and also a division in Viet Nam and we did due diligence again. He decided it wasn't quite what he wanted.

Another fellow I've known for a number of years, also very successful, showed interest immediately. We negotiated the terms for several months and approximately thirteen months from when I first began negotiating with the first interested party, the transaction closed to everyone's satisfaction on October 1, 2012.

A side note to relate how contract shops become and remain profitable is that they must develop a customer or account base that will bring in enough revenue to pay rent, employees, machines, benefits, taxes and allow the owner to pay his living expenses and hopefully develop a retirement program. Silicon Valley is an incubator for many hundreds of contract machine shops. Today a significant driver of the overall Silicon Valley economy is the Medical Device Industry. There are many medical device manufacturers here, making it a great industry. Many stories can be written concerning the benefit of these companies to the Bay Area economy.

In 2009, after a heart attack, I needed three stents inserted into the heart area, one artery was 97% blocked. When the surgeon was preparing to seal the femoral artery I asked him how he was intending to do that. He said he had several options. I asked him if he had the device developed and manufactured by Perclose Co. in Redwood City, CA and he said he had this device as an option. It was a hand-held device that sutured the artery. He proceeded to utilize this tool to close the artery. (Some time ago I had sold this company a new surface grinder.)

A few months ago, a dealer of solid carbide end-mills asked me to represent him to large successful contract machine shops. Since I know many shop owners, I accepted his offer. He and his staff had designed and produced very impressive catalogs of the products he represented.

He gave me catalogs and samples of the end-mills to present to prospective companies. I gave this opportunity a fair try. Soon I discovered that at this time, early 2013, the contract job shop business has some issues. I also discovered the large shops, since they have a lot of "clout", could virtually demand and obtain discounts. My company wasn't willing to deal that much and, with the high expense of fuel in driving, I only got paid when I made a sale and no expense money, so I terminated this relationship the end of February 2013.

There are two or three part-time ventures that I am still involved in. So that pretty much takes care of what my late jobs are now. At 86 years of age I am determined to stay active in sales; however, I want to be able to select my favorite venues.

Looking back over my work history, I am grateful to my Mennonite heritage for teaching me a solid work ethic, and to my God for granting me stamina so that I could feel satisfaction in the work I have accomplished.

Chapter 16
Mentoring

IN RETROSPECT IT HAS BEEN GRATIFYING TO RECALL THE RELATIONSHIPS WE
were able to develop and nourish with young men as a result of hiking events and
our contract shop business. It was important for me, a Mennonite Christian, to offer
fair benefits and pay as well as caring about their personal and spiritual development as they matured.

In 1969 I was invited to accompany a fifty-mile hike to help assist two boy-scout
leaders in charge of six high school-age scouts. My wife's cousin's husband was the
leader, their younger son, Mark, was one of the scouts. One of my assignments
was to lead devotion and prayer for each meal. We began this trek from Tuolumne
Meadows in Yosemite Park and proceeded to walk past Vogelsang Peak, climbed it
and on past Merced Lake and onto the Lyell Fork Pass. We hiked at least sixty-miles.

Mark Blalock, grade 8 in 1968.

Two of the six fellows were cross-country athletes and none of us could keep up with them. It was a joy to observe their accomplishments – they could hike! As a result of this week's experience, Mark and I became much closer.

Not long after this time it was my privilege to encourage him to accept Jesus Christ as his personal savior. Forty-three years later he is the husband of a fine Christian lady with four grown children. He is a great father and provider. The children are Christians and active in their respective churches. Their son, the oldest child, is married and has a good job. He is a college grad. The three daughters are fine Christian young ladies all in college. They have each done overseas Christian volunteer work.

There were many memorable experiences and vistas on our hike we could observe and explore. One view I'll never forget was of Half Dome from the top of Vogelsang Peak. Having observed Half Dome from many locations and angles, this view is like no other. Fortunately I had a fellow take a picture of Half Dome from the top of Vogelsang Peak. I happen to be in this view, which is a highlight of the hike to Lyell Fork. We rested at two High Sierra camps operated by the Yosemite Park and Curry Company, the first one was Vogelsang Camp, the nearest to Tuolumne Meadows. We adults asked the fellows to order milk shakes and they soon discovered they weren't available. (We adults were a little mean.) From there we continued to Vogelsang Peak and to Merced Lake High Sierra Camp.

*Harold atop Vogelsang Peak with Half Dome behind
him – Boy Scout hike in Yosemite (1969).*

On our way to Lyell Fork and Isberg Pass we were amazed at the High Sierra scenery. This trip truly helped me bond with Mark and we are very close.

When Carol and I developed our manufacturing business we employed a number of high school boys and they worked for us part-time most of the time. Every single fellow showed us much potential and it was an excellent opportunity to learn how to become an employer and a mentor to young men.

Ron, one of the young men of our Santa Clara church, asked me for a job when he was sixteen and bussing tables at a restaurant. He immediately caught on to my instructions, his work was very accurate and his production was very adequate. He stayed with us all through his high school years and then he enrolled at San Jose City College and studied Machine Technology, earning a two-year associates degree. He was very fortunate to study under Ron Witherspoon, who later developed a 100-man highly successful contract manufacturing company.

After Ron graduated from San Jose City College with a two-year degree, he decided to attend Fresno Pacific University in Fresno and pursued a degree in business administration. He completed the requirements for a BA in business and while he attended college he worked for us part time. When he graduated with a BA he had very little debt and in a short time, while he was employed with us, his debt was paid. He worked for us several years and left to broaden his resumé and obtained a good job with a floppy disc manufacturer. In a few months he was promoted to be the manager of the Model Shop. He gave us an opportunity to bid on work for his company.

To broaden his experience more he left for another challenge at an electronics manufacturer. He stayed there for some time and then he decided to start his own contract shop. This venture has been very successful. A few years ago he purchased a computer-controlled milling machine, which has broadened his capability. This business has made him a better-than-average income and has helped him pay for his son and daughter to get degrees in Architectural Engineering from Cal Poly at San Luis Obispo, CA. He has developed a very successful business and he and his wife are very active at Lincoln Glen Church in San Jose.

A neighbor boy we hired when he was still in high school made the most of his opportunity with us. He was bright, hardworking and stayed with us seven years. When we moved in 1980 he graduated from high school and he worked full-time. We taught him how to program computer-controlled machines and he was soon better than I was.

By this time we had hired programmer machinists so one day I decided to persuade him to leave our employment and get a college education. He was not happy. However he matriculated at West Valley Junior College and obtained his two-year degree. Then he enrolled at Cal Poly in San Luis Obispo and studied mechanical engineering. He graduated with honors and interned at IBM's large San Jose facility and then in fall was hired by Lockheed Missiles and Space in Sunnyvale. During the ten years he worked there they sent him to study in the Master's program of Mechanical Engineering at Stanford University in Palo Alto. He earned his Master's degree in Mechanical Engineering. Lockheed paid virtually all of his costs.

He invited us to his graduation at Stanford University and wrote a note thanking me for encouraging him to seek a quality college education in mechanical engineering.

Another young man who worked for us and has done well was Ed. He was well into his apprentice program with a large Santa Clara company and he was hoping to broaden his experience by performing more short-run work. He inquired at our company and when we had researched all of the possibilities the Apprentice Committee agreed to allow him to transfer to our company and complete the program with us. He turned out to be an excellent employee. We met him at a restaurant several years later after he had moved on and he was most cordial.

Another high school student we hired at our garage shop today has a 100+ man shop in Fremont. Doug has done very well. He keeps on growing his business.

A young married man, Chris, worked for us in Campbell and he was fortunate to be taught the fine points of machining by our excellent foreman, Steve. Chris stayed with us several years and definitely improved his position when a company that sells their own products hired him. He has done quite well.

Another fellow I helped connect with a successful small shop owner was also named Chris. He was a very bright fellow and he was a fast learner. I introduced him to my friend David and he took Chris under his wing and taught him machining and programming. He became very proficient both as a machinist and as a very competent programmer.

In the early 1980's we met a fellow who had a small shop in San Jose and since his business was lagging he asked me if I had any "surplus" orders and it turned out we did. It often is the practice of contract shops to contract out work when they are particularly busy. Through this contract Pete and I became life-long friends and eventually through my encouragement he became a Christian. He has a fine

Christian wife and they are active in their church and they travel the globe, volunteering on occasion.

A young man who worked for us a short time developed his own shop and he is quite successful. I see Mark occasionally and he is very happy in his work.

In the early 1980's we hired a young man who worked next door to our company. I had hired several experienced job shop employees that were looking for part-time work and one of them mentioned he knew of a beginning machinist who worked next door who was very good at setting up and operating Hardinge lathes. These are high precision lathes and we had several manual and two computer-controlled Hardinge lathes.

Our employee invited him to visit us and when he saw the computer-controlled machines he was very impressed. We stayed in touch with him and decided to make him an offer to set up, operate and learn how to write part programs for these machines. He accepted our offer but his present employer didn't want to lose him. We waited a bit and eventually he resigned next door and we hired him.

Jit was one of the finest employees that worked for us. After he was hired, we purchased a new computer-controlled milling machine and he learned how to program this machine as well. A few years later we purchased a new state-of-the-art Hardinge computer-controlled machine and the dealer provided programming classes that Jit attended. In the late 1980's Jit decided to terminate and he received a very good offer from Northrup Grumman Marine Division in Sunnyvale. This plant has some of the largest machine tools in the western U.S. Today Jit's title is Project Manufacturing Engineer Group Leader, CNC Programming Operations Engineering. Jit gave me a tour of this facility and I found it is very impressive. He said that to write a program for the most advanced machine requires three and a half months. Errors are not permitted.

The only fly in the ointment in the last story is that after he left our company, we hadn't trained a back-up programmer. One of our young men was learning but he had a way to go. Programming is not my strong suit so we couldn't continue our operation without another experienced programmer. I saw the "hand writing on the wall" and prepared to exit the business.

An IBM retiree we learned to know after we met his wife and family became a good friend. We had attended the same church with his family but he had not been interested in attending. Some years later they were considering selling their two-story home in San Jose and moving to southern California to be closer to their daughter. During this process I introduced them to a successful realtor and helped them stage the house and prepare the grounds since Brad could do no physical labor. During this time Henrique, a minister friend, invited several of us to a men's Bible study since Brad was now interested in the fellowship and study of God's word. He still wasn't a Christian but very open to discussing Christian issues. After several sessions I asked him if he had read Josh McDowell's books "More Than a Carpenter" and "Evidence that Demands a Verdict". He hadn't, and prior to our next session he had purchased the books. As I remember, with this information and Henrique's instructions and visits, he did accept Jesus Christ as his Savior.

Several years after they moved to Anaheim, his health deteriorated and they moved to a new retirement complex until his death. I drove south for his memorial with another couple that had ministered to him and his wife.

Another young fellow that I could help jump-start his career was the son of a good friend who has a successful job shop in his garage. He was a single parent and did not have an easy time raising his son, Philip. By the time Philip attended high school he had come a long way. Philip was so good at math that his high school encouraged him to take advanced math classes for extra credit at a community college.

In mid-1995 a friend approached me about a startup company that had a contract with the Siemens Company of Richland, Washington to design and manufacture a nuclear fuel rod detector instrument. The large fabricated base was built in Spokane, Washington. The Sunnyvale, California company that had the contract needed machined components and assemblies and didn't know how to contact and work with machine shops to manufacture the hardware they required. My friend worked close to that client and thus began years of interaction and a very satisfying relationship with Luke, the owner. The instrument he had designed measured the strength of nuclear "cold" non-radioactive pellets contained in zirconium alloy sealed tubes less than one half inch diameter and nine feet long contained in a square bundle eight to ten inches square, maybe sixty-four rods per bundle for boiling water nuclear reactors. The first week I worked with Luke I provided the preliminary hardware. As soon as possible they needed automatic loaders and un-loaders for the instrument and they were delivered several weeks later.

After we had contracted with competent suppliers to manufacture automatic loaders and un-loaders of the fuel rods, Luke suggested his key man and I fly to visit the Siemens facility in Richland, Washington. It was fascinating to observe the manufacture of nuclear fuel.

After several months of supplying hardware to Luke, he learned that my supplier had a teenage son who was very bright, attending West Valley College while still in high school at Westmont. He worked part-time producing auto-CAD drawings on a blueprint computer. He needed to obtain a work permit from Westmont High School and this was granted. When the instrument apparatus was assembled and then finally shipped to the Siemens facility, Philip was asked to join Luke in Richland, Washington. He worked on the project at Siemens, actually for Siemens, and also attended computer classes at a college in Richland. These classes were geared towards an electric engineering degree.

All of 2003 he worked for Versadyne in Campbell and later moved to Boise, Idaho. His job now is writing programs to design multilayered circuit boards.

I thank God for the opportunity to be a helper and guide to others, especially these young men who were able to forge a career from their part-time work. And I praise God for His leadership in my own life, so that I was able to lead several others into a personal relationship with Jesus!

Chapter 17
Our Churches

By Carol Siebert Voshage

As previously mentioned by Harold, his home church, First Mennonite in Mountain Lake, and its pastors had a profound influence on his personality and life. When I started teaching in that community, I immediately was warmly included in First Mennonite, even before our engagement and wedding.

While living in Mankato, Minnesota for a few months, we attended the Presbyterian Church of my college years, where we enjoyed the fellowship of my old friends.

As we left for our new life in California, Harold's mother mentioned that the local paper had stated that the former pastor of the Carson–Delft Mennonite Brethren Church had just moved to pastor the Clark Street Mennonite Brethren Church in San Jose, California. This church was located about 12 miles from where we settled in Sunnyvale, so on the very first Sunday after our California arrival, we drove to San Jose to visit this congregation.

When we met Pastor Bill Neufeld and his wife, Elvira, we were welcomed with open arms into the church family – singing in the choir and often partaking of delicious Sunday dinners and "faspas" in the homes of the church family! We never once considered trying another church, because we felt so completely "at home" from the very first visit!

From 1952 to 1955 we were very active at Clark Street. I taught a boys' Sunday School class, helped in Mary-Martha Fellowship, sang soprano in the choir, often sang solos, was in a trio with Elvira Neufeld and Martha Berg, and sang regularly on the Sunday afternoon radio broadcast on KEEN for one year. Harold sang tenor in the choir both at church and on the radio, as well as in Men's quartets and choruses. We were members of the "Young Married" Sunday School Class, where the prayers of our teacher, Hank Regier, were like hearing the voice of God Himself! His voice was *so* rich and his theology was *so* deep!

Our fellowship within the congregation was very special to this young couple just getting started in our married life. We had a Sunnyvale family who lived near us: Elmer and Louise Wiens and two sons, Larry and Jim, became our mentors and dear friends for a lifetime, teaching us by example and quiet words or actions how to shape our Christian home life. For example, Louise talked to me about how their family "tithed" according to Biblical principals, and yet they always had enough for the family "needs". At that time her advice went in one ear and out the other! However, in later years when we had a period of zero income, God reminded us of her example, and we decided to begin then as our income resumed. We found God to be faithful in supplying our needs, even though we set aside a "tenth" of our gross income each month to honor our God. Later it became our joy to be able to give *extra* to the Lord when He supplied abundantly!

Several other San Jose families became very dear to us: John and Alice Dick, Ernie and Frieda Berg, Harry and Rubena Berg, Hank and Eva Regier, Bob and Mary Wiens, Leroy and Marilyn Leppke and Henry and Katie Rogalsky all became lifetime friends. Our cup was full and even overflowing with their love.

When we abruptly left the Bay Area so that Harold could be hospitalized at King's View near Reedley, I was plunged into a different world of deep financial debt, no job, no transportation, and away from friends and family. Pastor Neufeld assured me that if I needed his help, just to call him and he would come. After an exhausting period of extreme heat, a new job, *no* money and extreme stress, I called him and he *did* come and helped to put me in the town hospital, suffering from heat exhaustion, and left me a check for $250.00 sent from our "Young Marrieds" class! That gave us *hope* amid a dark period of life! And when our friends would drop in for a visit, they would often press a $10.00 or $20.00 bill into our hand!

While we lived in Reedley, from 1955 to 1957, we made our church home at the Dinuba Bible Chapel, an outreach of the Dinuba Mennonite Brethren Church to migrant families. We worked alongside our new friends, Wally and Esther Loewen, and were greatly blessed by the friendships we made there. Pastor Wes and Ann Neufeld were the leaders while we attended.

Several years after we returned to Sunnyvale, a family from Dinuba Bible Chapel contacted us regarding their daughter's wedding. It would be held in an Orosi, CA church where there were *no* musical instruments. They asked that the Loewens provide their pump organ, that I would play the preludes, wedding processional, and the recessional on the organ, and that I would sing two solos with Esther Loewen as my accompanist.

I practiced the keyboard music on my piano using no pedal but rather connecting notes by careful fingering, all the while pretending to "pump" with my feet! I sent the vocal music to Esther so she could practice on the organ.

When we arrived at the Loewen home, we gals rehearsed with the organ. Esther was hesitant about the second solo, "The Lord's Prayer", as the accompaniment was all broken chords. I suggested that she play each measure as a chord and hold it for that measure; I marked the music for her. I reassured her that *if* she had any problem I would keep on singing to the end, and she could come in wherever she felt comfortable.

So the men moved the organ to the church, and we gals drove over to begin the wedding. The wedding party arrived late, so I had to play my 15 minutes of music over again and my "pumping legs" got *very* tired. I sang my first solo, and then started the second solo. All went well until almost the end, where Esther "froze": not playing any notes but still pumping vigorously! As I soared into the high notes of "Forever. Amen!" she found her place and played the chord. It came out as a *burst* of sound, and we finished together.

The wedding party insisted that we gals stand in the reception line, and so we frequently heard the comment: "That *ending* was just *so* effective!"

In late 1957 we moved back to our Sunnyvale house and again attended the Clark Street Church. In late 1958 we sang in the choir at the dedication of the new "daughter" El Camino Mennonite Brethren Church (later "El Camino Bible Church") in Santa Clara, and felt God prompting us to transfer our membership there. It was much closer to our home and had a young, vibrant spirit. I played piano, taught Sunday school classes, helped start a Mary-Martha Fellowship, and later I directed the church choir and also a Ladies Triple Trio; I was on the Worship Committee and played the organ. We both sang in the choir. Harold served on the Board of Trustees, on the Church Council, worked with the city and Cabral family to purchase adjoining lots and he arranged the installation of curb, gutter, sidewalk and fence between the church property and the neighboring school.

We enjoyed many new friendships in this congregation: Booth and Margaret Kugler, Cliff and Emma Payne, Marvin and Lorna Gerbrandt, Johnny and Betty Gerbrandt, Eldon and Marcella Claassen, Abe and Lydia Konrad, Al and Ann Dueck, Dick and Lillian Falls, Cal and Marian Ewert, Bob and Lillian Frey, Lenard and Betty Funk, Cliff and Laura Wiens, Ron and Arlene Mack, Arnold and Nellie Bergen, Walt and Mary Franz and many others over our years there.

The Bob Frey family: Lill, Bob, Janelle, Mike, Janet and Jerry at Big Basin Park.

A large group would often go camping together at Big Basin Park nearby. One time we set up camp in a circle around the table and fire pit at group camp. Johnny climbed up in the surrounding trees and put a nylon parachute over the central area. That night as we were ready to go to bed, one couple arrived late, ate supper at the table, and then we all retired to our tents and trailers in a circle around the table. Harold and I had only a tarp laid on the dirt with our two sleeping bags and pillows on top. As we nodded off, I heard a noise at the table, and so I crawled out of my sleeping bag with a flashlight and shone it at the table. I found that the late group had left food out on the table in sealed plastic bins, and raccoons were breaking them open! As I yelled and shone the light on them, they scattered. But I heard a loud "crack" nearby, and suddenly the whole parachute came down on the campsite with a broken tree falling on top of it! I screamed and everyone came running. We called to Harold to see if he was OK, and his muffled voice said he was all right. The men had to cut that tree in half before they could lift it off. Harold crawled out and we uncovered the sleeping bags. A branch had poked into my pillow where my head had been!

Camping in Big Basin, 1972, with Marvin Gerbrandts,
Eddie Kalfayans and others; children fishing.

Being interested in Bible studies and discussions has always been a need in our life. In 1981 we inquired of our pastor at El Camino Bible Church in Santa Clara if we should endeavor to teach a Sunday school class on Proverbs. Pastor John produced a book on Proverbs written by Charles Bridges. He wrote this book in the mid-1800's and it is 745 pages long. It is a Proverbs classic. We decided to teach as a team and we two studied Proverbs like never before. We were amazed at the wisdom that emanates from every verse. Israel's wise men said, "Real wisdom can begin only with recognition that God is the ruler of all life." Chapter 1 verse 7: "The fear of the Lord is the beginning of knowledge." Chapter 4: 5-7: "Get wisdom, get understanding; do not forget my words or swerve from them. Do not forsake wisdom, and she will protect you; love her and she will watch over you. Wisdom is supreme; therefore get wisdom. Though it cost all you have, get wisdom."

We were blessed by the leadership of fine pastors there: Dan Goertzen, John J. Gerbrandt, Robert Radtke, Al Kroeker, John Matson and Jon Anacker.

In 1986 we transferred our membership back to our original San Jose church home, now in a new location and called Lincoln Glen Mennonite Brethren Church. It was joyful to resume fellowship with all of the old friends and to meet many new ones as well. We became active again in choir and on the Mission Board and I led an adapted version of a Ladies Class on "Proverbs".

Pastors who blessed us with their leadership were: Werner Kroeker, Larry Albright, Travis Reimer, Wink Farrand and Bruce Porter.

We remain very thankful for the years we have spent in this warm and loving congregation both as a young couple and as older members!

*Congregation of our beloved Yosemite Chapel
outside for benediction, June 1984.*

We sold our Saratoga home in 2007 in order to move into a cottage at Lincoln Glen Manor, founded by Lincoln Glen Church and located adjacent to the church property. Since my walking has become more limited, Harold attends early service alone at the church, and later joins me for the joyous service at the Manor Chapel. Our chaplain, Victor Klassen, leads us in the familiar beloved hymns, sings uplifting solos, and shares thought-provoking messages with us. We thoroughly enjoy this blessed fellowship.

Carol Siebert Voshage

Chapter 18
Lisa

On an exciting day in February 1967, we received a phone call from our attorney who told us, "You have a happy and healthy baby girl!" When we first saw her, she was also beautiful and she still is to this day!

When we brought Lisa, our daughter, home from the hospital it completely changed our lives and also that of her grandparents. The first time Carol was caring for her, I remember Lisa looking at both of us. She was a darling three-day-old newborn, and her eyes met our eyes as if to say to us, "Are you going to take good care of me?" Needless to say she had us wrapped around her little finger.

Lisa Anne ready for church at 2 weeks (March 3, 1967) with Mom Carol and Dad Harold.

I was nearly forty and Carol, my wife, was thirty-seven. We had been married sixteen years with no pregnancy. Lisa's birth introduced a profound God-given purpose to our lives.

At the early age of 7 months, Lisa was developing a list of clearly spoken words. Her mother kept a diary of her rapidly expanding vocabulary. She loved music, enjoying her own little phonograph and records, as well as having us play classical music on our stereo for her. She soon was singing along and became a very talented vocalist.

Carol has often reminded me that when I came home from work, little six-month-old Lisa tried to get my attention so that I would greet her. When she was walking, she would stand by the screen door watching for me to drive up. When I walked in the house she wanted to be picked up and hugged. What a privileged Dad I was.

*Harold carrying 8-month-old Lisa in back-
pack at Kings River Park, Cedar Grove.*

6 Month old Lisa celebrating her final adoption day with her Daddy, Harold.

When she was three or four she would sit on a stool in my shop and she would draw pictures. She has always had a talent for art. She also has developed an excellent ability in making beautiful ceramic objects on a potter's wheel. Some of her glazes are outstanding.

A few years after she was born, I worked full time in my contract manufacturing business out of our detached garage and she often would observe my production and also amuse herself. When she was in grade school, I taught her how to operate a drill press and to perform basic operations on a high precision Hardinge metal-turning lathe. Lisa has always had an amazing range of aptitudes.

We had a lot of fun playing Ping-Pong, basketball, softball and volleyball, etc. In kindergarten, she often begged me to go to the nearby schoolyard to play. She wanted to show me how agile she was in exercising on the rings, and she really was good. I taught her to catch and bat a ball and she really can hit the ball well. She also could beat a lot of boys in Ping-Pong.

Lisa's special joy was her calico cat "Coonie", who lived with her for twelve years. There was not a mean bone in Coonie, but just fun and a desire to be with Lisa, cuddling and purring. Coonie usually shared Lisa's pillow at night!

We enjoyed watching Lisa's talents develop as she grew: a love for reading, music (singing, piano, flute, viola), bike riding, roller skating, ice skating, swimming, tumbling, gardening, and art (both pottery and painting). As a child she loved to go on rides with me at the County Fair and to drive up in the mountains to cut down our Christmas tree – and then she loved to decorate the tree! She enjoyed "The Nutcracker", her loving grandparents, birthday parties, but NOT braces!

We took Lisa on many trips, visited cousins and relatives in Mountain Lake, Minnesota and dear friends in Omaha, Nebraska.

In 1974 we swung north through Canada, where we three walked around to the back of Lake Louise and hiked up through several snowfields to the "Teahouse of the Plain of the Six Glaciers" at Victoria Glacier for a snack, before retracing our steps back to the hotel – a trek of 7 miles for a 7 year old!

Another high point on that trip was the beautiful Butchart Gardens of Vancouver Island. Lisa relished the colorful blossoms both on that first trip and again when she was a teenager.

Lisa loved camping! When she was in grade school I taught her how to make a bonfire so that she could light it with one match.

Yosemite Valley was our favorite place to camp. When Lisa was little she rode a burro (Dad leading and Mom pushing!), walked up the Mist Trail to Vernal Falls, and enjoyed the scenery and wildlife. She rode in a stagecoach up at Wawona. She watched rock climbers on El Capitan. During teen years she hiked with a group from Tenaya Lake over the top of "Clouds' Rest" (during a hail storm) down to the valley floor. The three of us hiked from Glacier Point down to Illilouette Falls, up to the Panorama Cliffs, across to Nevada Falls, and on down past Vernal Falls to the Valley. She has camped there in sunshine, rain, and snow. And once we three had a room at the Ahwanhee Hotel that faced the view of Half Dome! We share many happy memories of camping, hiking, campfires, and beauty!

One of Lisa's pleasures was to join her friends from all over central California at Hartland Christian Camp in the Sierras each summer, enjoying the outdoor life, making crafts, and making many new friends.

She attended Valley Christian School six years through high school graduation and was an excellent student. She made many friends, sang in the choir, played "bells" and sang in a mixed ensemble. They toured out of state to give programs.

Later she took driver education at her school, received basic instruction and she earned her learner's permit. On weekends I took her to a very large parking lot at West Valley College. She caught on quickly. I'll always remember when she had her license and if I remember correctly, she hadn't "soloed" yet. I gave her the last of a number of driving instructions and I told her, "You are on your own." I had a sporty small Dodge D-50 pickup with a 5-speed manual transmission and I said, "I'll see you when you return." This was her solo ride. She felt she was ready and I concurred. Less than thirty minutes later she returned; beaming she said, "I only killed the engine once." Lisa has become an amazingly proficient driver. In the mid-nineties, when she moved to California from Indianapolis, Indiana, she drove a large moving van and towed a car-carrying trailer over Donner Summit on Highway 80! When she was attending Azusa Pacific University she drove alone many times uneventfully over the Interstate 5 Grapevine Route.

She attended Biola University at La Mirada, California her freshman year of college and sang in the choir. She enjoyed that a lot; they sang classic sacred music.

She stayed home one year after her freshman year, working at Manpower Agency and attended local West Valley College. She matriculated at Azusa Pacific University at Azusa, California and graduated with a major in communications with honors. She sang in the College Choir the year they traveled to London to record their work with the London Symphony Orchestra.

When Lisa graduated from college she was hired at several very interesting companies. One of her first hires was at a Medical Device corporation. She was sent to Atlanta to put together meetings with doctors. This was a new experience for her and she managed this assignment virtually without a hitch.

One of her longest-tenured occupations was her responsibility as Director of Development for Arts Council Silicon Valley. Her charge was to obtain money to both run the organization and to provide funds to award grants to worthy recipients. She did this job nine years very successfully.

One of her accomplishments there was to organize and direct the Awards Banquet, which one year especially honored Irene Dalis, the former Metropolitan Opera mezzo-soprano diva, now finishing her career as director of Opera San Jose. David Woodley Packard presented Miss Dalis the award, and both were honored by a standing ovation of the entire audience. Lisa, who was in charge, handled the luncheon seamlessly.

In April 16th – 30th, 2008, Lisa and I had the distinct privilege to visit Paris, Barcelona and Madrid. We had a great trip to celebrate our birthdays (40 years apart). We visited Normandy, the Eiffel Tower, Versailles and many sights in Paris. In my travels of nearly sixty countries, I have never seen a city quite like Paris.

Lisa and Harold in Paris at the Eiffel Tower celebrating birthdays 40 years apart.

Lisa is an excellent traveler; the one facet I'll always remember is that I kind of relied on her in keeping me on schedule. In Paris when we were waiting to board our high speed train to Marseilles, the train was late so I wandered away to explore, and when the train arrived and passengers were boarding, I was nowhere around; Lisa couldn't locate me. Fortunately I showed up in time but not before I got an earful! I had it coming.

We had an amazing experience on the high-speed train; they served us the same as on an airplane, from aisle carts. We enjoyed Marseilles. The highlight of our trip after leaving Paris was Barcelona. For me probably the epitome of that city was visiting the Cathedral Gaudi designed and built. It is amazing architecturally, inside and outside. Barcelona is a very grand city.

We experienced one disturbing event in Barcelona: we were robbed! As we walked along the street, suddenly a liquid was "spilled" over us, and people rushed out with towels to "help" us clean ourselves off. Lisa refused help and managed by herself, but I allowed them to wipe me down. It wasn't until we returned to our hotel that I realized that my billfold was gone from my upper body pocket! So my small amount of cash, my driver's license, and my charge card were gone! Luckily Lisa had her *own* charge card and could use it for the rest of the trip. What embarrassed us was the fact that we had read the warnings in Rick Steve's books about this exact same type of robbery! I immediately called home and had my charge card cancelled, so I was *not* out any large amount (only the odd cash I was carrying). And we both *still* felt Barcelona was *beautiful*!

We toured Madrid and Toledo also. When we completed our tour of Spain and arrived at Paris to board our Air France 747 plane for SFO, the layover was very short, less than one hour. Lisa and I had to scurry and almost run to make our connection for the flight to San Francisco. We had very little time to spare.

Our only regret on this trip was that we did not have more time to spend in the cities that had so much to offer, particularly Paris and Barcelona.

When I was gone on my travels, Lisa often spent time with Carol on "mini-vacations" at Carmel, Mendocino, Little River, Big Sur Lodge, and most often at a B&B in Cambria. These are "girl-time" trips!

Lisa Cole seaside in Cambria, CA (2013).

Lisa was a joy to raise; she was happy and had such a pleasant manner. Her dress, appearance and surroundings were always tasteful and yet stylish. In spite of hardships and illness, Lisa kept a positive attitude and has emerged from several difficult years with fortitude, grace, and trust in God! She has been a model of Christian conduct to us, her parents! She is not only a beautiful woman, she also has a lovely manner and is thoughtful and considerate to others. We love her as our daughter, as an adult woman, as a Christian, and as a friend!

She is a fine Christian young lady. At the River Church in San Jose she helped lead a young people's Bible study. She loves God's word. She has a beautiful high soprano voice. At our fiftieth wedding anniversary Lisa sang two solos: "Our Love is Here to Stay" and "Always."

These forty-six years of our daughter's life have enriched my life immensely. We go out for dinner together as often as we can and call each other often.

I thank God that we are very close. I am grateful for the God-given privilege I've had to share the continuing pleasure of interacting with my lovely daughter, Lisa. I really believe that the way she has enriched my life has added additional days to my eighty-six years, and that my good health is because of my wife and daughter, who continually reward me with joy and blessings!

Chapter 19
Family Adventures

By Carol Siebert Voshage

IN TODAY'S WORLD WE USUALLY HEAR IN THE MEDIA ABOUT THE BAD EVENTS that happen. Yet in many quiet and ordinary Mennonite homes embracing the Christian faith we would be likely to find *good* events occurring that bring about joy and family unity.

Being parents in a Mennonite home necessarily brings great emphasis on "family life", just as our parents and ancestors found this to be of high importance. This includes not only love, Christian nurturing, music and reading, but also just plain "fun" times spent together. We found that camping and travel drew us closer, in spite of the often-heard "Are we there yet?" complaint!

Over the years, our camping setup evolved from "on the ground", to "in the car", then a tent, later a teardrop trailer, next a travel trailer, then a Lance camper on a one- ton truck and finally a motorhome.

Early days found us often camping at Big Basin in our nearby mountains. Lisa and her friends enjoyed deer, raccoons, campfires, hikes and playing "house" inside hollowed out redwood trees using acorn cups as "pretend" dishes.

Big Sur also was a favorite campsite with hikes up the Ventana trail and very hot, sunny treks up Mount Manuel. Harold and I plodded up Mount Lassen two times, resulting in severe sunburn! Harold and his cousin, Vel, backpacked to Lake Seville in the Sierras, and once Vel hiked with us to the Boole tree, overlooking the Kings River Canyon.

Our "second home" for years was Yosemite National Park, where we camped and hiked and backpacked. Harold and I walked UP for 13.3 miles in one day to camp at Merced Lake, where we enjoyed the high country and helped rangers bury a marauding bear! We also backpacked up to Vogelsang Pass, but gave up due to severe altitude sickness.

Camping in Little Yosemite Valley en route to Half Dome in 1963: Vel Teichroew, Harold & Carol Voshage, Betty & Johnny Gerbrandt, Carol Gerbrandt.

Harold and I, with Vel and friends, spent several days in Little Yosemite valley, where we hiked up Half Dome; I quit just below the cable ladder (sick!), but Vel and Harold made it to the top! Since then, Harold has trekked to the top of Half Dome nine more times, once *without* the aid of the cable ladder! He also has hiked up to the crest of Cloud's Rest (higher than Half Dome) two times alone.

Going up the Cable Ladder on Half Dome.

*Harold atop Clouds' Rest (Yosemite) with Half
Dome behind him at left (1992).*

He has hiked up past Yosemite Falls to Yosemite Point several times, also observing rock climbers on Lost Arrow pinnacle traversing across on ropes!

Lisa also hiked from Tenaya Lake up over Cloud's Rest (in hail, fog, rain and lightning!) with a church youth group.

Later, we three took a bus up to Glacier Point and hiked down to Illilouette Falls, up to Panorama Cliff, and down to Nevada Falls and on down the steep trail to the Yosemite Valley floor. A few years after, Harold's cousin Elaine and I drove to Glacier Point, watched "hang gliders" take off (to soar in space and land on the valley floor), and hiked down to Illilouette Falls, only to almost become trapped in a forest fire as we climbed back up to Glacier Point. Our car was one of the first to leave, and as we drove through Washburn Point area, the fire was already burning across the road. Any people on Glacier Point without a car were ordered to leave "on foot" down the Four Mile Trail! Harold and Lee (Elaine's husband) saw the fire from the top of Half Dome and walked out under the canopy of heavy smoke to the valley floor.

Of course Harold and I were both fascinated by Alaska, and so Harold has been there fifteen times and I a few times less! We enjoyed Southeast Alaska and the Inside Passage both when we worked at Echo Ranch Bible Camp and on numerous cruises. Later we made two summer-long trips to Alaska and Canada by motorhome. The first time we made a side trip to Inuvik in the Northwest Territory, and Harold flew to Tuktoyaktuk on the Beaufort Sea of the Arctic Ocean. The last time we came home via Yellowknife, on the north shore of Great Slave Lake, also in Northwest Territory. This area is unique with rocks everywhere, gold mining in town and bison roaming free along the remote roadway.

On our way north through Alberta's Peace River area, we visited High Level and La Crete, a Mennonite settlement. Harold enjoyed speaking Low German with the shop owners here. This is the northernmost wheat-growing area in North America.

And we drove back once on the alternate to the Al-Can highway: the Cassiar. There is only one native settlement in this two-day section: two-lane road with one-lane bridges. At the southern end we drove west to Prince Rupert on the Pacific Coast, where Harold took a floatplane ride to Kincolith, B.C.; a native couple were flying home with their groceries and supplies from shopping in Prince Rupert.

Other types of adventures have been day trips to the Pacific Coast where we watch for whales migrating; two car trips with Lisa up into the Rockies of Canada and to Vancouver Island; a train trip to Lustre, Montana for the Schmeckfest (lots of fresh delicious cracklings); frequent stays at B&Bs in Cambria and Mendocino and many summer trips back to our "roots" in Minnesota, visiting our extended families and enjoying the reunions with favorite ethnic foods. Closer to home we go each year to the Mennonite Central Committee Sale in Fresno for the pancake breakfast (German sausage), quilt auction (also comforters, afghans, baby covers and wall hangings), ethnic food stands, and most especially meeting old friends from all over the state!

Carol & Harold backpacking in Tuolomne Meadows (Yosemite) in 1964.

These are a few of our "close to home" adventures over the past sixty-two years of marriage. Life is never dull around here!

Carol Siebert Voshage

Chapter 20
Faith Without Works is Dead
(James 2:14-26)

Mennonite Service Organizations

THERE ARE MANY REASONS THAT I AM A GRATEFUL MENNONITE. FOLLOWING are some of the reasons for this gratefulness that become clearer as I grow older.

The Mennonite heritage is biblical. Menno Simons and the early leaders of the Anabaptist movement stressed the need to return to a belief and practice of the word of God in faith in Jesus Christ; 1st Corinthians 3:11, "For no one can lay any foundation other than the one already laid, which is in Jesus Christ." Verses Mennonites also practice are James 2:17, "Faith by itself, if it is not accompanied by action is dead." Part of verse 18 says, "I will show my faith by what I do", Verse 24: "You see that a person is justified by what he does and not by faith alone", and verse 26, "As the body without the spirit is dead, so faith without deeds is dead".

A senior pastor of the Mennonite Brethren denomination was raised as an Assemblies of God member by parents who were successful overseas church planters. I asked him what attracted him to Mennonites and he replied that we stress belief in Jesus Christ for salvation and eternal life, as do the large evangelical denominations, but we also stress helping people in the various programs that we provide.

MCC/Mennonite Central Committee

Edgar Stoesz, Matt Adrian, Harold, and Ben Adrian at Machu Picchu, Peru.

(A lifelong friend and dear brother who wrote the following pages is Edgar Stoesz of Akron, Pennsylvania. He held executive positions with MCC for 35 years. He has probably traveled to more than seventy countries. He was chair of the board of Habitat for Humanity for four years. He is a friend of former President Jimmy Carter. Since his semi-retirement he had worked for Tourmagination, a Mennonite-operated travel agency that hosts tours in Mennonite settlements worldwide. It was my privilege to tour South America with him a few years ago. He has traveled and studied and reached the many Mennonite settlements in Paraguay numerous times. He was the resource person on the trip I was privileged to attend in April of 2002).

About MCC

MCC was organized in 1920 predominately by Swiss Mennonites to minister relief to Russian Mennonites who were at times starving in Russia in the aftermath of the

Lenin-led revolution. It resulted from the consolidation of six relief committees, and thus the name "Mennonite Central Committee". Literally thousands of lives were saved through this effort. Many later immigrated to Canada, Paraguay, Brazil and Uruguay.

Once that need had been ministered to, MCC went into hibernation. Warnings of an approaching war were beginning to be evident as the decade of the 1930's was coming to a close. Wanting to avert the bad treatment given to Mennonite Conscientious Objectors in World War 1, Mennonite leaders felt compelled to work out an alternate program with the government. For this a "central" committee was needed. So the connection was made to MCC, which ended up administering the Civilian Public Service program (CPS) through which 5,000 men served for the duration of the war.

(Author's note: In 1945 I was one of the last Mountain Lake men to be drafted. I was assigned to CPS camp #64 in Terry, Montana. It was a very well managed and administered camp with an outstanding project: constructing irrigation canals, leveling land and operated by the Soil Conservation Service and Bureau of Reclamation. It was a very successful project and was completed. I worked as an engineering draftsman.)

When the war was over, MCC was in the natural position to respond to the horrendous refugee need and help rebuild a war-torn continent. This it did in a major way. Large feeding programs were organized with food collected in the USA and Canadian Mennonite constituency. A PAX program was organized through which young men built houses in Germany. Five thousand six hundred refugees were resettled in Paraguay and Uruguay on four large chartered ships.

Then MCC, under the visionary leadership of Orie O. Miller, took note of the refugee problem resulting from the portioning of Palestine. Next it was widespread starvation in India. All the while MCC stood with the new communities in Paraguay and Uruguay. So it was that MCC was drawn by need to be an instrument of the Mennonite churches in the U.S. and Canada to minister to a needy world "in the name of Christ".

William T. Snyder succeeded Orie O. Miller in 1958 and under his leadership MCC phased from predominately relief ministries to prevention emphasis, better known as "development". Seeing the approaching end of colonialism and with it the need for education programs, MCC initiated the Teachers Abroad Program, directed especially to the African continent. More than one thousand years of service were rendered through this program, mostly in the 70's and 80's.

So it was the MCC we were now joining was maturing, growing and stretching to adjust to the changing needs of the world. This also involved positioning itself within the larger framework of the worldwide Mennonite church.

Mennonite Central Committee is now a multimillion-dollar international non-profit organization that works alongside local churches in 50 countries including Canada and the United States to carry out disaster relief, sustainable community development and justice and peace building, especially in regions torn by war or armed conflict.

MCC also is at the forefront of sustainable programs to provide adequate water supplies at affordable levels.

MDS/Mennonite Disaster Service

Harold wearing his MDS cap.

(Written by Kevin King, who is the Executive Director of Mennonite Disaster Service (MDS) Canada and the United States.)

About MDS

Mennonite Disaster Service (MDS) www.mds.mennonite.net coordinates an organized response to disasters for the Mennonite and other related Anabaptist churches. In keeping with their biblical and Christian service theology, MDS responds to the needs of those affected by disasters in Canada and the United States. The major contribution of MDS is supplying personnel for cleanup, repair and rebuilding operations. As per our mission statement: **Mennonite Disaster Service** is a volunteer network of Anabaptist churches that responds in Christian love to those affected by disasters in Canada and the United States. While the main focus is on cleanup, repair and rebuilding homes, this service touches lives and nurtures hope, faith and wholeness.

MDS places special emphasis on helping those least able to help themselves – that is, the elderly, widowed, handicapped and disabled; people with low incomes; people who are uninsured or families with a single parent. MDS regional and bi-national offices are organized to assist its 50 local units in Canada and the United States in the effective operation of disaster programs.

Although the major thrust of our traditional disaster assistance is in the areas of post-disaster residential cleanup and home building repair and rebuilds, MDS personnel are willing to consider expanding their areas of involvement where there is a need and when a sufficient number of volunteers are available, e.g. assisting municipalities with sandbagging in a flood situation. MDS is primarily a recovery and not an emergency response organization; it provides:

- **Cleanup of residences** after flood, fire and wind damage

- **Recovery assessment** and both **physical and emotional support** to clients

- **Minor/major repair and complete rebuilding of owner-occupied homes** after floods, windstorms and fires

MDS leaders and workers are volunteers *who serve without pay.*

They carry out their disaster assistance activities, supported by the larger regional and bi-national network, in a spirit of cooperation with the various agencies of the government, other non-governmental disaster service organizations, e.g. Red Cross, Salvation Army, World Renew and St. John Ambulance, churches and Interfaith. MDS actively supports the formation and functioning of community-based long-term recovery committees to carry out client casework and bring to the table all agencies with recovery resources.

The MDS organization does not provide resources for housing materials or heavy equipment, anticipating that these will come from other sources. MDS will require no fees for services provided, although support via other charitable organizations, local Interfaith, etc. toward food and lodging assistance for volunteers is welcomed and appreciated.

MEDA/Mennonite Economic Development Associates

(*A brief overview of MEDAS's history* – Written by Wally Kroeker, Editor of "The Marketplace", published by MEDA)

About MEDA

For nearly 60 years MEDA has been a mechanism for Mennonite business folk and others to share their skills and resources with the less fortunate. Sometimes described as a "mission arm" of the Mennonite business community, it has redefined the nature of ministry and whole-life stewardship as it helps people in poverty to build livelihoods that last.

It all began in Paraguay in 1953. Mennonite refugees from Europe had come to Paraguay after World War II. MCC did a great job of helping them with food and shelter, but was not equipped to provide them with capital to establish businesses.

The banks were of no help because they wouldn't risk giving credit to homeless refugees who had no collateral or credit history.

Orie Miller, the head of MCC, knew all about business and the need for working capital. He owned a successful shoe business back in Pennsylvania. He knew how important it was to have productive enterprises to provide an economic foundation for a community. He decided to recruit other Mennonite business folk from North America. He organized trips for several of them to visit Paraguay and see for themselves what could be done. These visitors immediately saw the need, and just as quickly saw a way for them to fit in.

In late 1953, a small group got together in a Chicago hotel and formed Mennonite Economic Development Associates (MEDA). The purpose was to provide capital funds to help individuals in need become self-reliant and economically self- sufficient. Loans would be made at low interest. As they were repaid, other projects would be initiated and new loans made. Board members were assigned to sponsor projects and to visit their partners to provide ongoing counsel.

The first project was the Sarona Dairy in Paraguay's Fernheim Colony. If you go to Paraguay today, and eat breakfast at a four-star hotel in Asuncion, you may be served yogurt or chocolate milk from one of the numerous Mennonite-owned dairies. Today, two-thirds of Paraguay's dairy production comes from the Mennonite colonies.

The next project was a tannery, to make leather from cattle hides. The third project was a shoe factory to make shoes, boots, saddles and motorcycle seats from the leather from the tannery.

Soon MEDA found itself working in various countries of Africa. Eventually there would be more than 100 projects in places like Tanzania, Zaire, Somalia, Ethiopia, Ghana, Kenya and Nigeria, working with the poorest of the economically active.

In 1981, the new MEDA aimed: (1) to help business people see their work as a form of ministry, and thereby integrate their faith with their business and (2) to use the skills and resources of business people to provide business solutions to poverty.

Today MEDA operates numerous programs designed to Create Business Solutions to Poverty. These include financial service programs, production and marketing programs for rural producers, a trading company and an investment arm.

MEDA has also been a force to redefine ministry in daily life, for we see daily jobs as a great place to model what it means to be a follower of Jesus.

Other Mennonite Service Groups

The Mennonite Churches not only preach the Word of God, they also provide several types of services to both Mennonites and to the general public, some worldwide.

A partial list of these other services would include:

- MCC Relief Sales

- Ten Thousand Villages

- International Gift Faire

- Mental Hospitals

- Universities/Colleges

- MCC Thrift Shops

- School Kits

- Retirement Communities

These are the ones that I am most acquainted with.
Following is information about these services.

MCC Sales

Each year, in a number of locations across the country, a sale is held to supply funds for the Mennonite Central Committee (MCC) to pay for its projects.

Our area holds the Sale at Fresno Pacific University the first weekend of April. A huge auction of quilts, comforters, afghans, wall hangings, lap robes, baby covers and other items are sold in the gym. Meanwhile, inside and outside, there are sales of used books, baked goods (zwieback and fritters), dried fruit, ethnic foods, homemade ice cream, German sausage, hand-crafted toys and things too numerous to list! Usually there are some antiques sold or auctioned off as well!

This year, I heard that the quilt auction sales totaled $75,000, and the entire Sale netted over $200,000 for MCC coffers!

Ten Thousand Villages

Ten Thousand Villages creates opportunities for artisans in 30 developing countries to earn income by bringing their products and stories to our markets through long-term, fair trade relationships.

Men and women around the world have a simple dream – to earn an honest living, provide a home, food and education for their children, and to be gainfully employed in a job that brings dignity and joy. Ten Thousand Villages partners with thousands of talented artisans in a healthy business relationship.

Ten Thousand Villages is a non-profit program of Mennonite Central Committee (MCC), the relief and development agency of Mennonite and Brethren in Christ churches in North America.

"Ten Thousand Villages is a nonprofit job creation program of the Mennonite churches of North America," explains a volunteer from San Jose. "We market folk art from 30 Third World countries. Our sales provide full-time, year-round income for fifty to sixty thousand very poor Third World artisans and their families."

The artisans rely on their creative skills for income for many reasons. Some are refugees, while others are the spouses of "disappeared" human rights workers. Sometimes the artisans are illiterate, landless or homeless. What they have in common is a determination to make a better life for themselves and their children. This also helps better their villages.

International Gift Faire

Each year before the Christmas season a sales event is held at Lincoln Glen Church in San Jose, CA to display the handmade wares of artisans around the world supplied by non-profit Ten Thousand Villages. These might be toys, candles, coffee beans, jewelry, pottery, and other hand-crafted items too numerous to mention. These are set up and sold by unpaid volunteers of the church and other interested friends. What a treasure trove for a Christmas gift shopper!

The International Gift Faire is an organization that helps third world crafts people establish their manufacturing ventures by purchasing their products, thereby creating a ready cash market for their goods and providing a livelihood for them. Their products are purchased wholesale and sold retail. Shipping, venue's rent, setup, repacking and shipping unsold items is covered by the price spread.

The only financial benefit for the local church consists of a lunchroom staffed by the church women to raise money for Women's Ministries. We usually have breakfast there, enjoying fresh hot fritters (portzelky) or rolls (zwieback) or home-baked cookies.

This two-day event is one of the largest and most successful in the country, grossing over $80,000!

Mental Hospitals

When Mennonites served as CO's during World War II, they revolutionized the care of mental patients in hospitals where they served. As a result, not only did care become more humane in existing hospitals, but the Mennonites opened their own mental hospitals in the U.S. I was fortunate to seek help for my illness at Kings View Hospital outside Reedley, CA.

This ministry is a blessing to those seeking help for mental illness, especially since this help is very difficult to find in the secular world, due to political choices of state government. Thanks be to God for people who care about those who are suffering in this world.

Universities/Colleges

There are many Mennonite colleges and universities in the U.S. and Canada; our nearest one is Fresno Pacific University in Fresno, California. This excellent school has gained a reputation for its superior training for teachers. School systems are eager to hire graduates into their staff, as they are well prepared for the work. This university is also well known for its math instruction, called AIMS (Assisting Integration of Math and Science).

MCC Thrift Shops

In various towns in the U.S. and Canada are small thrift shops selling used goods that are donated, to be resold to raise funds for MCC relief work.

These stores are called by many names, but the purpose is the same, to bring in funds for relief work around the world.

School Kits

Each year, churches, retirement communities and individuals sew cloth bags and assemble school kits to put inside. These include pencils, eraser, colored pencils, ruler and notebooks to provide the essentials for students to use in school. These kits are distributed to needy students in the U.S. and all over the world.

Retirement Communities

One aspect of Christian life is the care of our elderly. Mennonites have excelled in this area by building many retirement communities to house, feed, and provide care as needed for those who no longer wish to remain in their homes.

We are fortunate to directly benefit from this heritage of care. In 2007 we decided to sell our home and downsized from a large house to a "cottage" (one half of a duplex) at Lincoln Glen Manor in San Jose, CA. The Manor was initiated and built by the Lincoln Glen Church as a place for senior citizens to live without the responsibilities of home upkeep, cooking, cleaning, and with help available when needed. There is *no* expensive "entrance fee" and *no* restrictions as to any religious affiliation. We simply pay rent each month, which includes basic utilities, and are free to enjoy the fellowship of other seniors who have now become our friends, such as our dear duplex-mates, Atlee and Twyla Stroup.

We appreciate the dedication of our executive director, Loren Kroeker, and his caring and helpful staff.

Chapter 21
Volunteering

Service to Others

VOLUNTEER SERVICE IS A MAJOR COMPONENT OF MENNONITE TEACHING. THIS quality of Christian life is *not* focused only toward other Mennonites, but reaches out to mankind in general. Mennonites extend help to the poor, the ill, those devastated by loss or disaster, and to those who are in need of Christian love or just a shoulder to lean on.

I was influenced by the Mountain Lake community and especially by my parents, who were models in giving help to others.

So volunteering gradually became a part of my life over the years and has expanded my world and widened my circle of friendships greatly.

Following is a chronological overview of my years spent in volunteer assistance to those around me and around the world.

I. MONTANA (CPS)

The first time I took advantage of an opportunity to perform meaningful volunteer work was in the fall of 1945. Having been drafted into Civilian Public Service (CPS) in August to Camp #64 in Terry, Montana between Miles City and Glendive near the Yellowstone River, we were invited on a long weekend to install an in-ground water system at the General Conference Mennonite Church, Cheyenne Indian Mission at Lame Deer, Montana. Rudolph Petter had translated the Cheyenne language into English. Alfred Habegger and Malcolm Wenger also were missionaries at this station.

CPSers installed a water system at Lame Deer, Montana (1945).

II. MOUNTAIN LAKE, MINNESOTA (First Mennonite)

The next opportunity to provide labor for a project was in 1948 in Mountain Lake, Minnesota. The new Eventide Home needed beds and a number of beds were available that needed to be repainted. A group of young people, including Melroy Penner, Marvin Bartel and Lila Penner of the First Mennonite Church, accepted this challenge and we subsequently stripped the old paint and varnish and prepared the beds for their new coat of paint.

First Mennonite Youth refurbishing beds for Eventide Home:
Lila Penner, Marvin Bartel and Melroy Penner (1948).

III. CALIFORNIA MENNONITE DISASTER SERVICE PROJECTS (MDS)

Felton Grove, California was the first MDS project I participated in in California. It was a very rainy winter and the local river had overflowed and a number of homes were flooded. Members of Lincoln Glen Church and others mucked a lot of sand from basements and first floors of low-lying homes. This was back breaking work; we removed a lot of wet sand in wheelbarrows. This group (MDS) has been helping people for over sixty years.

IV. COALINGA, CALIFORNIA (MDS)

In the early 80's Coalinga, California was hit with a damaging earthquake. Volunteers from Lincoln Glen Church helped clean up and then rebuild homes that had little or no insurance.

This was the first MDS project where I actually participated in reconstruction.

On January 2, 2013, Carol and I finished breakfast at a local restaurant and before we left a group of several families left and the last of their group stopped to visit with us. He had lived in Coalinga when we had helped clean up and reconstruct. He was so grateful even now that he almost cried as he thanked me! He mentioned that we were unique among volunteers in not taking advantage of victims. Again I was reminded to be grateful to my Mennonite heritage that this mission was to be of assistance to all hurting people of all or no faith and of all nationalities and race.

V. YUBA CITY, CALIFORNIA (MDS)

Yuba City was severely flooded several times. In October of 1997, levees containing the Feather River failed. The farmhouse where we were billeted had been flooded 2-3 feet deep in the upstairs bedrooms.

VI. FERNDALE, CALIFORNIA (MDS)

In Ferndale in northern California (Eureka area), I worked on several projects at different times. The last time we worked on constructing a new home in Ferndale, building a home from foundation to roof; the original home had been destroyed in an earthquake.

VII. SAN JOSE, CALIFORNIA (Lincoln Glen)

In 1988 and 1989 Eddie Feil and Ted Thiessen of our congregation were instrumental in working with a Hispanic church called "Iglesia Los Hechos" in east San Jose. They asked me to perform routine renovation and refurbishing of their first church buildings. We did carpenter work, plumbing, electrical, and carpet-laying. It should be noted that Eddie and Ted each had a heart for people to hear the gospel. Today the church is thriving and has outgrown its facilities and has planted several other congregations.

VIII. WATSONVILLE, CALIFORNIA (MDS)

MDS restored many homes in the Watsonville area (most in the city) after the Loma Prieta earthquake in 1989. The project continued for several years. A number of new homes were constructed.

Watsonville had many older 2-story Victorian homes with no actual foundations. The houses merely rested on large timbers or beams. When the quake hit, the homes slid off the beams and the houses were nearly destroyed. Most could be salvaged. MDS contracted with Fresno house movers to crib up the houses that could be rebuilt.

Several of the MDSers were expert in concrete work and one fellow who had a lifetime of professional concrete construction experience headed up crews that set forms around the perimeter of these large Victorians and installed rebar, poured concrete and mud sills with bolts attached. The houses were lowered onto the mudsills and bolted securely. Utilities were connected and new porches, steps and entries were installed. Most of the damaged Victorians thus could be salvaged, better than new!

We also rebuilt homes in outlying areas north of Watsonville. One of the highlights of these projects was observing the presentation of the keys and a Bible to a single mother and her son. She now had a washer and dryer for the first time (donated by Mennonites).

IX. HOMESTEAD, FLORIDA (MDS)

In 1993, working with Amish in Homestead, Florida was a great experience. The volunteers lived in a house restored after Hurricane Andrew. Several carloads of young Amish men arrived from Amish settlements in Pennsylvania and roomed with us and worked on projects together. I was amazed at their aptitude for construction skills. They were in their late teens and early twenties and they understood "how to take hold". We enjoyed our off time with their lively men a lot. It was one of the highlights to work with these very capable Amish brethren. In February the Mennonite Disaster Services All-Unit meeting (U.S. + Canada) was held in the temporary dining hall of a church that would accommodate 100 diners. Just a handful of expert cooks fed all of us very well and promptly.

X. REDWOOD ESTATES, CALIFORNIA (MDS)

In 1993, several years after the Loma Prieta quake, Joe and Kay Dozier contacted MDS and asked us to help build a new house for them in Redwood Estates, between Los Gatos and the summit. Their house, having been astride the fault line, had been destroyed. They were allowed to build if they could obtain a lot more away from the fault. A lot was available but they had to locate the previous owner. This required several years of title searches. Upon a successful title search and discovering the property was available, they purchased the property and were issued a permit to construct a 2-story house.

Joe had hired a carpenter and they constructed the foundation and we helped with the sub-floor. MDS asked me to assist them and I called people at the church where they were members. A good number of men responded and a number of carpenters and former contractors and working electricians from Lincoln Glen Church (my church home) also responded. We built the 2-story home, completing nearly everything except shingling and plumbing and taping and texturing.

We MDS volunteers received much unsolicited attention during this project. The San Jose Mercury News published front-page stories with photographs of the workers, and we were also interviewed by Bay Area television stations as we worked! Later San Jose Mayor Susan Hammer commended our local MDS volunteers at a city council meeting, and presented a plaque to us.

Harold leading MDS volunteers build a house in Redwood Estates (1993).

XI. NORTHRIDGE, CALIFORNIA (MDS)

In 1994 when disaster relief organizations were assembling at Northridge after that devastating quake, Wilmer Lichty and I were asked to assess damage at Sherman Oaks. We were amazed by what we observed. Numerous houses collapsed, people had died, and cars were flattened. At this headquarters we observed the Southern Baptist set up a feeding program: they brought in semis, tents, fork lifts, portable gas stoves – they could feed literally thousands in just hours.

When the projects got underway, I also worked at Fillmore and later at Piru rebuilding homes damaged in the same earthquake.

An event that really impressed me was observing the meeting of MDSers and Red Cross and other disaster relief workers from all over the U.S. It was "old home week" in action.

XII. REDDING, CALIFORNIA (MDS)

In the winter of 2000 there were several MDS reconstruction and new home-building projects in northern California after devastating wild fires. Several of us from Lincoln Glen Church helped build a new house in the Bella Vista and Palo Cedro area near Redding. We were billeted in a house that had been graciously provided for us by the owners. The extremely high temperature of summer forced us to start work at dawn because the roof of the house, as we put on the shingles, would burn our feet through the soles of our shoes.

XIII. JULIAN, CALIFORNIA (MDS)

Eddie Neufeld and I and others assessed the terrible devastation caused by wildfires in the Julian area east of San Diego. In 2003 we were absolutely amazed by the extensive destruction. One large trailer park was completely devastated. Only charred metal remained. In one area, where a community had some stores and houses, people were living in tents. It is difficult to imagine what affected people must endure.

MDS damage assessment at Julian, CA (2003).

In the winter, Eddie Neufeld and I delivered two trucks to the project that had been established. MDS had the use of a Catholic campground facility. The accommodations were very good. There was 4-6 inches of snow on the ground, by morning there was five inches more.

ALASKA
(Background of Volunteer work there and worldwide)

After liquidating my manufacturing business in 1990, I had worked for Ken Friesen, a general contractor and fellow member of Lincoln Glen Church in San Jose over three months helping complete a 4,000 sq. ft. 2-story home. After completion, Leo Warkentin, a former member of Lincoln Glen Church, then living in Auke Bay, Alaska, was visiting friends and relatives in the San Jose area. His wife Blondina had recently passed away. When we met, I asked him if sometime he could show me the interior of Alaska. He said this could be arranged and we flew there in November. Even though it was -30 and -40 degrees at times, this trip "hooked" me on Alaska. He knew people at Haines Junction; these folks had a mission church and knew John Tieszen, a good friend of mine in our class of '45 at Mountain Lake, who was a long-time missionary with his wife in Ecuador. Leo knew people at Glen Allen, Alaska Bible College; we stayed overnight here. Then we had lunch with people he knew at Wasilla.

Driving to Anchorage, we stayed with the Lowneys and they graciously allowed us to use their place as base and we visited Cooper Landing and Seward. Before returning home we visited Harry Reimer at Fairbanks. This was the beginning of a great relationship with Harry and Adeline Reimer and Bob and Lois Franz, all originally from Mountain Lake, Minnesota.

In exploring the Juneau area, Leo showed me the Echo Ranch Bible Camp forty-five miles north of Juneau at the end of the road, adjacent to the Lynn Canal. Gospel Missionary Union, now Avant, operated this successful Bible Camp for children. Leo and Blondina Warkentin had volunteered many hours, donated vehicles and supported this camp for years. The camp had an aluminum boat that could carry vehicles and named it the Blondina.

Dean and Alice Diller of Pandora, Ohio were camp directors for thirteen years. They were members of a very vibrant Mennonite Church, USA in the countryside of Pandora called St. John Mennonite Church.

XIV. ECHO RANCH BIBLE CAMP, ALASKA (GMU)

In the spring of 1991, Leo called and said they needed construction people to help erect a fairly large 2-story apartment and office building. Carol, my wife, said, "Lets go!" We took the Alaska Ferry at Bellingham, Washington and worked there for two weeks. It was a great experience. When I worked for Ken Friesen, he had taught me how to hang Anderson double-pane windows. Leo gave me a crew and we hung windows on both floors.

Harold & crew installing windows in office/apt. building at Echo Ranch, Alaska, facing Lynn Canal (1991).

Working on the 2nd floor, next to Echo Cove off Lynn Canal, we would occasionally see whales cavorting and we would stop and take pictures with cameras on tripods. It was an amazing location.

Jake Hoffman of Lustre, Montana, a community of Mennonites who homesteaded land in northeast Montana a few years after 1900, was a pioneer minister and church planter in the area just north of Juneau. He came there in 1964, organized the Auke Bay Bible Church and was the leader of the founding of the Echo Ranch Bible Camp. This camp was operated under the auspices of the Gospel Missionary Union. He was a leader with a vision – winning adults and children to the Lord in the Juneau area.

Jake Hoffman also was instrumental in organizing a church on Douglas Island just west of Juneau. An interesting sidelight I heard about in the closing months of 2013 is the story of how a Lustre, Montana rancher bequeathed a portion of his estate to help the Hoffmans navigate smoothly during their later retirement years.

When Henry Franz, a cousin of my mother, passed away awhile ago, he bequeathed a goodly portion of his estate to the Hoffmans of Auke Bay adjacent to Juneau. My wife and I had the privilege of visiting the Hoffmans. They have since passed away.

Henry Franz was a bachelor who developed a wheat and cattle ranch in the Lustre, Montana area. I visited him several times. After he died, an auction was held; I was not able to attend. However, my uncle Peter Teichroew of Mountain Lake, MN and Harlan Teichroew, his son of Yankton, South Dakota attended the sale. It is not unusual that bachelor ranchers have accumulated many vehicles and machines. They seldom trade in a used piece of equipment, truck, tractor or combine. They simply let it set outdoors, seldom indoors. Since in northern Montana it is seldom humid, these items exhibit very little corrosion. Franz had a few Ford model A combines, a huge Altman-Taylor fuel-driven tractor. It was quite an auction.

This story reinforces my gratefulness for the Mennonite heritage that I have been privileged to live out. Henry made a huge difference in the lives of the Hoffmans. As was previously mentioned, the Hoffmans' vision in establishing Echo Ranch Bible Camp has exposed thousands of youngsters to the gospel of Jesus Christ, and many have responded.

Dean and Alice Diller spent time in the area and at Echo Ranch Bible Camp in 1976, 1978 and 1981. In 1984 they were appointed camp directors at Echo Ranch and they served well into 1996, nearly thirteen years. The original camp consisted of 160 acres donated by the McMurthy family, 80 more acres were donated later and today 60 more acres have been donated. 125 children from southeast Alaska attend each 2-week session during summer vacation. A hundred a year accept the Lord as Savior; 30-40 rededicate their lives to Jesus. In the 13 years the Dillers served, 10,000 campers attended and 2,000 accepted the Lord.

Over 400 young people from Ohio have worked as counselors at Echo Ranch during the years that the Dillers served. Alice Diller passed away in the spring of 2008 in Ohio, and 200 cards were received and 468 Gideon Bibles were given in her memory.

Dean Diller told me of a boy, Carlos Boozer, who had attended Echo Ranch Bible Camp as a child. Later Dean found by chance a New Testament that inadvertently had not been presented to Carlos. He recognized that Carlos was now an accomplished professional NBA player. So when Dean saw that he would be playing at a scheduled game in Cleveland, Ohio, he brought the Testament with him and managed to convince the security people that he wanted to speak briefly to Carlos. When they met, Carlos remembered Dean and told him that he was still living a Godly Christian life. He had accepted the Lord as a boy at the camp and continues to walk with God!

XV. PAPUA NEW GUINEA (NAZARENE CHURCH)

When Carol and I visited Alaska all summer in 1992 with our motorhome, we enjoyed tremendous times of fellowship with Harry and Adeline Reimer in Fairbanks.

As it turned out, Harry Reimer was in charge of assembling work teams for the Nazarene Church all over the globe. He was gathering a team for a project of constructing four buildings for married student housing at the Nazarene Bible College at Mount Hagen in the highlands of Papua New Guinea. These teams were called "Work and Witness Teams". He needed twenty people and could only obtain eleven. He encouraged me to consider this since I had construction experience. I was reluctant as I had never traveled overseas and had no passport. My wife, however, encouraged me to accompany the team and help them. After prayer and soul-searching I agreed (this was the first of nearly twenty overseas trips). I boarded a Delta Airlines plane to Los Angeles from San Francisco. There another volunteer and I boarded a Delta Lockheed L1011 wide-body for Anchorage.

After refueling and restocking, we left for Hong Kong. From Hong Kong we boarded an Air Niugini on an overnight flight to Port Moresby, arriving after breakfast. Our luggage wasn't on our plane. After customs we took a smaller jet to Mount Hagen in the highlands of New Guinea. Our luggage arrived a day later.

Upon arriving by land vehicles at the Nazarene Bible College, Rene Mauldin, a contractor in Fairbanks, checked out the lumber that was supplied for us, and also the slabs that had been poured, anticipating our construction. Monday morning Rene organized the material, tools and workers. He was so organized that his crew was soon ahead of schedule. All of us visited an outlying Mission station by twin propeller plane. One end of the runway dropped off to a canyon! After this visit, Roger McPeak and I flew to Ukarampa over a hundred miles east of Mount Hagen. Ukarampa is a village of 700 Wycliffe Bible translators and support staff. It is a virtually self-sustaining village. We remained for two days. On the return trip a native owned a large van and we paid for our return to Mt. Hagen. He would yell at villagers regarding his service, and after stopping at a few villages, the van was full. Approximately halfway to Mt. Hagen, 50 to 100 natives were running in the bush and ditches toward us with various primitive weapons. They were very agitated. The driver stopped the van, backed up a short way and stopped. Soon he continued. We later discovered that a neighboring tribe had killed one of this tribe and now they were attempting to get even – "payback". This system is *not unusual* in Papua New Guinea. If a foreigner has an auto accident and a native is injured, the foreigner must abandon the vehicle and run for his life.

One weekend the Nazarene staff and their assistants created a Muaum for us. They dug a six-foot 2-3 foot diameter hole to cook a meal with hot rocks laced with different meats, sweet potatoes, carrots, etc. It was a feast to remember.

Natives preparing a Muaum feast for volunteers in Highlands of Papua New Guinea.

Papua New Guinea native tribes speak over 500 languages, probably more than anywhere in the world. In addition to Wycliffe Bible Translators, New Tribes Missions are there and today I believe Lutheran Translators also labor there.

One weekend we visited a nearby Nazarene general hospital operated by them at Kudjip. They have buildings for the natives to stay while a family member is cared for. The facilities for patients are primitive. There is a large plate glass window to the operating room so that family can observe their loved ones undergoing surgery. This hospital is widely recognized and respected in Papua New Guinea.

On the day that the four houses were dedicated, a man in native garb happened to walk through the grounds, and after he observed the gathering, he requested that we take his picture with me, hence the picture on the cover of this book.

Kidron, Ohio MCC Sale

In 1991 when Carol and I volunteered our services to Echo Ranch Bible Camp, we met numerous volunteers including John and Carrie Miller of Pandora, Ohio. They attended the same church as Dean and Alice Diller, camp directors.

Several years later Carol and I took a trip to visit them and during this visit they casually mentioned that one of the largest regional MCC relief sales was occurring soon and if we would like to accompany them. This large sale is an annual event at the Mennonite School at Kidron.

After discussing this possibility we decided to travel east to Kidron and enjoy this MCC sale. John said a personal friend had established a thriving well-organized homemade ice cream concession that he took to auctions and various popular community events, and we could help! He had set up three five-gallon ice cream freezers and one large ten-gallon freezer. He used an old-time gasoline engine for power and he had designed a transmission and clutch apparatus that was very ingenious. He had a trailer that contained the ingredients of the ice cream, including large sacks of dry vanilla pudding mix that helped the ice cream firm up. Several women were in charge of preparing the ingredients. The big blocks of ice were stored in a small, refrigerated truck, and on the ground was an ice chipper, electric-powered, that broke up the ice for the freezers. Of course we also used lots of rock salt.

On the first day of this widely attended sale, a Friday, we made and sold over 215 gallons of delicious vanilla homemade ice cream. Since one of my weaknesses is homemade ice cream, I really put into practice the verse in Deuteronomy 25: 4 that reads, "Do not muzzle the ox while it is treading out the grain." It was a very pleasant day, just a little on the warm side and people really enjoyed the ice cream. Saturday, the final day of the sale, the weather turned overcast and chilly for that time of year. We weren't very busy, now people were buying coffee instead of ice cream!

XVI. ECHO RANCH BIBLE CAMP, ALASKA (GMU)

In June of 1996 another opportunity presented itself to assist in constructing a large equipment building at Echo Ranch Bible Camp north of Juneau, Alaska.

My wife and I again took the Alaska Ferry MV Columbia from Bellingham, Washington to Auke Bay just north of Juneau, Alaska. We worked there two weeks, I in construction and Carol in the camp kitchen. Dean and Alice Diller were camp directors (their final year).

Carol & Harold on Alaska Ferry offshore Auke
Bay and Mendenhall Glacier (1996)

After approximately a week of work, a Dungeness crab fisherman from Juneau asked Dean if he could supply one man to help him set the first pots of the season. He had a good relationship with the camp and they had allowed him to store his pots in a protected place on camp property on shore. As it turned out, we were ahead of schedule, and Dean asked if I would be willing to help with his two diesel boats, bait the traps and set them each with a marked buoy so his were all identified.

The first day we baited and set all his pots and several hours later the kitchen staff asked us if there might be enough Dungeness crabs for the evening meal. We checked the pots and sure enough, we must have caught enough to almost fill a forty-gallon container. The women prepared melted butter. The first crabs of the season were very delicious!

XVII. KLAIPEDA, LITHUANIA (MB)

In the fall of 1994, Ted Thiessen challenged me to consider investing some time in Klaipeda, Lithuania to construct dormitory furniture for a 5-story building that Art and Leona DeFehr and Dennis and Rene Neumann of Canada had obtained. Klaipeda was the location of an emerging Christian College. This Mennonite Brethren venture was renting space from the local college.

This college was named Lithuania Christian College. The administrators and instructors were recruited from Canada and the U.S. Many were retired and willing to volunteer their services to help establish the college in Klaipeda (the administration in 1994 was headed by Len Loeppky; Peter Enns and Henry Dueck worked in administration).

The idea for a Christian College in Lithuania was generated during a summer evangelistic mission in August 1990 led by Johannes Reimer of Logos in Germany. It resulted from a discussion with the Vice-Minister of Culture and Education. The City of Panevezys was aggressive in its invitation to establish an independent educational institution and a three-way Protocol of Intent was signed on that visit. The idea was to begin with a pilot project consisting of a Summer English Institute in the summer of 1991, then plan for a repeat Summer English Institute in 1992, with the hope of moving to a more complete college program in the fall of 1992.

In the summer of 1991, Lithuania Christian College functioned as an English Language Institute with instructional staff of 14 plus 4 persons involved in various roles such as administration and future planning. Several very capable Lithuanian staff acted as translators, administrators and general support. There were a total of 100 students: the majority being Lithuanian English teachers from the secondary school system, and several community professionals. The balance consisted of recent high school graduates hoping to enter the College in the future. The City provided the building and other facilities.

A Winter Language Institute was held from October 1991 to June 1992. Forty-five full-time students were enrolled and the emphasis was on improving English levels in preparation for the first year college classes.

Lithuania Christian College (LCC) moved to the City of Klaipeda in July 1992. This decision followed months of discussion with Lithuanian officials both in Panevezys and in Klaipeda.

In a visit to Lithuania, Art DeFehr, together with Otonas Balciunas, leader of the Christian Charity Fund of Lithuania (CCFL) thanked the City of Panevezys for the many areas of cooperation for the 1991 and 1992 Language Institutes. It had become clear in discussions that the long-term objectives of a Christian college could best be developed on the campus of Klaipeda University (KU).

The City of Klaipeda is an old port city, formerly known as Memel when it was part of Königsberg. It has Anabaptists in its ancient history and a continuing strong Lutheran presence. Population is 208,000 with a substantial "old quarter". The balance of the City has pleasant tree-lined streets with buildings on a quiet scale compared to more modern Russian cities. Klaipeda is the largest seaport in Lithuania with expectations of considerable growth as trade with western countries increases. The Baltic beaches provide an excellent setting for relaxation and future tourist growth.

Klaipeda University came into existence in September 1991 as a fully accredited and independent institution sponsored directly by the Lithuanian Parliament. It had a total of 4,000 day/evening students. It intended to develop a western orientation to benefit from its port location and to create a competitive distinction from the other Lithuanian Universities. KU was anxious to have a strong English Department and desired to develop a western style management program.

A Protocol of Agreement was signed between KU and the CCFL in early March 1992 to establish an autonomous college on the campus of KU. The College offered a bachelor's degree in either English or Christian Studies. Through cross-registration students could obtain degrees from either institution.

The 1992 Summer Language Institute in Klaipeda ran from July 6th to August 7th. Thirty-three western volunteers ranging in age from the 20's to the 60's ran a well- organized, high-energy program. Senior secondary school students, secondary school teachers of English, Klaipeda University students and professors, as well as professionals, made up the student body of 292 eager individuals, desiring to improve their English skills.

Lithuania Christian College (LCC) officially opened its doors September 12, 1992 and offered students a B.A. program with either an English major or a major in Christian Studies. Thirty students enrolled in first year college studies. The majority of these students reached English proficiency at the college entry-level by studying at our Language Institutes in the past years.

Forty-two students enrolled in the one-year, non-credit Language Institute program in the fall of 1992 to prepare for college entry-level English proficiency. In addition, LCC offered evening community courses in both English and Computer Skills.

A dedicated team of eleven staff members, under the leadership of Ernie and Elfrieda Reimer, were involved in LCC's first year as a college.

The 1993 Summer Language Institute registered 185 Lithuanian students as well as one student from Riga, one from St. Petersburg and one from Kiev. Included in the student body were post second students, English teachers, professors and professionals including doctors, engineers, librarians, social workers and secretaries. For the first time classes were formed on the basis of an oral and written examination. The staff of 33 included 25 Canadians and 8 Americans. Two Lithuanian-born North Americans were part of this summer team. One was the librarian, born in Panevezys, and the other was a Texas pastor who taught the Bible elective.

The opening of the 1993-1994 academic year saw a dramatic increase in both student and staff numbers. Twenty-one teachers from both Canada and the United States committed themselves to teaching a full time student body of 126. Of these, 55 were enrolled in the Language Institute, 37 in first-year college and 26 in second year. Klaipeda University students numbered 23. In addition to these full time students, the staff taught adult and community ESL to 357 individuals a week. For the first time, German was also being offered to both college students and the community.

Some of the Organizations/Colleges Affiliated with Lithuania Christian College:

- **Mennonite Brethren Missions and Services (MBM/S)** has participated from the early stages of Lithuania Christian College's life in providing teaching staff.

- **LOGOS** participated in the original 3-way Protocol of Intent signed with the Lithuanian government and the DeFehr Foundation, and has assisted in purchasing furniture, equipment and supplies.

- **Mennonite Central Committee (MCC)** has donated funds for the purchase of computers, has provided teaching staff and participated in recruiting personnel for renovations.

- **Eastern Board of Missions (PA)** sponsored teaching staff as well as participating in recruiting personnel for the dormitory renovation.

- **Fresno Pacific College (CA)** participated in the organization and implementation of the Summer Language Institute program.

The 5-story building that was obtained had been a Russian naval dormitory. Volunteers from Canada and the U.S. rewired, plumbed, built all furniture for student rooms (such as double bunk beds, tables and desks), new double-paned vinyl windows, installed new boiler for heating, new roof, new stucco and steps and porches. The project was quite successful.

Harold at work on the Delta Unisaw building dormitory furniture for LCC in Klaipeda, Lithuania (1994).

Since the building was of cement block construction, a groove had to be chiseled near the ceiling to contain the new electrical cables. John Braun and I were good pals, and when he and his helpers were each working on step-ladders checking grooves to accommodate cables, I would in jest call him the "resident electrician-archeologist." I did not envy these men. They wore masks to keep the cement dust from their noses - this was not a pleasant task!

My work was to build, assemble and install student furniture for the dormitories. John Braun, a skilled brother from Canada, and I made a good team. We also installed large sheets of a brown Masonite type of material for the dorm room floors. The material for the furniture was manufactured in Klaipeda. It was 5/8" thick

Masonite-like 5'X 9' sheets. We operated a new 10" Delta Unisaw and Unifence table saw with extension tables. The saw was in operation at least 8 hours a day until we had assembled and installed the furniture in all five floors.

Dorm room furniture after installation.

There was an eleven-story building across the street from the dormitory building and the volunteers and their support staff was housed and fed in one entire floor of this building. It was a great time to become friends of volunteers from Canada and the U.S. The married fellows' wives provided excellent food and they graciously did our laundry.

Sunday, we worshipped in the local evangelical churches, Baptist and others, and also visited the Russian Orthodox where we stood for the entire service. One Sunday a group of us were invited to the home of a Lithuanian mason, Harry, who was hired to work on the dormitory. He lived south of Klaipedia in Silute near the small Russian state of Kaliningrad, a small area between Lithuania and Poland. He cooked a delicious hot noon meal for us. We had worshiped at a Lutheran Church that Harry attended. They were without a pastor and John Braun, our electrician, was asked to bring the message in German. There were less than thirty in the large church and it was not heated. We warmed up when Harry served us the meal. Later he showed us a large concrete and block house he was building, it was over fifty percent complete.

Enjoying a meal in the home of Harry (a mason): Harold,
John Braun, unidentified couple and Rueben Holland.

Reuben Holland, a brother of Leona de Fehr, and I became fast friends. He remained on the project through its completion. He was the purchasing manager and he knew where to get material and supplies to refurbish the five-story building. He had a large truck so he could pick up and deliver throughout the country and area. We had many good times on the weekends. I worked at the college for two months.

Henry Dueck, Reuben Holland, Harold, Mr. & Mrs. Ernie
Enns, and Maria Dueck (Klaipeda 1994).

The invitation to the twentieth anniversary of the inception of Lithuania Christian College University brought back many delightful memories of my two months' volunteer work in September and October of 1994.

When Dr. Merrill Ewert (then president of Fresno Pacific University) heard of my pending trip he also was interested in attending this anniversary. We gladly traveled together and he is a delightful travel companion. (Actually prior to the anniversary event, after I had arranged all my logistics, including airfare, etc., I decided at my age this trip could tax me excessively. I cancelled all reservations and since it was for medical reasons there were no cancellation charges.) With the possibility of traveling with Merrill I successfully initiated the reservation process again. We had a great satisfying trip.

During our time in Klaipeda, we had a little free time and we visited the Hill of Crosses at Siauliai. Acreage of an estimated 30-40 acres is covered with thousands and thousands of crosses of all sizes. It is very touching. The Soviets during their reign bulldozed the hill; the Lithuanians again placed crosses on the hill area and they have not been disturbed again.

The Hill of Crosses at Siauliai, Lithuania.

We also visited the Jewish Holocaust Museum at Kaunas. It is very impressive; the Jews created a large memorial statue-like edifice.

The Jewish Holocaust Museum at Kaunas.

I enjoyed my time in Klaipedia at the reunion. The programs, banquet, and a group walk to the festivities were most memorable. This event was a highlight of my life. In case it hasn't been mentioned previously, the Mennonite Brethren have planted six churches in Lithuania.

Prior to this event, a businessman who lives on one of the Channel Islands, whom I had met on a Ukranian tour, invited me to visit him when our schedules coincided. Since Dr. Ewert was traveling with me, the host graciously invited Dr. Ewert also. As guests we were made very welcome and enjoyed our stay very much.

Our host is the non-executive chairman of a company, O3b Networks. This company was scheduled to send 4 satellites into orbit aboard a Suyoz Rocket from French Guiana on June 24, 2013. Arianespace will launch the first 8 satellites in 2013. Due to weather, this launch was delayed, and *did* take place successfully on June 25th.

O3b Networks delivers broadband connectivity everywhere on earth within 45 degrees of latitude north and south of the equator. O3b's vast coverage includes emerging and insufficiently connected markets in Latin America, Africa, the Middle East and Australia, with a collective population of 3 billion people.

After we departed the Channel Islands, Merrill and I enjoyed a walking tour of London. Returning to the air terminal at Gatwick and departing for home, this was one of my most memorable trips.

XVIII. DRESDEN, GERMANY (MB)

Ted Thiessen presented another challenge to me in the summer of 1995. He was a dear brother who, when he presented a project that could use one's assistance, we always enjoyed his gentle "arm twisting". He had a way of presenting a project so you knew it would not be easy to sleep well if he was turned down. Ted was a gifted leader.

Ted and Marylene Thiessen worked in Dresden, Germany on the construction of a new structure for the Evangelische Mennonitische Freikirche being built on the corner of two busy four-lane roads – one leading to the Autobahn. The property the M.B. Conference had located was part of a cemetery that needed income. It sold a well-constructed masonry structure and allowed a new meeting building to be built adjacent so they could be utilized as one unit.

In September I worked all month – several weeks working on this and other interesting projects. Lawrence and Selma Warkentin allowed me to live in their travel trailer on their rented property. Lawrence was the Pastor and also the project coordinator, where he did much work. I'll always remember when he asked me to help him for a few days to do inside wall plastering. Lawrence was a skilled plasterer. It was a joy to work with him and also Rudolf Reim. As a consequence of this project, Rudolf and I became lifelong friends. For a few days I helped him installing radiant heat plumbing – he was a skilled pipe fitter who was unemployed.

Exterior of Dresden Church (1995).

It was always a joy to worship with Lawrence and Selma, to sit under Lawrence's vibrant preaching, to hear the good music and to meet many Christians from various countries. These two planted churches in Austria and Germany for many years until their retirement, and even after have made many trips to encourage those congregations.

Several Saturdays I went hiking with church families in the German Swiss hills. One time Rudolf and I drove to the Czech Republic and hiked. Another weekend Rudolf and I took the train and visited Vienna.

Harold hiking with church families.

In 1997 it was my privilege to worship with these dear folks again. The church was nearly full. In 2005, when I could visit them, they were considering planting another nearby church – this one is maxed out and it is not feasible to add to the buildings.

Worship in the church in 1997 visit (Lawrence Warkentin in pulpit).

In 2005 I also visited Paul, Lawrence and Selma's son, and Ina Warkentin in Bielefeld. This church seats 400 and was packed. They now have two services.

XIX. VIZCAINO, BAJA, MEXICO (Missions of Baja)

In Vizcaino, Baja, Mexico, I had the opportunity to do construction work at the Vizcaino location of Missions of Baja. Carlos Freyre of Norco, CA and his wife, Celia, developed this mission to the impoverished Mexicans of northern Baja Sur on the Vizcaino desert. This location was inland from the cove where whales, wintering from Alaska, come to calve.

Ophthalmologists, optometrists, dentists, chiropractors, nurses, nurse practitioners, kitchen staff, construction and mechanics would fly in for long weekends and serve the indigenous population.

Pilots of private single engine and twin-engine planes would fly volunteers from Colorado, Texas and Northern and Southern California. They would transport donated and purchased medicine and supplies plus food for the volunteers. Volunteers were housed in mobile homes. The majority of medical assistance was usually dentistry. We would fly in Friday a.m. and the doctors and construction people would begin work early Friday p.m. We would work all daylight hours and medical staff would often work until 1:00 or 2:00 a.m. Sunday, beginning at sunrise Saturday morning. The food and fellowship were outstanding. On one occasion we set up and showed a Jesus film outside.

An airline captain of American Airlines, Jim Nielsen, flew us down from San Jose, California. He had a twin 8- place "411" Cessna. We would fly from South County Airport in San Martin, south of San Jose, to Los Angeles in just over 1-1/2 hours, and usually pick up more volunteers at Torrance. Jim is an outstanding pilot.

He now commands a Boeing 777 for American on a Tokyo run. It was my privilege to work here five times.

Jim Nielsen & Harold ready to fly in Jim's plane to Mexico.

After a number of trips there, the Mennonite Brethren Missions and Services Intl. were establishing a church in Tijuana, Mexico, located just south of the U.S. – Mexico border, south of Chula Vista.

XX. TIJUANA, MEXICO (MB)

Here in Tijuana we constructed a substantial frame structure with 16' side walls and we manufactured roof trusses on site. I was privileged to spend more time there than any other volunteer. We also erected temporary living quarters for the pastor and his family.

Crane lifting trusses onto M.B. Mission Church in Tijuana, Mexico.

The property was located just above the large public school. Before we began construction, hundreds of squatters moved in above the church property, and even a few moved onto the property. We dealt with a leader of some of the squatters and we built a small shack for his family and he convinced the ones on our property to move.

The squatters had no water, no electricity, roads or sewers, and they lived in shacks constructed of pallets, or some lived in derelict campers, etc. As we commenced construction, we observed the squatters' children walking past on an adjacent primitive road to school – they were neatly dressed and shod.

XXI. JUIGALPA, NICARAGUA (Missions of Baja)

Carlos Freyre of "Missions of Baja" organized a short trip to Juigalpa, east of Managua, Nicaragua. Dentists, an ophthalmologist and other medics helped indigenous poor people of Juigalpa. We worked in a hospital. I assisted the ophthalmologist set up a portable microscope he needed for cataract surgery. I took pictures and he took pictures. We in North America often don't realize how fortunate we are to have been born here with much better opportunities and health care and a more caring government and infrastructure.

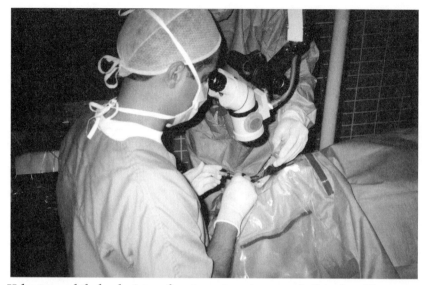

Volunteer ophthalmologist performing cataract surgery in Juigalpa, Nicaragua.

XXII. LA ESPERANZA, BAJA, MEXICO
(Mexican Medical Mission)

Mexican Medical Mission invited pilots and medics and support people to volunteer dental, optical, chiropractic and other disciplines at La Esperanza, approximately 75 miles south of Ensenada.

Mexican Medical Mission has developed a facility to help the migrant laborers from as far as southern Mexico. These poor people live in shanties made from corrugated roofing set up vertically, with a makeshift roof, one spigot outside for washing and drinking, a sheet for the door and temporary toilets. These people come from various states and don't even speak the same language. The owner of the plantation lives on a high bluff in a palatial white mansion. He does not permit any photographing of the migrants' "accommodations".

A truck was set up to show the Jesus film one evening and some of us helped show it.

XXIV. CAMPBELL, CALIFORNIA (Habitat for Humanity)

In the late 1990's I learned that Habitat for Humanity had obtained six lots for homes in a good location on Campbell Avenue, only two miles from our home. They needed volunteers to construct six modest single-family homes, and so I helped on this project for two weeks. It was an enjoyable experience.

Observations

The very well organized and superb effectiveness of MDS Unit #1 in eastern U.S. demonstrates the Eastern Mennonites' experience and their superior organizational management skills.

It was a wonderful privilege to observe and participate with the Eastern Unit #1 of Mennonites and experience first hand their setup of the logistics of housing and feeding of the volunteers and providing project directors for the numerous sites. One man was in charge full-time checking out tools and equipment and maintaining them. This was his assignment for the duration of the project. The tools and equipment virtually filled two forty-foot semi-trailers. Being a Californian, it had been my goal to work with the Eastern Mennonites in an MDS disaster relief project. It was truly amazing how professionally well organized they were!

I will always remember working with a carload of young unmarried Amish men. It was a treat to observe how they could undertake any task the project leader assigned them. To work with these great men was one of the highlights of my project time in Homestead, Florida.

I should note that women are often part of MDS work crews and are quite adept in construction, repair, "mudding", painting and other tasks!

It needs to be mentioned that just a few women could feed a hundred or so men so efficiently and seamlessly that it had to be observed to be believed. They were amazing! Our sleeping arrangements at that time were in renovated houses that were eventually utilized by families; when we used these places the finished floor coverings were not yet in place.

It has been very gratifying to me to observe how the various agencies work so well together after a major disaster. Cooperating with each other are Mennonite Disaster Service (MDS), Red Cross, FEMA, Salvation Army and Baptists, to name those I recall. It is heartwarming to see all of these groups reaching out to those who need help, regardless of race or creed – only a need for help!

A few years ago a settlement of Mennonites that had migrated to Seminole, Texas from Mexico 25 – 30 years previously hosted the Mennonite Disaster Service Annual All-Unit Meeting in their community. These folks are Old Colony Mennonites and other Mennonite congregations. I had the distinct privilege to be billeted in the new home of a young vibrant family with four young children. Their three daughters were in the early grades at school and their son was four. I will always remember his lively spirit as we talked up a storm in Plautdietsch; this was a real treat for me. The father had a business erecting commercial and industrial steel buildings. On Sunday I had the privilege of worshiping with the family at an Old Colony Church; they gave me a book of the history of Old Colony Mennonites in Canada, a fascinating book.

A very poignant facet of my appreciation for the Mennonite faith has been the privilege I've had to volunteer on various construction projects initiated by Mennonite agencies in Tijuana, Mexico, Klaipeda, Lithuania and Dresden, Germany.

Observing the enthusiasm and professionalism and energy that people like Lawrence and Selma Warkentin of Abbotsford, British Columbia demonstrated when I helped them build a Mennonite Brethren mission church in Dresden, Germany in 1995 has left an indelible memorial in my personage.

Invited to Lithuania Christian College University for a September 21-25, 2011 20th Anniversary Celebration, Merrill Ewert, then the President of Fresno Pacific University in Fresno, California and I enjoyed the festivities of this celebration. The university now has a beautiful campus with numerous new beautiful buildings. The school's reputation is impressive. An interesting side note; the campus is entirely debt free. This achievement is in no small part due to the foresight and overall oversight of Dennis and Rene Neumann, Art and Leona De Fehr and the entire board of directors. This has been very gratifying.

Last year when I toured the Baltics, the group I was with visited Tallinn, Riga, Klaipeda and Germany. The twenty people in the group wanted to visit Lithuania Christian College University. Dennis Neumann, a real estate developer and an early founder of Lithuania Christian College University arranged a tour of the University on the group tour so that Dr. Marlene Wall, the president of the school could show us the school. She is an amazing administrator. Dr. Wall gave us an excellent tour. The entire group was very impressed with Dr. Wall, the campus, and its mission!

To sum up my history of volunteerism, these experiences have really multiplied the gratefulness that I have of my Mennonite heritage. It has been brought to my attention that Mennonites are unique in their history of practicing what Menno Simons wrote: "True evangelical faith cannot lie dormant; it clothes the naked, it feeds the hungry, it comforts the sorrowful, it shelters the destitute, it serves those that harm it, it binds up that which is wounded, it has become all things to all men."

I often read II Peter 1:3-11 and also James 2:14-18. James 2:17: "Faith by itself, if it is not accompanied by action, is dead".

Chapter 22
Love of Flying

ANY MEMOIR OF MY LIFE MUST INCLUDE THE INNATE DESIRE I HAVE TO SOAR into the sky; and the desire for adventure has over the years aroused my interest in flying! My many trips for volunteer work and visiting Mennonite communities worldwide has further drawn me into the air. Following is a glimpse into my experiences in this facet of my life.

My first airplane ride occurred during a Mountain Lake, Minnesota fall Pow Wow Celebration. This was an annual event put on by Mountain Lake's merchants to promote the village businesses. They even had a free beef barbecue for many years. Carnival rides were available and they raffled off a new car. It was a great festive day.

I was probably seven or eight years old, possibly younger, and had heard that a "barnstorming" pilot had given my Uncle Abe Teichroew and his daughter Velma a ride. This pilot apparently had landed in a stubble field. Velma recently told me that she and her next younger sister were taking naps (they were both pre-school). She was awakened when a "barnstorming" pilot had landed on their farm and wanted to give her father and her a ride in an open cockpit bi-wing plane. When I heard this story I was terribly jealous that my cousin had gotten an airplane ride. I could hardly live with myself until I too had an airplane ride.

My father had given me a dollar when we arrived at the Pow Wow festivities and he told me this dollar was to last me all day. Those were the days when popcorn was still sold by Henry Buller at the corner of the park for a nickel a bag and hamburgers were probably only twenty-five cents.

As soon as I lost my Dad in the crowd I walked west of town where a "barn-storming" pilot had landed in an oats stubble field. He flew a fabric covered Taylor Craft tandem two-seater. This was a highlight of my young life. After we landed and I walked to the Pow Wow I was really walking "tall in the saddle." When I returned to the Pow Wow I was literally overjoyed – walking on "cloud nine." Since my money was gone, I could not get any ride on the carnival concessions, nor could I buy any eats. As I remember the occasion, it didn't matter because I had an airplane ride!

After my ride, I was really pumped! That was easily the most momentous event in my life up to that point.

Frankly, I don't remember the next airplane ride. I was a senior in high school; a classmate of mine, his girl friend, her sister and I got a ride on an amphibian plane. This was a lot of fun. I also rode in one with my future wife in 1950.

I don't think I got many rides until we moved to California in 1952. I met Wally Loewen in Reedley in 1955 and he had a Schweizer Glider. Before this he had been part-owner of several planes. He gave me a ride in the glider and what a thrill!

In 1955 he took me to Adelanto, George Air Force Base for a glider meet. A Bi-wing Stearman towed the gliders. I talked to the tow-plane pilot to have him take me up as a passenger and he said it was not allowed because of possible additional weight restrictions. We discussed this with Wally and they agreed to let me catch a ride because the Stearman had a lot more power than most tow planes. I strapped on a parachute and we were off! This was my first ride in an open cockpit bi-winger. What a treat!

Often Wally had his own plane in addition to his glider. When Burt Rutan, an aeronautical engineer at Mojave, had designed a two-seat rear engine plane constructed of Styrofoam and fiberglass, Wally decided to buy a kit and made plans for building this plane himself. He built this kit plane in the upstairs of their large two-story home in Reedley. It took him several years. To extract the finished product, he had to remove some windows and disassemble the plane. After this was achieved he took the new plane to Reedley's Great Western Airport, north of town. He rented a hanger space and reassembled the plane; and eventually he took the Vari-Eze up for its inaugural flight.

Esther & Wally Loewen and his home – built Vari-Eze plane, "Elijah's Chariot".

The plane is very light and fast. It cruises over 180 miles per hour. When Wally and Esther took long trips they traveled very light. I was privileged to fly with Wally and it was a treat! Wally and Esther's son Paul completed a successful career as a crop duster pilot and he said if I wanted a ride to remember he would take me up in the Vari-Eze. However, he quit his crop duster flying and developed health issues and didn't want to fly anymore. Wally subsequently sold the Vari-Eze and also his Cessna 180 since he couldn't pass his physical.

Years ago on one of our visits to Minnesota I learned that airline captains on holidays were giving rides in antique planes based at Flying Cloud Field, outside the Twin Cities. I talked to a fellow who was giving rides in a Stearman, a powerful radial engine bi-wing plane used to train pilots in World War II. Before we took off I asked him if I could take the controls after we were at cruising altitude and he said I could. I asked him how the plane handled and he said "Like a tractor!" Another of my giddy life experiences!

One winter approximately forty years ago, a cousin had completed her Wycliff short-term assignment in Mexico and she visited us before she went home to the Midwest. I suggested that I could have a three-place Schwizer 232 glider take us on a ride over the Mt. Hamilton Range of southern San Jose. A Tow plane got us airborne and when our pilot could catch some good waves he released. As soon as he released he noticed some strong, nearly silent wind currents lifting us higher and higher. He said he had never experienced such a strong winter wave over any other mountain. We continued to gain altitude and amazingly the flight was as smooth as glass. Often in the summer gliders like to catch thermals and ride them as high so they have lift and they can be turbulent. These waves were different – very calm, but tremendous lift! The pilot had such a great time until he realized it would take him some time to get back to the base. He had to virtually perform dives to lose altitude rapidly enough to get to his base expeditiously. What a ride we had!

In 1973 a friend of mine offered me a ride to Yosemite Park; in those days it was permissible to fly at an elevation of a few thousand feet over the park. It was exhilarating.

In November of 1990 a friend took me on my first visit to Alaska. After touring the interior of Alaska (my first of fifteen trips there) we returned to Juneau to prepare for my departure and it was snowing. I had an extra day there. It quit snowing and the weather turned pristine. Leo, my companion, suggested we contact his good friend Glen Cave, an electrical contactor, and see if he might have time to take us over the Mendenhall Glacier area. He did and what gorgeous pure white snow. We saw a cow moose and her calf. What a fitting end to my introduction to Alaska!

Several years later when Carol and I volunteered two weeks at a Bible Camp north of Juneau, Glen Cave gave me a ride from the beach. He landed and took off from the camp road on the shore. Another amazing experience!

In 1992 when Carol and I returned from Alaska we drove the Cassiar Highway south in Western British Columbia. When we arrived at Prince Rupert I decided to catch a ride on a floatplane. We found the dock and I hitched a ride on a Beaver to Kincolith, a settlement that relied on boats and seaplanes. My pilot was a wizened older pilot. He was so proficient that I felt no sensation on take off or landing. It was a supreme treat to ride with him!

In 1998, on another RV tour of Alaska, Carol wanted to see Glacier Bay and stay overnight there. This is amazing from the standpoint that Carol doesn't care to fly at all, but she wanted to stay at Glacier Bay and take side boat trips from there to see whales, etc. She saw an ad for this excursion on the bulletin board of the RV campground where we stayed. We got a ride on a six-place plane and when we looked out the windows with peaks of Davidson Glacier above us, we felt we could nearly touch the snowfields just below us. Needless to say, our boat trips at Glacier Bay were outstanding and from a native boat on Icy Strait we saw humpback whales!

Both in 1992 and 2010 I was privileged to fly over the Glaciers of Mount McKinley. In 1992 we took off from a small private landing strip behind Petracach RV Park, and changed to another plane at Talkeetna Airport. We flew over the glaciers but were unable to view the peak due to afternoon clouds. In 2010 I flew from Talkeetna up to the drop-off level on the glaciers for mountain climbers at 7,000 feet altitudes and landed there to experience the vast snow and ice of this huge mountain.

Also on our "trip of a lifetime" we flew in a 10-place passenger twin-engine commercial plane from Prudhoe to Barrow. Most of the flight was on instruments and we weren't even certain if we could land at Barrow; however, it cleared adequately so we could land uneventfully. When we returned to Fairbanks and Anchorage, the Alaska airliner carried 50% cargo and 50% passengers. The only other time I've flown a "combi" airliner was returning from China to SFO in 2001 on a China Air 747.

Van tour group flying from Prudhoe Bay to Barrow, Alaska (instrument flight with fog), (Carol & Harold to right of door).

In 1994 when I built furniture for a five-story dormitory for students at Lithuania Christian College in Klaipeda, Lithuania, my friend Ruben asked me to join him one Saturday to shop at a large flea market at the city. When we arrived in his truck we noticed a large radial engine bi-wing airplane in a cow pasture. We didn't know what was going on, so we inquired and discovered the plane was giving rides. It was a 12-15 passenger Russian Antonov AN-2, the largest bi-wing airplane ever built. It had a large powerful radial engine and it could take off and land in a very short distance. We got our ride and we were duly impressed. The landing strip was merely a small bumpy cow pasture!

An aspiration that has for many years gnawed at me was that I wanted a ride on a fast World War II P51 fighter. A very powerful Rolls Royce V-12 cylinder engine powered this plane. A few years ago I caught a ride in Hollister, California in a Raceworthy P51 – what a treat; however, I was disappointed that he didn't "wring it out" because I had told him I had had three stents inserted in my heart arteries (so he didn't give me my money's worth).

Approximately a year ago my wife and I were invited to take a ride in an airship based at Moffett Field. The field has three enormous hangers built to house dirigibles. The last years Goodyear Blimps have been used as advertising venues or floating billboards for Goodyear, Farmers Insurance and other companies. A close friend of my wife, Louisa Beeler, chartered several rides on the airship to fly from Moffett Field past the Hoover Tower at Stanford University. I readily accepted, however, Carol declined. It was a very quiet and smooth flight. I took lots of pictures and the view of the cities of Silicon Valley and also the long runways and large hangers and wind tunnel facilities were spectacular. The engines are very quiet, the entire ride was very quiet – a real treat.

Some years ago two widowed men from Ohio wanted to tour Hawaii. Since Carol had no interest in visiting the Hawaiian Islands, I was pleased that I could accompany these men. We flew to the islands and then toured the islands aboard a Norwegian Cruise line ship. We also rented a car for a day. We wanted to observe the lava flowing into the sea, so we chartered a helicopter so that we could get a very good view of that spectacular sight.

Elvin Olfert's plane (Air Ambulance) Lustre, MT.

Before I forget, I've received several rides in the Frazer-Lustre area of northeast Montana from Elvin Olfert – what a treat. A number of years ago another cousin's husband, Wilmer Reddig, took me up in a Piper Cub that he had recently restored. When we were cruising and observing his son's cattle, he pointed out a dry lake and suggested we land on the dry ground. As soon as we touched down he said, "Harold, can you lean back?" It turned out the bed wasn't completely dry – the wheels got stuck in the soft dirt but the plane didn't nose dive. He had a radio and he asked his son to bring some planks so we could walk the plane onto dry land. When we were on dry ground he took off and he landed on dryer ground and picked me up.

*Harold & Wilmer Reddig by Wilmer's plane on
a "dry" lake near Lustre, Montana.*

When we flew back to the home place and we came to the house, our wives were laughing and laughing. They were surprised we had left the radio on, so they had heard all of the conversations on the radio. He and I had hoped we would keep this episode to ourselves but this way the women had a great story to tell.

Commercially almost all of my flights have been uneventful. The only really rough flight that I, my wife and our daughter, Lisa have had as a family was on a take off from MPLS to SFO in the month of September. The weather was calm but cloudy, with no rain or wind. The takeoff was smooth, and the first minutes were quiet and uneventful. But just after takeoff, as we entered the cloud cover, it got so rough that I thought the engines would break loose. The plane would shudder, bounce and one time dropped hundreds of feet – it was terrifying. Lisa's eyes were huge and wet with tears and Carol sang, "Great is Thy Faithfulness", all three verses five times until the turbulence was past. The captain apologized for the awful turbulence and he said incoming pilots had warned of the roughness and he had "avoided the worst of the turbulence!" We wondered what the worst could have felt like.

After this flight it has been very difficult to get Carol on a long airplane ride; she has never flown overseas. Amazingly though she has encouraged *me* to fly overseas. At my first opportunity to perform volunteer construction overseas, she convinced me to accompany Harry and Adeline Reimer and a group from Fairbanks, Alaska to Papua New Guinea.

This was a long flight. Delta airlines took me to LAX and there I boarded a 1011 wide-body for Anchorage. At Anchorage we refueled and landed at Hong Kong. Then we boarded an Air Niugini for Port Moreseby, flying all night east, somewhere in the Philippines. Then we passed customs and awaited our luggage, which didn't arrive until we flew to Mt. Hagen, our destination. The luggage showed up the next day.

As we know, commercial flying has its stories. A few years ago I joined a Heritage Tour to Omsk, Siberia. Needless to say it was a long ride. We also had spent ten days in Uzbekistan learning about the Silk Road. When our tour was complete, we awaited our boarding of the Delta plane at Moscow for SFO, changing planes at Atlanta. We left Moscow nearly three hours late because the crew didn't appear! They finally arrived and the flight to Atlanta was routine, except I missed my connection to SFO. It took me over an hour to be proactive to catch another plane. When I finally reached the gate for SFO there was only one agent standing there and he told me they were already boarded. I ran to the plane and the door was still open and they had two seats left.

When I arrived at SFO it was 2:00 a.m., I called my shuttle for San Jose and he was almost full and dropped off a family in Los Gatos. When I arrived home, I caught a few hours of sleep, showered and repacked for my flight to MPLS for my Mountain Lake, Minnesota High School reunion.

When I settled in my seat, I immediately fell asleep. This is unusual as I have a difficult time sleeping on an airliner. Renting a car, I was on my way to Mountain Lake via Shakopee and Mankato. As soon as I felt comfortable on the through highways I fell asleep again. Twice I nearly drove in the ditch sound asleep. I rolled down the windows and did my best to stay awake, which (thank God) I did.

One of my most comfortable overseas flights was from Miami to Sao Paulo, Brazil on a Boeing 777. It was an economy red-eye flight. The 777 is a very nice ship. I couldn't sleep so I got up to wander forward. The business class passengers were asleep and so were the attendants. I kept walking forward and observed the first class seats that convert to a bed; what a comfort! I vowed then and there that if I flew any more overseas trips before I died I would buy at least one time a business class fare.

My volunteer construction work in Mexico was at Viscaino in the desert near the northern border of Baja Sur. Carlos Freyre, an evangelist of Norco, southern California and others had established a mission and needed dentists, ophthalmologists, chiropractors as well as cooks, carpenters, tile setters, plumbers, etc. Sometimes five or six planes came with professionals to help. People flew in from northern and southern California and from as far as Colorado.

We had a great time helping people.

I was fortunate to ride with Jim Nielsen, a captain for American Airlines, who owned an eight-place Cessna Twin 411 with auxiliary wing tip tanks for additional range. It was a very good plane and I had many round trip rides with Jim. We also worked at La Esperanza several times. On one of my last rides, when Jim landed at Torrance on our return, there were just the two of us. After he cleared the mountains and set his heading for San Jose South County Airport (our home field), he proceeded to fall asleep. He and a dentist friend had worked late into the night into the early morning and then played guitars and sang, so he was tired. I said, "Jim, do you want me to take it in?" He said, "Harold, I'll set the instruments for you and as long as you maintain the heading, let me sleep." As soon as I was comfortable with the settings, he went to sleep and I woke him as I saw south San Jose approaching.

Several other times when we were alone he asked if he could perform barrel rolls. I was overjoyed to agree. He did two rolls in succession. What a treat!

My pilot friend, Jim, strongly urged me to take flying lessons, he even recommended an instructor. He said it might be insurance if something happened to him, then I could safely bring the plane down to a non-eventful landing. One reason I never took lessons and also never wanted to have my own plane was that I really didn't have need of a plane and I couldn't justify the expense; I considered it a luxury.

On March 20th of 2013, Wally Loewen emailed me that his son Paul had died in an accident at his home in Reedley, California.

I have many fond memories of Paul. Years ago he had a good friend who liked motorcycles. In talking to Paul I suggested he consider purchasing a Harley-Davidson Sportster, I had had several and they were a joy to ride; they were fast. He purchased one and he and his buddy had a great time; they rode and camped a lot.

About this time he was driving a big rig refrigerated van loaded with peaches, plums and nectarines for three or four large stores in Los Angeles. He asked if I would join him in the evening ride and unloading the fruit. I agreed and we proceeded to have a great time. He needed to make four office drops and he was scheduled to meet "swampers" at each stop to unload each store's order. At the third stop, the swampers didn't show up. We waited and waited and I suggested we could use the store's pallet jacks and fork lifts ourselves. The store allowed us to unload their order and we just barely arrived on schedule at the next stop. At this stop the swampers were prompt.

Paul's boss had given him money to pay the swampers, so that when they didn't appear at the third stop, he could keep that money for himself. Paul had received meal and expense money; this was a bonus. Years later when Paul and I would reminisce about this experience it still cracked him up.

Paul became a crop duster. He was an excellent pilot; he never had an accident. Some years later a crop-spraying company that utilized turbo-prop engines in large "Ag Cats" employed him.

Toward the end of his career, Paul was completing an assignment and as he was looking to land at his base, he became disoriented and, thank God, he finally could summon all of his experience and made a successful landing. He took the keys and handed them to the business owner and announced he was summarily resigning.

After Paul's resignation, he had not flown on an airplane again. He told me before he resigned that when it suited both of us he would give me a ride in Wally's Vari Eze that I would never forget. Wally made the initial flight and then Paul strapped on a parachute and gave the plane a serious test flight. Paul enjoyed aerobatic flying.

Paul pronounced the plane very airworthy and since then Wally flew many hours in his pride and joy; it was christened "Elijah's Chariot". They made numerous cross-country trips; one disadvantage, there was very little space for luggage. Wally gave me rides and they always were memorable.

Paul and I were lifelong friends and brothers in Christ. He loved God's word and he loved to pray. Carol and I drove to Reedley, California to attend Paul's memorial on April 1st at the Reedley Mennonite Brethren Church.

Chapter 23
Horological Tours
(2001-2013)

THE VOLUNTEER TRIPS I WAS PRIVILEGED TO ENGAGE IN FOSTERED BOTH MY love of flying *and* a love of world travel!

I accepted a friend's invitation to a tour of the "Henry B. Fried Memorial Horological Tours", led by Nick Lerescu of Advantage Tours International of Glenwood, New Jersey. Nick is a Romanian who experienced communism under Nicolau Ceausescu. He is very knowledgeable concerning world history, and with each tour he provided pertinent history lessons regarding the tour.

These tours sometimes followed a theme: watch manufacturing, unusual clocks, clock museums and mechanical instruments or music boxes of all sizes.

Gold clock that belonged to Catherine the Great (Milan, Italy).

Our transportation mode was varied: ocean cruises on the Mediterranean, Atlantic, East and South China Seas, and Adriatic; river cruises on the Danube and Yangtze River; and numerous motor coach trips.

We visited many countries: China, Denmark, Thailand, Italy, Malta, Greece, Turkey, Sweden, Iceland, Newfoundland, Switzerland, Czech Republic, Austria, Germany, Romania, Okinawa, Taiwan, Vietnam, Singapore, Estonia, Latvia, Lithuania, Croatia, Slovenia, Dalmatia, Montenegro and Albania. But the Baltic nations filled me with gratitude for my Mennonite heritage and the outreach it makes in our present world!

Harold on the Great Wall of China.

In 2012 we were privileged to tour the Baltic countries of Latvia, Estonia and Lithuania. The trip into Lithuania was nostalgic for me, as I worked there in 1994 building dormitory furniture for Lithuania Christian College.

Our first stop was at the Hill of Crosses at Siauliai. This hill is covered with an incredible number of crosses of every type and size, placed there as a symbol of Lithuanian nationhood and deep religious faith.

When Nick learned of my association with LCCU, he asked me to introduce him to Dr. Marlene Wall, president of the university. She explained to our group the origin and mission of the school, and gave us a tour of their beautiful new campus.

I was very thankful for my connection with LCCU and the fact that I had attended their 20th Anniversary in 2011. Recalling my two months of work there as a volunteer, and now observing the new campus and hearing of the accomplishments of the graduates, helps to make me a very grateful Mennonite to have been involved in their successful mission, which was created, financed, and staffed by North American Mennonites.

Following this tour, I rented a car and visited Lichtenstein, then Speyer, Germany to tour a large technical museum, co-founded by a friend of mine, on to Belgium and to Bielefeld, Germany, where I visited friends.

I continued to Vahlbruch, my Grandfather Voshage's birthplace, then on to Dresden, my favorite city of all Germany. I was fortunate to volunteer here in 1995, and return whenever possible. In 1995 the Lutheran cathedral Frauenkirche (the Church of our Lady) was in total ruins. After an appeal for restoration contributions, I have seen this huge church be rebuilt over the years. Now I was privileged to attend a service in the fully restored building! The congregation sang the song "Grosser Gott Wir Loben Dich" and I was really touched – we sang this very same song in my home church often. The name means: "Holy God, we praise thy name". After, I walked up the long spiral staircase to the 360 degree viewing area and had a panoramic view of this beloved city.

Restoration of the Frauenkirche in Dresden.

Later I attended a concert at the large Catholic Hof Kirche on the "Silberman" pipe organ – what a treat! I even called my wife on my cell phone and she could hear it (at 2:15 a.m. in California!); so we were able to share the blessing.

On Sunday I worshipped at the Evangelische Mennonitische Freikirche, which I helped build in 1995, and enjoyed fellowship with many old friends there. Rudolf and Dorothee Reim invited me to their home in nearby Lichtenberg for Sunday dinner, and on Monday took me to Bautzen, a neighboring city that has a unique "Sorb" ethnic culture.

Rudolf and I have had many great times together. In 1995 we hiked one Saturday at the Saxony Swiss area; another time we toured Vienna via train. On one of my trips we toured Krakow, Poland and Auschwitz and Birkenau, German concentration camps – very revolting!

A few years ago, Rudolf and Dorothee visited us in San Jose. They had landed at Calgary then "camped" their way in our National Parks. We hosted them at a local motel (since we were recently moved into the Manor and didn't yet have our furniture), and drove them to Santa Cruz and along the coast, where Rudolf had a chance to plunge into the Pacific Ocean!

Chapter 24
Holland – Poland
Study Tour (2001)

IT WAS MY PRIVILEGE TO TRAVEL TO POLAND AND HOLLAND ON A MENNONITE study tour led by Dr. Peter J. Klassen, Dr. Paul Toews and Mr. Alan Peters. This was the first of two consecutive Holland-Poland study tours that the Ungers of Conference World Tours had organized. Their collaboration with brothers Klassen, Toews and Peters assured the wide appeal and unqualified success of this mind-broadening study of the Mennonite sojourn and history of the Mennonites after they left Holland in the fifteen hundreds.

We took a day trip to Kulm (Chelmno) area; visiting Mennonite sites farthest away in Tragheimerwerde villages, and lunched in Marienwerder.

On Saturday we toured Werder Delta Villages, former Mennonite communities, including Ladehopp, Orloff, etc; lunch in Elbing (Elblag), visited Rosengart; returned via the Museum of Werder Village Life in Nowy Dwor. We visited Baerwalde, birthplace of Johann Cornies the acclaimed leader in Chortitza, Ukraine.

Sunday we had a free day in Gdansk. Some walked to the morning Pentecostal service at the former Mennonite Church. A later bus took a Mennonite village route including a stop at Sxtutowo (Stuthof, WWII concentration camp for Jews). A dear friend of mine from our Lincoln Glen Church (MB) in San Jose California knelt at the entrance to the first camp building and prayed and I joined him. This was the third holocaust museum I had visited; years earlier I had visited Dachau in Germany and Kaunas in Lithuania. A dear Dresden friend and I visited the huge concentration camp in Krakow. I will never again want to view man's inhumanity to man.

In Poland we were fortunate to visit an "arcaded" house the Mennonites had constructed many years earlier. A highlight was a meeting that Peter Klassen had arranged with Polish teachers and academics. Thanks to Dr. Klassen, significant numbers of Poles have learned of the Mennonite presence, history and future aspirations in Poland. Across the alley a number of cemetery monuments were collected in a museum. I found a name not very common in Mennonite circles, "Behrends". My father's oldest sister, one of seven, Minnie, was married to Leo Behrends.

A wooden "arcaded" Mennonite home in Poland.

We visited a church in Gdansk that the Mennonites had built many years ago. It was restored after World War II and is now the meetinghouse of an Evangelical Pentecostal congregation. Their adjacent building that the Mennonites used for assisting people of need has been restored and they are effectively using this building. Dr. Klassen interviewed the Pastor and Associate Pastor; the latter was fluent in English. At the rear of the meetinghouse is a large brass plaque to commemorate the Mennonite construction and operation of the Mennonite Congregation. It is gratifying to experience the continuing evangelical presence in Gdansk that the Mennonites began years ago.

Pentecostal church (formerly Mennonite) in Gdansk.

After visiting the former Mennonite church in Gdansk, now a thriving Pentecostal church, again I thank God for the Mennonite faith that began in Switzerland and Holland in the early 1500's. I am grateful for these forebears who developed a biblical theological faith that today resonates around the globe.

We toured the University of Singel Seminary, which houses a Mennonite Library. We met Mr. Piet Nisser, the Dutch Mennonite historian and librarian.

We visited Mennonite churches in Westzaar, Haarlem, and Friesland; and later visited Menno Simons Monument and the hidden Mennonite Church in nearby Pingjum.

Westzaar Mennonite church in Holland.

As an aside to this Holland adventure, my father's mother came from Gronigen, northern Holland, near Menno Simon's roots. In 1994 returning from two months of volunteer work in Klaipeda, Lithuania, I rented a car at Frankfurt and met my cousin Lowell, who was a professor at a college in Utrecht. We toured Amsterdam one day and on Sunday worshiped at the historic Mennonite Church in Amsterdam; a real treat!

During the communist rule in Poland, no churches were closed. There was a lot of solidarity in the general population in Poland opposing communism.

A sidelight of the Poland trip was occasionally observing large stork nests on utility poles. Thirty percent of the European storks live in Poland. They leave on August 28th every year to winter in Egypt. Storks mate for life. When one dies they remain single until death. There is a stork census every three or four years.

At the time of the Poland tour, I was not aware of the fact that my wife's great-grandfather had lived in Pastwa, *Poland*; we had assumed he was from Pastwa, Ukraine! Therefore I did not attempt to visit that area. But we learned through both family letters and this tour how the Holland Mennonites came to the Vistula River delta and developed dikes and levees in order to expand productive agriculture. There again I am grateful for the Mennonite heritage of development of worthless swamps into rich farmland.

Restored Mennonite house and barn in Holland.

My Teichroew ancestors could have been a part of this history, since their name means "dike preserver"! And in the letters from Carol's great-great-grandmother to her son in America, she writes of the floods and the constant need to repair the dikes and levees in order to save their farmland! Therefore, we *both* are grateful to be part of this awesome history of our Mennonite ancestors.

Chapter 25
South America (2002)

In 2002 I participated in a Tourmagination trek of five South America countries, led by Edgar Stoesz and Wilmer Martin.

Edgar has made numerous trips to Paraguay, more than twenty. Having grown up with him on adjacent farms three miles south of Mountain Lake, Minnesota and riding ponies to District #33 country school in the thirties with Edgar and his brother, Harvey, I have many fond memories of the rural years at Mountain Lake and our friendship.

This eventful tour of the countries that we spent the most time in (Paraguay, Bolivia and Peru) really was an eye-opener, especially the Mennonite settlements in Paraguay. Edgar is a masterful storyteller; and since he has been in Paraguay many times and visited upwards of twenty Mennonite colonies and also is fluent in German and Low German, he is an ideal resource leader.

We took a bus from Asuncion to Filadiphia, in the Chaco, on the highway that Harry Harder of Mountain Lake and PAX men had constructed. This project took five years; Vern Buller and his equipment of Richey, Montana created over sixty-two miles of improved roads in 1953.

Then in 1957 Harry Harder returned to Paraguay to complete the highway construction from Fernheim colony to Asuncion, the capital. He, his wife Anne, and two teenage children spent five years there to construct this lifeline.

The Trans-Chaco Highway is a marvelous monument to the foresight of the Mennonites in Paraguay and the United States, to the Paraguayan government officials, and to the dedication and devoted expertise of Vern Buller, Harry Harder, and the volunteers in PAX (founded by Cal Redekop) who built the highway. The achievements of these wonderful Christian brothers are amazing!

Modern truck near an ox-pulled cart.

It seems to me, from what I have read and observed, two overriding factors that were very instrumental in the physical success of the Mennonite colonies hinged on programs that really made a difference in the success of the Mennonites' lives in Paraguay. One was that William Snyder and others developed opportunities to qualify for low-interest long-term loans to help the colonists develop the land and buildings and business. Second, the construction and completion of the road from Fernheim to Asuncion was a godsend to allow the western colonies to deliver produce and products to developed markets much more efficiently. Before the completion of the highway it took weeks or longer to herd cattle to Asuncion. The shrinkage in weight was a great loss in final revenue. With the completion of the highway, trucks could deliver cattle and produce and products in a matter of hours. Praise God!

Kilometer 81 Leprosarium

One of the greatest achievements accomplished by the settling of Mennonites in Paraguay was the vision that leprosy sufferers could be helped and possibly cured. To me, a grateful Mennonite, this achievement ranks next to bringing the saving gospel of Jesus Christ to the Paraguayans, including of course leprosy patients.

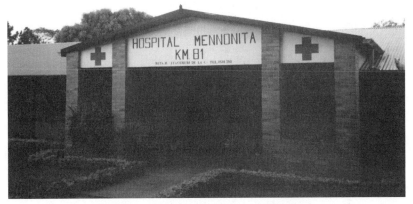

Kilometer 81 Mennonite Leper Hospital.

In Edgar Stoesz's seminal work on the Mennonites in Paraguay (I am quoting): "Leprosy in the Bible – The Bible contains many references to leprosy, though the word as it's used in Scripture means something different from its meaning today. In the ancient world, many dermatological conditions were called leprosy. Associating leprosy with uncleanliness or divine punishment, as some do, adds to a stigma that can be as painful as the disease itself. Leprosy is no more a curse than any other disease. Someone with leprosy should never be referred to as a leper".

Probably no trip I have taken has so vividly showed me what the Mennonite faith has produced, and has made me more grateful to have experienced the Mennonite faith and practices in my life. These observations show how God has given Mennonites a vision and resources to make a huge difference in countless people's lives in Paraguay.

When Edgar introduced us to Kilometer 81, we were introduced to Dr. John R. Schmidt and his dear wife Clara. They had lived in Mountain Lake, Minnesota when they received the call to help leprosy patients in Paraguay. He studied at the leprosy clinic in Carville, Louisiana, before closing his Mountain Lake clinic.

Edgar Stoesz visiting with Dr. & Mrs. John R. Schmidt (founders).

The Schmidts arrived in Paraguay in October of 1961. They lived in Asuncion awaiting the completion of the construction of their house near the new Leprosy Hospital.

When Edgar introduced us in 2002 to the Kilometer 81 Leprosy Hospital, Dr. Carlos Wiens, the Medical Director, guided us. He was born there when his father served there as Chaplain. John Schmidt attended his birth. He grew up on the grounds of the hospital and in playing with neighboring children, became conversant in German, Low German, Spanish, English and Guarani. He graduated number one in his class at Asuncion Medical School.

Wiens served as medical director and resident surgeon at KM 81 from 1988 to 1991 and again from 1994 to 2003, when he took a post as Paraguay's Director Medico Del IPS under Paraguay's President Duarte.

The hospital also provided prostheses and custom-made shoes for deformed feet and limbs. The hospital treated 425 patients for leprosy in 2006.

The patients exposed to the physical healing arts have received healing of the soul as well. Services are conducted in a beautiful chapel on the grounds. A number of patients have said they found Jesus through their treatment at the clinic. The first baptisms were conducted in 1959. Because many patients take a newfound faith with them when they return to their home communities, the extension work emanating out of the KM 81 base has also resulted in the establishment of a network of churches. Dr. Schmidt insisted from the outset that the KM 81 project should belong to the Mennonite Churches of Paraguay, not to the funding agencies. The churches not only own it, they also have supplied much of the staff. They support it financially through an offering taken one Sunday each year in all German Paraguayan Mennonite churches. Very few if any leprosy missions anywhere enjoy such a strong support base.

In completing my recollection of the touring of Paraguay, it was impressive to visit their large cooperative retail stores.

In the Chaco, buildings are designed to collect rainwater in cisterns. That reminded me of southwest Minnesota where houses have gutters installed to direct rainwater into cisterns so that soft water is available for laundry.

Robert and Myrtle Unruh began working in the Chaco at Fernheim in 1951. Both had been raised on farms, Bob in Montana and Myrtle in Kansas. They were recent graduates of Bethel College in North Newton, Kansas. Myrtle worked with women and assembled the first Paraguayan cookbook, "Fed by Mama". This modest book came to grace most Mennonite kitchens of that generation. It helped improve the family diet and consequently increased health and morale. Each section included a feature on feeding the soul as well as the body. She taught women better home management. She gave cooking and canning demonstrations to a new genera-tion of Chaco women through a course in the local high school. The hot sun that burned their crops was harnessed to dry fruits and vegetables. Always the concen-tration was on using available resources in the Chaco, such as the sun.

Robert Unruh experimented with various crops and egg production; he decided that cattle raising and milk production could be the most viable. His experiments proved his ideas as being singularly successful. Today Mennonites provide most of the milk and dairy products of Paraguay and a lot of meat products as well.

Adjacent to the Fernheim settlement is an Indian settlement called Yalva Sanga. They have farms, schools and churches; it is amazing how well they are doing. Under a large permanent canopy we were treated to a delicious lunch and serenaded by a combo of Paraguayan musicians.

It was my desire to speak Low German, my mother-tongue, to an Indian. Lo and behold, the bass fiddle player was as fluent in Plautdietsch as I am. In the earlier years of the settlements, Mennonites had adopted infants who had been abandoned by natives who couldn't care for them. What an amazing story!

Leaving Paraguay, we visited Machu Picchu and Lima, Peru and also a Mennonite settlement in Bolivia.

Harold and native girls at Lake Titicaca, Bolivia.

In Lima we visited several local industries that produced ceramics and various products that they sell to a Mennonite organization called "International Gift Faire". Churches including Lincoln Glen Church in San Jose have annual events selling these hand-crafted products. The proceeds go back to local artisans. My gratefulness of being a Mennonite took another boost observing how we endeavor to help people worldwide.

Chapter 26
Mennonite Heritage Cruise (2002)

(Kiev to Odessa Via Crimea on the General Vatutin)

I JOINED THE 2002 (9ᵀᴴ) MENNONITE HERITAGE CRUISE ORGANIZED BY MARINA and Walter Unger who also accompanied this memorable cruise. The Ungers are outstanding cruise organizers and in accompanying the tours, nothing is left to chance. In my opinion, they are easily as good as any in the business, if not the best. Their reputation is without equal.

To tour the fatherland of my maternal Teichroew clan, it is difficult to *not* be proud of my Ukrainian roots. This visit really inspired me to be grateful to Almighty God, my heavenly Father, for having Mennonite roots emanating from Neufeld, Goossen and Teichroew families.

In the Kiev area, we visited a Jewish holocaust site at Baba Yar, and the complex of monastic buildings known as Pechersky Lavra. Observing this enormous ravine where countless Jewish people were buried, some reportedly not quite dead, is a poignant example and reminder that evil men held sway in various awful historic times. The Mennonites I am related to have experienced their share of persecution unto death for their faith.

Our Kiev cruise prologue included a command performance by the outstanding Boyan Male Choir.

Sailing the great Dnieper River we had the distinct privilege to hear ten lectures and to observe many presentations by Paul Toews that cover Mennonite history, architecture and genealogy.

Dr. Paul Toews giving Mennonite history lecture.

We got ahead of the ship and took buses to Dnipropetrovsk, an Imperial Russian Centre well known to our ancestors. It was formerly known as Ekaterinoslav. A walking tour of the old city centre reminded me of the influence of entrepreneur and mayor Johann Esau, politician Herman Bergman and other Mennonites in this region. We saw the Thiessen mill and the Red Cross Hospital where many Mennonite men trained for and served in the Sanitatidienst in World War I. Around the corner are the infamous KGB dungeons.

We also saw sites associated with the anarchist Nestor Makhno. In April 1918 German troops briefly occupied Ukraine. Desperate Mennonites met them joyously at the railroad station hoping it would bring an end to the years of chaos and anarchy that followed the revolution. However, it was an enormous tactical blunder. Local Ukrainians saw them welcome the enemy – and never forgot.

Six months later when Germany withdrew, Ukraine became the central battleground in the ongoing revolution. Banditry was worse here than anywhere. Warlord/anarchist Nestor Makhno became the scourge of the Mennonites. He and his 30 thousand troops (some estimated 100,000) attempted what was originally a conservative breakaway attempt. All the Mennonite colonies fell under his brutal occupation. On the west bank of the Dnieper River in 1919 his men engaged in a series of killings, hundreds died in the massacres. 143 men, women, and children were killed in two villages at Borozenko, some were raped and beheaded. A formal dedication ceremony was attended in October 2002 of the previously unmarked

mass gravesite of 67 of the Borozenko victims. (It may be that Makhno was seeking revenge for having been mistreated as a young man while working for Mennonites).
- from a lecture by Dr. Paul Toews

An emotionally charged room in the local museum is devoted to the millions of people who perished under Stalin. Representative photos of faces, including a Mennonite face, form a candle-lit pyramid.

We saw the Fast mill, seven stories tall with large concrete silos to store grain. One of the flour mills the Mennonites had constructed is still in use.

At Zaporizhia we visited the Maedenschule (girls' school). This was a distinct event to help us develop our gratefulness for our forefathers' foresight to educate both girls and boys. Visiting this school was one of the highlights of my tour of Ukraine.

We also saw the Koop house and large factory. Mennonites manufactured wagons (the best of their time), rudimentary machine tools, farm machinery, etc. Some of their factories provided employee housing. In my opinion, one of the amazing benefits that the settlement provided in their hey-day was good care for developmentally challenged people. The business people and farmers helped fund these care-providers and establishments by paying adequate taxes to take care of all of societies' unfortunates. This appears as another benefit of the Mennonite presence being a virtual independent society within the Russian state – a state within a state.

We took bus trips to personal-preferred locations in the Chortitza and Molotschna colonies via bus routes that reflected our individual choices. We visited Halbstadt, founded in 1804, and saw the Willems house and Willems Mill, now a dairy-products factory.

At Alexanderwohl we learned that the entire congregation had immigrated to Kansas in the 1870's. We visited a cemetery at Tokmak.

There was a monument to 131 orphaned, mentally challenged children, murdered by Germans in 1941. We saw a church building and a school for gymnasts, where Mennonite archives had been stored upstairs until 1917.

We stopped at Jushanlee, the Reimer Estate at Kleifeld. We saw remains of a Mennonite Brethren Church at Alexanderkrone, and we saw Fridensruke in the distance.

We were invited to Maria Pankratz's house. She is nearly 90 years old; she lives with a daughter and family. We gave a donation to her. She wanted someone to pray a blessing in Low German, and though there were two pastors in the house, they didn't know Low German, so I volunteered. Believe it or not this is the first time (and probably the only time) that I have attempted a public Low German prayer. It wasn't easy. Mrs. Pankratz is a treasure. The house is orderly and nice and she is taken care of very well. She is happy and content.

Visiting Mrs. Pankratz in her home with her family.

Johan Cornies, as Paul Toews writes, was a Mennonite phenomenon. He revolutionized Mennonite standing in Russia. He was highly respected in St. Petersburg. He was a wealthy, well-connected farmer, innovator, planner and keen observer and amateur anthropologist. At one time he initiated the silk industry. Many mulberry trees were planted. The industry appeared somewhat successful for a time until overseas competition forced the Mennonites to discontinue the silk industry. Cornies developed a plan to plant windbreak trees and fruit trees and he established a large tree nursery that we visited. His farming ideas, such as strip farming of grain to conserve moisture, were successful. He was on a first-name basis with government officials in St. Petersburg and received at least one medal for his leadership. Though his education was modest, the efforts he introduced definitely succeeded. The brightest, most promising young people were sent to Switzerland, Holland, Germany and St. Petersburg for advanced education. This program was quite successful.

We visited a Cossack open air equestrian event on Chortitza Island. Needless to say, the Cossacks are expert horsemen. While I was sitting in the stands I observed a fellow with a large notepad was glancing at me often, and when the program was over he offered to sell me a picture he had sketched of me. He had also sketched one of Jake Epp of Canada. I did buy mine for $10.00 and found it was flattering.

The Romanov's Livadia Palace has a lot of history. This is the palace where Roosevelt, Churchill and Stalin met on February 4, 1945.

Several years prior to this meeting, these three leaders had met there to strategize the logistics of the German invasion of Russia and the pending defeat and eventual retreat from Stalingrad. When they met in 1943, Stalin convinced Roosevelt and Churchill to force the Mennonites that would trek to Poland and Germany without documents, passports, etc., to be "repatriated" (returned to Russia). According to

Dr. Paul Toews, of the 35,000 people who mostly walked on the awful "Great Trek" across Poland to Germany, Hungary, Austria and Romania, only 12,000 made it. 23,000 were "repatriated" by the Soviets. Of the 40 million displaced during World War II, 12 – 15 million were ethnic Germans and they, like the rest, became helpless victims of the war.

I happen to know several women who traveled on this 2 year "Great Trek". Justina Neufeld of North Newton, Kansas is one. Another woman, Anna Franz, wife of Delbert Franz of Mountain View, California, was on this trek with her sister, Helene, and her mother, Amalie Bergen. She has amazing stories to tell of this very difficult sojourn.

As a grand Mennonite epilogue, we saw a special exhibit from the Peter Braun archive, miraculously rediscovered, and the Board of Guardians Archive, displayed for us on the ship. For me this was one of the highlights of this entire trip. To see the amazing examples of work that school students had achieved was for me mind-boggling. These examples of students' work and advanced professional architects' drawing, etc., were astounding. I couldn't have had a more fitting culmination of this incredible cruise as the Braun Archive Introduction in the Ship's Music Room. What a fitting benediction.

The Peter Braun Archive.

It seems to me I need to recognize the Mountain Lake, Minnesota group I met with numerous times when we had photo ops: Lorin and Becky Epp, Eldean and Deanna Ratzlaff, Quentin and Bee Neufeld, now of Oregon, Bill Hiebert, now in Illinois, and Harold and Eleanor Franz, Kansas (she was a Laker). These nine folks ate together virtually every meal and they had a great time!

One of the most important facets of the trip was helping support the Mennonite Centre in Ukraine, which has a mission to aid needy people in troubled times. We were asked to fill a large suitcase with personal needs items and clothing, etc., to leave at the Centre, which a lot of us did. Part of this organization's mission is also to rehabilitate the Maedenschule (Girls' School) in Halbstadt, Molotschna Colony. The Centre develops programs in home-care assistance, small business, and agriculture and community development. Priorities now are youth and seniors.

The Mennonite Centre in Ukraine, restored by Canadian Mennonites.

All through this tour I was deeply impressed by the sophisticated society of the early Mennonite settlers in the Ukraine, and their sufferings under the Russian regime later. I am thankful to be of Mennonite faith and lineage.

Chapter 27
Mexico (2007)

In March 2-11, 2007 David Friesen and Dave Worth led a very memorable tour to Mexico. This tour visited the Old Colony Mennonite Church in Gnadenfeld where we worshiped beginning at 8:00 a.m. The men filed in one door and the women in by another to the benches. The men sit on one side and the women on the other side of the church. Several men sat facing the congregation on one side of the church and they were the "for sanger" who lead congregational singing in unison. The church leader preached from a written sermon that he read. The singing and sermons were in High German.

Later after the service ended at 10:00 a.m., we boarded our bus and drove to the Blumenau Mennonite Church (affiliated with Mennonite Church Canada) to join in their 10:00 to 12:00 service. David Friesen, one of our tour leaders, had been asked to deliver the sermon, which he did mostly in German with a few English phrases and thoughts interspersed. Following this service we were invited to accompany them to their school gym where a carry-in lunch was being served. The vegetable noodle soup was delicious.

The following Monday we boarded the bus and had a delicious Mexican style breakfast at Motel Tarahumara in Cuauhtemoc. Then we left for the Swift Colony settlement that had been established in 1922 by Manitoba immigrants. More immigrants arrived later from Swift Current, Saskatchewan. Driving to Gnadenfeld (part of the Manitoba colony) we toured this village, which was laid out in the traditional Russian style. The homes with a barn and small acreage were surrounded with low stone or concrete fences, divided by wide laneways.

Children and elders in Mennonite colony.

We toured a cheese factory, which is an important part of the community's survival. We had ample opportunity to sample and purchase their cheese. We returned to the Old Colony Church where we had worshipped on Sunday, to have more questions answered. Lunch was enjoyed at the La Huerta (apple) Restaurant, which is owned by a family in the apple orchard business. We observed numerous apple orchards and many had provision to keep birds off the trees, with large netting arrangements.

We also visited the Rehabilitation Center for alcohol and drug addicts. John Bixler led the group in several songs to encourage the residents. When we left we saw farmers preparing their fields for planting. Then we drove to Cuauhtemoc for a delicious meal of Chihuahua-style beef. After supper we went to the Mennonite Historical Museum where we observed a video of the Mennonite settlements in Mexico.

Then we traveled to the Copper Canyon to board the train on the very scenic railway. The views were dramatic. The mountains are heavily wooded, mostly pines. Near villages are apple orchards. Cowboys herded cattle on open ranges. There were stellar jays and meadow larks in the open meadows and forests. Clear streams were observed that indicated higher water run off.

When we arrived at our scenic Hotel Mirador for the night, on the rim of the Copper Canyon, the Tarahumaras had their wares spread out on the walls and steps and the women sat among their wares and continued to weave their baskets. We enjoyed observing many hummingbirds that enjoyed feeders hanging from the patio. The views of the canyon were amazing.

Harold & Mexican guitarist at Copper Canyon.

Three Tarahumara men performed dances representing deer and donkeys. They then ran a race while kicking wooden balls. In their native culture they sometimes race for 36 hours. Two young women then ran a race with hoops representing some of their traditional races.

At mid-morning we boarded the bus for a sightseeing tour of the canyon rim. Our first stop was the balancing rock along the Orinique Canyon. The 50,000 Tarahumara people who live on the hillsides and in the valley live off the land, raising corn, beans and fruit. They are Catholic and were preparing for the Easter celebration with their own unique rituals. We stopped at another lookout where we could view three canyons, which along with four others make up the Copper Canyon system.

Harold at the rim of Copper Canyon.

We drove through two small towns and observed how the local folks live. They grow most of their own food and supplement their income by working in the tourist industry.

Eighty-five years ago on this day, the first Mennonites arrived at the train station in what is now Cuauhtemoc and gave thanks for their safe journey, the privileges the government of Mexico promised, and for their new homeland. Our tour group felt a real sense of connection to those courageous Mennonites as we stood under one of the poplar trees (which is one of three remaining from 85 years ago) at the same train station and listened to David Friesen read the words of Harry Leonard Sawatsky from his book *"They Sought a Homeland"*. Singing, "Now Thank We All Our God With Heart and Hand and Voices", we could feel their gratitude on this 85th anniversary.

At the Mennonite Museum the group admired the replica of an Old Colony home complete with kitchen where a family of a dozen or so would eat and work and visit. David Friesen showed us an old German Bible printed in 1941 in Mexico. The type had been set, painstakingly, by a fifteen-year old girl. She lived to be an old lady and died several years ago. David's family donated furniture and farm equipment to the museum. One corner cupboard has a secret drawer and to this day David doesn't know where it is! His father's iron-wheeled wagon with a wooden box sits in front of the museum. David remembers that if that wagon would be backed up the wheels would begin to loosen and fall off.

Later we visited the Blumenort School, which was in session. Our group divided into three separate sections and visited classes where children were separated by age, not grades. In the 6-7 year old class, 13 children sang for us in German, sounding much like the chanting we heard in their church on Sunday. The teacher, Lena Funk, was from the Swift Colony. The instruction was done in Low German, but in the two older classes High German, Spanish and some limited English was studied. In the middle group, the children did a reading lesson in unison in a sing-song voice in German. They read from a storybook run off on a copier. Blumenort was a "Committee School" rather than a school run by the Old Colony Church. Desks were not individual, but one long desk and backless bench to accommodate several children who were all well-behaved, clean and neatly dressed.

Children in school at Cuauhtemoc.

Sometime later we came to Steinrich, a daughter-colony to the Manitoba Colony and the setting where David Friesen began teaching where he pastored a church and where some of his family is buried. Isaac Bergen, President of the Bible School, welcomed us and told us about the school, which has a mission statement to ready young people with low education or literacy skills. Here all are accepted when probably they wouldn't be able to go to another college. The school presently runs for three months with about 250 students from Mexico, Canada, the USA, Bolivia and Belize. In the dining hall, the students were having a good time washing dishes while we ate our lunch of mashed potatoes, meatballs, coleslaw and apple pie, the same fare the students enjoyed. Many of these students were in the choir, which sang at the second service we attended on Sunday morning.

The second cheese factory we visited was a large establishment called "Lacteo Mennonitas de Chihuahua". A young woman (their chemist) dressed in a white lab coat, explained the cheese-making process from the time the raw milk is trucked in until the finished product; the cheese is shipped out all over Chihuahua. This factory is state-of-the- art and meets all of the government requirements. Our guide impressed us with her artistic flip charts used in training the cheese makers in hygienic practices. They treated us to tasty samples of their products, plain or pepper. A lot of us liked their products so much that we walked next door and purchased cheese to take home with us.

The cheese factory at Gnadenfeld.

Cheese

Another highlight of the trip that really helps us to obtain the "flavor" of these settlements was an invitation we had received from a Kroeker family who lived on a successful farm. This was at Campo 2B in Gnadenfeld and the "Faspa" was served by Mrs. Kroeker and her four daughters. The tables were loaded with buns, meat, cheese, jam, pickles, butter and cookies and sweet breads. Homemade potato and sausage soup completed the sumptuous "Faspa". The farmyard was like a petting zoo with rabbits, chickens, cows, goats, pigs, ducks and dogs in their enclosures on the perimeter of the farmyard.

We also visited Hofsnung Heim, a residential facility for persons with developmental disabilities, a cooperative venture of several colonies. Presently thirty-four adults are served. This was an impressive ministry to the greater Mennonite community in Mexico.

The Kleine Gemeinde family, in the El Valle Colony, raise primarily cotton to be exported to Japan. They also grow corn, peppers and wheat. They gave us a tour of the Cotton Gin where the harvested cotton is cleaned by four large mills and then pressed into large bales, covered with plastic and stored outside, until it's picked up by the buyers. The seed is processed into oil and meal. The cotton yields about 500 lbs. per acre or about $728 per acre. Water is found in very deep wells. The colony has been operating for seventeen years and has a small airfield and a plane to spray the fields. There are about 200 people living in the colony.

I was very impressed by the way the Mennonites in this area of Mexico have established a viable way of life. They provide a good living environment for their families, and carry on many traditional customs and usage of the Low German language. I enjoyed my fellowship with these brethren in the faith.

Chapter 28
Moscow - Omsk, Siberia - Uzbekistan (2010)

At Fresno Pacific University, Dr. Paul Toews and Walter and Marina Unger held a meeting about a coming conference to be held in Omsk, Siberia in 2010. I became interested after attending; my impressions of the proposed trip to the conference astounded me.

I made up my mind immediately to go to Omsk if my health and checkbook did not complain too much. I simply had to attend this academic conference in Omsk. Also at this Fresno meeting I met John J. Friesen, who with Hans Werner edits "Preservings", a magazine that discusses the Old Colony Mennonite history. Having visited several Old Colony settlements in South America and North America, I was immediately ready to subscribe to this magazine; it is a real treasure! Hans Werner also was to attend the Omsk Conference; he is an amazing resource on Mennonite culture and history.

This area of Siberia, Russia had been established about one hundred years ago, to become a successful wheat-growing industry of the Mennonite settlers.

Starting our tour in Moscow, we toured Tratjokov Gallery, had a general city tour, and met street vendors who were selling tickets to a concert. We agreed to be vulnerable and purchased the tickets. Our faith was rewarded; we attended the concert and enjoyed it. Also someone recommended a business that sold cinnamon rolls; we found it and they were very good!

Colorful architecture in Red Square, Moscow.

We took a one-day trip to Vladimir and Suzdal; this was a tour of villages a way from Moscow, giving us a window into how rural people live.

The Conference on "Germans of Siberia: History and Culture" was held in Omsk June 2-4, meeting in the Omsk Regional Government Building, the Ibis Sibir Hotel and the Marx Scholarly Center of the F.M. Dostoevsky Omsk State University (OMSU).

In addition to the scholarly reports covering Mennonite history, language, education, relationships with other nations and religions, families, vacations, violence, war, and migration, we were entertained by city tours, dinner and a folkloric performance. There was also a meeting with the Rector of the University.

On Saturday we drove to Waldheim, a Mennonite rural settlement and we were privileged to be billeted by the Pauls family in their very modern house. In order for us to "qualify" to stay in a village family's home we needed to be fluent in Low German, Plautdietsch; thank God I am fluent in Plautdietsch; it is my mother tongue. I didn't speak a word of English until I was six.

We were invited to attend Saturday evening services in their village church, which was within walking distance from the home. It was a real blessing to be able to enjoy the worship service. The preaching was inspirational. There were upwards of forty or more young people providing vocal and instrumental music for the worship. These young people were very good musicians. It was a lengthy service. Sunday morning we worshiped with them again. The young people were again very inspirational. The quality of their singing and playing was excellent. We learned that some of the musical expertise has been self-taught.

Waldheim Church interior.

At lunch in the birch forest (the Wald) a number of young men entertained us with brass instruments and they too were very good. Apparently they noticed these instruments on the way to recyclers; they obtained them and refurbished them and taught themselves to play.

"Recycled" brass band.

A former senior pastor was interviewed for us after we partook of a delicious lunch, more like a dinner, and he described his five years in a gulag, a prison before glasnost. We Americans find it difficult to appreciate what price our Christian brothers and sisters have paid for their faith. Today leaders and others are witnessing to ethnic Russians about their faith with some success. This was one of the most gratifying stories of this week, another reason I am a grateful Mennonite!

Mother and child at picnic in the forest.

Saturday I received a tour of a large mechanical and maintenance garage to repair and maintain even their largest trucks, combines and equipment. They could weld and perform necessary mechanical work, and a large metal cutting lathe made it possible to manufacture their own items.

Walter Willems and his wife of British Columbia, Canada have been instrumental in assisting the Waldheim settlement in wheat growing and related business. He has built a flour mill that is operating and also shipped in a large Caterpillar blade road grader, donated by a Mr. Block; the outgoing roads need help. Mr. and Mrs. Willems have donated time, expertise and resources to really improve the lives of the Omsk, Siberia Mennonites.

One vignette I would like to include was observing the dairy cows returning home before dark to be milked. The system the Mennonite farmers employ here is somewhat similar to the system they used in the Ukraine. The families cooperate in using a large pasture that is supervised by a herdsman. On the way to their respective barns the cattle are herded down the road and they know what driveway they need to turn into and enter the barn and their stalls for their evening milking. The lady of the house does the milking, with machines, the children help with preparing and cleaning machines, it only takes minutes and the operation is complete. We were all very impressed with the satisfaction of their position all the people exhibited. Many mothers, housekeepers and sometimes milkmaids were a jolly, very happy people.

Cattle in home lanes.

The houses are very modern, maybe almost ultramodern; the Pauls' house had a sauna that I used. They had recently installed a new bathroom; it included a bidet. We observed all modern convenience except television.

For Sunday morning breakfast Mrs. Pauls included cracklings in her servings. Len Loeppky and I felt like royalty!

Since the Gorbachev years, the Mennonites have had a lot more freedom; they are enterprising and thriving.

"Silk Road Tour"/Uzbekistan – June 7-18, 2010

The next portion of our tour was in the famous "Silk Road" area of the Middle East. We travelled through the country of Uzbekistan and its major cities. The term was coined by German geographer von Richthofen, the uncle of the Red Baron.

The name "Silk Road" brings to mind caravans crossing the world's highest mountains and barren deserts, but it originated as a complex network of land and sea routes between China, the Middle East, the Mediterranean and Europe that was in operation from the 1st century B.C. to the A.D. 15th century.

Harold with a Silk Road "Camel".

The two main routes that entered Central Asia from China were: 1) the northern route, which passed from western China into what is now Kazakhstan and went through or near what is now Alma Aty (Kazakhstan), Bishek (Kyrgyzstan) and Tashkent (Uzbekistan); and 2) the southern route.

Silk was prized as a trade item and was ideal for overland travel because it was easy to carry, took up little space, held up over time, weighed relatively little but was high in value. By weight silk was worth as much as gold.

The silk carried on the Silk Road came in the form of rolls of raw silk, dyed rolls, cloth, tapestries, embroideries, carpets and clothes.

The Silk Road stopped serving as a shipping route for silk around 1400.

When we left Waldheim, we were driven to Omsk again and then flew to Moscow. There we flew to Tashkent; we explored this modern capital of the Republic of Uzbekistan, and enjoyed a sightseeing tour of the "Old Town", where we visited the Barak-Khan Madrasa, a late 16th century Islamic seminary housing the Sunni Mufti of Central Asia. At Madrasas the young Muslim men studied Islamic theology.

A Madrasa (school).

We visited the Museums of Decorative and Applied Arts and viewed the antique "suzani" (silk embroidery). Then we went to the Bazaar, a marketplace where you can buy anything from pomegranates to local handicrafts. I asked a bazaar clerk what the spices tasted like, and he licked his finger and dipped it into a bin of cinnamon and tasted it; I did likewise and found it delicious. I should have bought some!

Bazaar in Uzbekistan.

As we drove to Bukhara, we visited Serabulak village, a site related to Mennonites. There are a number of abandoned buildings where I believe some Mennonite families had once lived. These Mennonites refused to accept collectivization, so Stalin deported them to Kazakstan.

On a personal note, when I volunteered in Dresden, Germany, I helped to build a Mennonite Brethren mission church for Mennonite emigrants from Kazakstan. While there working, and on subsequent visits in later years, I again visited this church, worshipping with them. Many of them became my dear friends. I shall always cherish my memories of helping to provide a church for them in their new home.

How this Uzbekistan visit justifies my book's title, "A Grateful Mennonite": when viewing the buildings that Mennonites had occupied before moving on, has given me renewed appreciation of the history my forebears have experienced in their search for religious freedom and better economic opportunities, and more political privileges.

Siberian Mennonites are strong and vibrant, surviving many years of hardship and persecution. When I heard of the gulag experience of one of their pastors, I felt proud of their staunch firmness of faith and perseverance under trial. May we, as grateful Mennonites, also remain true to our Christian faith in the years to come!

Chapter 29
Ukraine Dnieper River Heritage Cruise (2010)

THE LAST TOUR I HAD THE PRIVILEGE TO PARTICIPATE IN WITH A GROUP OF approximately 180 pilgrims occurred on October 1st – October 16th, 2010; the final of fifteen tours that Marina and Walter Unger organized and hosted on the Dnieper River between Kiev, Odessa, Sevastopol and Yalta ("Grand" Mennonite Heritage Cruises). We congregated at Odessa and boarded the Dnieper Princess ("Jewel of the Dnieper River/Black Sea Fleet").

Marina and Walter Unger, of Toronto, who accompany each cruise, created the Mennonite Heritage Cruise. Marina is an experienced travel agent, specializing in Central and Eastern Europe and the Middle East. Walter joined her in the travel industry in 1994 after a diverse career of 37 years with the Canadian Broadcasting Corporation. Their primary focus is the Mennonite Heritage Cruise. In 2001 they added a Poland-Holland study tour. It was my distinct privilege to travel with them on their inaugural Poland-Holland Tour of May 21, 2001 – June 4, 2001. Dr. Peter Klassen was the tour director in Poland and Dr. Paul Toews was the director in Holland.

It may be necessary to define "Russian Mennonites" at this juncture. Dr. Toews says that on Easter Sunday, 1788, fifty persons with wagons and possessions departed from the village of Bohnsack (near Danzig) in what is now northern Poland. They were the vanguard of the Mennonite migration to New Russia. After five weeks of trudging along muddy roads they reached Riga. From Riga they followed the Duna River to Dubrovna, where they wintered. Others soon followed and by the spring of 1789, there were 220 families ready to follow the Dnieper River southward to their new homeland in what today is the country of Ukraine. (Quoted from Dr. Paul Toews).

The term "Russian Mennonites" or "Northern European Mennonites" is used to differentiate between the people and their descendants mentioned above and the "Swiss Mennonites", including the Amish, who had a much different history of immigration. The "Russian Mennonites" originated in the Netherlands, then some fled to Poland to escape severe persecution and later settled on lands granted by the Imperial Russian Tsars, notably Catherine II. Still later they acquired more lands in various parts of the Russian Empire, including Siberia. The mother colonies and some daughter colonies were located in present day Ukraine.

Dr. Paul Toews and Mr. Rudy Friesen are founding and continuing leaders of the cruise. Mr. Alan Peters is the leading Mennonite genealogist resource leader.

Rudy Friesen is a practicing and award-winning architect in Winnipeg. His parents immigrated to Canada from Russia in 1926. He received his architectural training at the University of Manitoba and has been active in numerous professional organizations.

Mr. Friesen is the author of the important 1996 Mennonite book, "Into the Past" and "Buildings of the Mennonite Commonwealth". An even more popular version of the book, "Building on the Past" was published in spring of 2004. It is currently being translated into Ukrainian. He has written over a hundred articles on Russian Mennonite Architecture and visits to the area for "Der Bote." On the most recent cruises Rudy presented a series of definitive illustrated lectures on Northern European Mennonite architecture, having also traveled to the Netherlands and Poland. He has since given versions of these lectures to various Mennonite Colleges and Universities in Canada and the USA. He is a founding board member of the Friends of the Mennonite Centre in Ukraine, having himself supervised the renovation of the historic schoolhouse, which housed the Centre.

Along with historian Dr. Toews and genealogist Mr. Alan Peters, Mr. Friesen has helped create the international prestige and reputation of the cruise.

Dr. Paul Toews is Professor of History at Fresno Pacific University. He is also Director of the Centre for Mennonite Brethren Studies, Mennonite Brethren Biblical Seminary and Fresno Pacific University. He is the author of many articles and books on diverse aspects of Mennonite history including "Mennonites in American Society, 1930-1970", and "Modernity and the Persistence of Religious Community", published in 1996. Like other leading Mennonite scholars today, he is involved in archival research projects in Ukraine. Currently he is leader of the international team, which is creating the new Siberia Mennonite Archive and supervised a major international scholarly symposium in Siberia in 2010, in association with the Russian Academy of Sciences. He has spent a year in Ukraine as a Fulbright exchange scholar. Dr. Toews gives four major illustrated lectures and hosts other significant cruise events. His presence on the cruise is much respected and universally loved. Passengers often comment that he uniquely symbolizes the spirit and excellence of the cruise.

Mr. Alan Peters is the master Mennonite genealogist. He is acknowledged by his peers in the genealogical world as having done more work in tracking the Dutch/ Prussian/Russian/North American Mennonite stream than anyone else. The GRANDMA project, officially sponsored by the California Mennonite Historical Society and Fresno MB Biblical Seminary, is based on his work. That project alone now includes genealogical information on well over a million people out of this northern European Mennonite strand. In addition to researching in Mennonite records, Alan has worked in the civil records and state church records of Prussia/ Poland and Russia/Ukraine. Alan brings his laptop computer on the ship and presents family trees to passengers who have requested genealogical researches.

On the last ten cruises Alan has presented computer-assisted seminars on genealogy that had passengers riveted for two hours – thanks to his profound knowledge of Mennonite genealogy and familiarity with genealogical software. Alan is an accomplished litanist and has helped shape many of the reflective occasions on the cruise. Genealogy has become a mainstream interest for many people and Alan has always been "ahead of the curve". Having retired after a distinguished career in California Social Services, Alan is much sought after for workshops in genealogy.

Our tour began in Odessa, and was a "reverse" of my 2002 trip!

We had opportunity to climb the great Potemkin Staircase and walk around the city to shop for souvenirs.

On the 4th through the 6th we began our tour of Crimea. For three days we were docked at historic Sevastopol. Here we saw a high-energy musical revue by the Fleet musicians, singers and dancers.

We were docked within twenty minutes drive to one of the world's great panoramas – depicting a day in the Crimean War (1853-56). We were also close to the site of the tragic Charge of the Light Brigade.

Crimea is a fascinating place with a varied geography. Most of the peninsula is flat, fertile, arable land, much coveted by 19th century land–starved Mennonites from the Molotschna. We visited the former Mennonite villages; we stopped at Spat and Tschongrau.

As we left Crimea, we were privileged to update our knowledge of Russian Mennonite history with historian Dr. Paul Toews and architect, Mr. Rudy Friesen.

On October 7th we were again on the Dnieper River to make a short stop at Kherson to enjoy a rustic outdoor picnic lunch and crafts sale on a Dnieper delta island. The Mennonite lectures concluded.

Harold at Kherson Crafts sale (Ukraine).

From October 8th – 11th we were docked at Zaporizhia. We saw famous Chortitza – Rosenthal, now a suburb of Zaporizhia, including the famous oak tree, the Maedenschule and other well-known sites. From Zaporizhia we visited the parent Chortitza and Molotschna colonies via bus routes reflecting passenger requests. On a trip to the Tokmak area adjacent to Fuerstenau, where my Teichroew and Goossen forebears lived, it was dark when we were returning to the ship so we didn't stop there. I was told the settlement has been nearly obliterated.

New MB Church built on foundation of an abandoned church.

One of the most touching aspects of the entire tour is observing the candlelight memorial service in memory of passengers whose family members died in the World War I holocaust. It was not easy to keep from shedding tears. It is another example why I should be grateful for my Mennonite heritage. My forebears have shed *their* blood from the 1500's until at least World War II. The memorial service commemorated the disappearance during the Soviet terror of 30,000 Mennonite men, women and children.

The cruise ended in Kiev. We visited old Kiev Hiel, St. Sofia Basilica and the Jewish holocaust at the ravine at Baba Yar, where many Jews lie buried.

We heard the renowned Harlytsa Ukraine Folk Ensemble, then the gala Captain's Dinner received our undivided attention. We were favored to a command performance by Ukraine's outstanding professional Boyan Male Chamber Choir. This was an example of their new fall program which they then took on the road for an extensive autumn tour of Western Europe. The singers love to perform to appreciative Mennonites from North America.

Dances by a folk ensemble.

From here I traveled to Vienna prior to leaving Europe for my home in San Jose, California.

It has been thrilling for me to retrace the steps of our Mennonite forebears during these six Mennonite history tours! I have been impressed over and over by their tenacity, their clinging closely to the faith, their excellent farming practices, and the way the Mennonite customs and language have continued on, generation after generation.

I am thankful that I am a part of this unique heritage, and that my wife and I have been fortunate to carry on much of this rich Mennonite heritage in our home!

Chapter 30
Our "Super Alaska Trip"

By Carol Siebert Voshage

WE HAVE DONE MANY TRIPS TO ALASKA: HAROLD BY AIR AND PICKUP TRUCK, then both of us twice by ferry to the Inside Passage and many cruises to southeast Alaska, as well as two motorhome vacations for three months or more all over Alaska and western Canada. A few of these trips involved volunteering, but *all* enlarged our fellowship with new friends.

In late summer of 2010 I planned a five-week journey (with much assistance from our travel agent-friend Susan Reimer Stewart) so that we could cover a wider area of Alaska with a minimum of air travel (for my sake).

Amtrak took us by rail north to Seattle, where we rode a Princess bus to Vancouver, B.C., Canada. We boarded the "Island Princess" cruise ship there for a sail to the "Inside Passage", with stops at Ketchikan, Juneau and Skagway. Here we took a day trip by bus up the White Pass into British Columbia and the Yukon Territory, where we visited Caribou Crossing and Carcross.

Back on the ship we saw many beautiful glaciers emptying into the Pacific Ocean. We sailed on to Whittier, Alaska, where we transferred to the Alaska railroad for a ride through Anchorage to Talkeetna, where we got on a bus for the Princess Wilderness Lodge perched on a mountainside facing Denali Park.

While there, Harold went into Talkeetna to visit a friend, and to catch a plane ride to the glaciers of Mt. McKinley. At the airport he ran into Todd and Sarah Palin, who were also flying in to film a "Discovery" segment on the Alaska wilderness. Todd graciously took a picture of Harold and Sarah before they all "took off" in their planes. Harold's plane landed at an approximately 7,000-foot elevation on a glacier, where climbers are flown in to climb Mt. McKinley ("Denali").

Harold by the plane on Mt. McKinley / Denali Glacier.

For one entire day we were privileged to enjoy full sight of "Denali" from the lodge – usually enshrouded in clouds!

Then we transferred by bus to the Princess lodge at Denali National Park. While there we took a day trip by bus through the park, past Mt. McKinley, past Kantishna Roadhouse (where we had visited in 1992), to the end of the 95-mile park road and back. We saw much wildlife and sometimes the bus had to "crawl" behind a caribou or moose that had decided to "meander" down the middle of the road ahead of us.

Next the Alaska RR took us past the coalmine area of Healy to Fairbanks, where we relaxed at the Princess Riverside Lodge. While there we rented a car and spent a day at Chena Hot Springs, where we had lunch. Harold bathed in the outdoor (*very* HOT!) hot spring pool, while I photographed a meandering moose until a ranger warned me to keep more distance!

Moose at Chena Hot Springs, Alaska.

We also cruised in the boat "Discovery III" on the Chena River, visiting a typical native "fish camp" on the shore.

Now we joined a small tour group to travel by van north on the "haul road" to Prudhoe Bay. We were limited to one *small* bag each, so we shipped our luggage to Anchorage to be fetched later.

We first followed the oil pipeline up the Steese and Elliott Highways past the Tatalina River to stop at Joy, Alaska (Mile 45) where our friends, the Carlsons, have lived and raised their large family for many years. They built two-story log buildings and serve as a "rest stop" for travel groups.

On north and west onto the Dalton Highway, still following the pipeline. We crossed the mighty Yukon River, then the Arctic Circle and stopped for supper and night lodging at Coldfoot, a road service settlement and gold mining area.

Going north on the Haul Road to Prudhoe Bay alongside the oil pipeline.

The next day we visited the small, isolated community of Wiseman, where a group of Christians decided to settle. They graciously allowed us to tour their homes, chapel, museum, gift store and gardens. They are up-to-date, with computer access, in spite of their location off the highway by the Dietrich River Middle Fork.

On northward into the Brooks Range, through Atigun Pass, still alongside the Trans-Alaska Pipeline Utility Corridor, out through the "Gates of the Arctic National Preserve" onto the North Slope. We ended our journey at Prudhoe Bay on the Beaufort Sea (Arctic Ocean) among the oil wells, collection pipes and wandering wildlife.

Collector pipes from oil wells at Prudhoe.

Almost every building there is on skids or wheels, so that it can be moved. Our "lodge" would have required dressing and walking outside through mud to another building in order to use a bathroom (even in the "night" – always daylight), so Harold and I switched rooms with a pilot who was located in the bathroom building. While there, on my nighttime trek to use a toilet (which was located up a step onto an elevated platform), as I was ready to leave the cubicle, all of the lights went out! The window was blocked off and the emergency light did *not* work! I felt along the wall (after I remembered to step *down*), bumped into a sink, a towel dispenser and a large wastebasket) until I located the doorknob to the hall! I was lucky not to break a leg!

Oil well drilling at Prudhoe.

In order to get to Barrow, you *must* fly! So we climbed into an "Air Arctic" 10 seat 2 engine plane for the trip – not being sure that our plane would be able to *land* at Barrow (there was fog and Barrow airport has no tower to report conditions). But we safely landed (other flights could not!) and were able to enjoy two days there.

We were lodged at the "Top of the World Hotel", a 3 story building with a metal grating walkway on the second level outside, leading to "Pepe's North of the Border" Mexican Café! (Both of these places were prominently featured in the recent movie "The Big Miracle".) These were extremely well run and very popular and comfortable.

We took a local bus tour with a native whaling captain, Eli, as our driver. He drove us as far north as possible, past a "fishing camp" where I saw a rarity: two trees! However, these were man-made of an old wooden pole with "palm fronds" of whale baleen hanging from the top!

The end of the ride took us to a spot where we had the water of the Beaufort Sea to our east and the water of the Chukchi Sea to our west, *both* part of the surrounding Arctic Ocean. The water was very cold!

On our return to town, we stopped for ice cream cones at a little store/café. Outside the building Harold showed me a trap door in the ground. (He had been in Barrow in 1992 – catching rides on semis and flying over from Prudhoe, and he had seen this trap door and had investigated. The store's owner came out and accompanied him down a ladder into the ground, which had a scant layer of soil atop and endless depth of permafrost ice – it was the natural "freezer" for the store! It remains frozen year round!)

As a finale of our tour, we visited the community center, where the native children demonstrated their chants, instruments and dances. I especially enjoyed watching a small girl (in costume) attempting to do the correct movements alongside her older sister, who was trying to teach her what to do.

Then the entire group, with the help of the audience, brought out an old "retired" whale boat skin, unfolded it and had everyone grab the rope handles, in order to do a "blanket toss". I was fortunate to catch the action of a boy up in the air while Harold was helping to "toss" him up!

Visitors at Barrow, Alaska helping in the "blanket toss".

We left Barrow on Alaska Airlines, landing briefly at Fairbanks, where a mysterious dark-haired woman in a black cocktail dress boarded the plane. She would not speak to anyone and refused all help. She had no purse, no sweater, no luggage! After a time, an airline agent came out to the plane and quietly ordered her to leave her seat, and escorted her off to the terminal. We never saw her again!

After landing at Anchorage, we next day boarded a bus to Whittier, where we again boarded the "Island Princess" for a return voyage and a *reverse* route of the northern passage to Alaska, all the way back to San Jose.

- Carol Siebert Voshage

Chapter 31
80th Birthday

On April 2, 2007 God allowed me to celebrate my eightieth birthday with an open house at our place where we had lived for forty years. Here we had been privileged to raise our dear daughter, Lisa. We had operated a small manufacturing business full time from 1972-1980 and we had excellent neighbors.

We were in the process of selling our place. It would take several more months until the house sold and we moved into a duplex cottage at Lincoln Glen Manor, our church's retirement complex. In a five-year retrospect, we have been glad for the move. As it turned out, even though we had no idea the housing market and the country's economy was drastically slowing, we benefitted from the timing.

Having been a member of the Clark Street Mennonite Brethren Church and then a charter member of the daughter church in Santa Clara, it has been my privilege to know many people in both churches. Also in my work and travels I have had many opportunities to make extended friendships, all enriching my life over the years. God has graciously allowed me to expand my horizons to include many wonderful people.

A great number of these people helped me to celebrate my 80th birthday. As a grateful Mennonite, friends and family are precious to me. I deeply appreciate the love and fellowship of all of these folks.

Carol sent out invitations to the birthday event and suggested it would be a Sunday open house from 1:00 to 5:00 p.m. We anticipated a reasonably good response. To prepare, friends helped us hand-crank five gallons of homemade ice cream, a great recipe that our dear friend Zelma Heier gave us, and we bought bakery sheet cakes.

My three double cousins from Minnesota and Kansas came, a cousin and her husband from Sacramento, cousins from Portland and Fresno, and cousins from Castro Valley and San Jose. We invited church friends, men that had worked with me over a thirteen-year period in Palo Alto, former employees, fellow shop owners, Carol's family, and of course neighbors.

Harold's cousins help him celebrate his 80th birthday in 2007 at his Saratoga home (L to R) Laura (Wall) Lepper, Elaine (Teichroew) Unruh, Lillian (Wall) Neufeld, Ron Ross, Elena Ross, Vernette (Teichroew) Regier, Harold A. Voshage, Velma Teichroew, Lisa (Voshage) Cole, Royal De Laney, Elfrieda (Rempel) De Laney, Kay Tropiano, Karen Kallman Wolf, Charles Wolf, Myra Neufeld, Dwight Neufeld.

Our final count totaled 142 people. Since the open house was from 1:00 to 5:00 p.m., we assumed people would come and go. It turned out they came and *stayed* and all had a great time. I was so busy visiting I forgot to eat any ice cream. When I realized I hadn't eaten any (and I'm a homemade-ice-cream-aholic) I second-guessed myself and kept on "schmoozing".

Carol and I were very gratified for the turn-out. The response to her invitations was fantastic! When I look back, now that I'm over eighty-six years old, it is amazing that God has made it possible for me, a Mt. Lake, Minnesota farm boy, to move to California years ago and develop relationships with so many quality people. Almost daily I praise God for the many contacts we made in Sunnyvale, Santa Clara, Palo Alto, Cupertino, Reedley, Dinuba, Fresno and of course Mt. Lake and many places in Minnesota and the Midwest, Montana, the Pacific Northwest, and many people in Europe.

Here again it reminds me why I am a grateful Mennonite. The influence of the Mennonite faith in my life has been very gratifying and fulfilling and satisfying, almost a DNA in my being. I truly believe the Mennonite heritage and experiences related to the "Mennonite World", added to the Word of God, is what makes me "tick".

Chapter 32

Fresno Pacific University

ONE OF THE MANY REASONS I AM A GRATEFUL MENNONITE IS BECAUSE OF Fresno Pacific University, probably the largest Mennonite University or College in the world.

When Dr. Merrill Ewert and I participated in the twentieth Anniversary Celebration of Lithuania Christian College University in Klaipeda, Lithuania in September of 2011, I learned more of what made Fresno Pacific University such a successful Mennonite school. One of the key bedrock attributes I discovered was its devotion to God's word.

Attending the annual MCC sale in April, 2013 I noticed in the sidewalk adjacent to the dining room area on the way to the gymnasium auditorium a series of plaques of granite.

Each graduating class since 1998 had placed a granite plaque approximately 4 ft. by 4 ft. square very professionally created with the graduate class verse. I recorded the verses from each class – 1998-2011.

The verses follow:

> **1998**: John 16:13 – But when he, the Spirit of truth comes, he will guide you into all truth. He will not speak on his own; he will speak only what he heard and he will tell you what is to come.

1999: Proverbs 3:13 and 14 – Blessed is the man who finds wisdom, the man who gains understanding. For she is more profitable than silver and yields better returns than gold.

2000: Romans 15:13a – May the God of hope fill you with all joy and peace as you trust in him.

2001: Philippians 1:6b – That he who began a good work in you will carry it on to completion until the day of Christ Jesus.

2002: Colossians 3:12, 14 – Therefore, as God's chosen people, holy and dearly loved, clothe yourselves with compassion, kindness, humility, gentleness and patience. And over all these virtues put on love, which binds them all together in perfect unity.

2003: Galations 2:20b – The life I live in the body, I live by faith in the Son of God, who loved me and gave himself for me.

2004: Proverbs 19:21 – Many are the plans in a man's heart, but it is the Lord's purpose that prevails.

2005: Proverbs 16:9 – In his heart a man plans his course, but the Lord determines his steps.

2006: Hosea 10:12 – Sow for yourselves righteousness, reap the fruit of unfailing love, and break up your unplowed ground; for it is time to seek the Lord.

2007: Philippians 4: 11-13 – I am not saying this because I am in need, for I have learned to be content whatever the circumstances. I know what it is to be in need and I know what it is to have plenty. I have the secret of being content in any and every situation, whether well fed or hungry, whether living in plenty or in want. I can do everything through him who gives me strength.

2008: Romans 12:12-13 – Be joyful in hope, patient in affliction, faithful in prayer. Share with God's people who are in need. Practice hospitality.

2009: Colossians 3:33 – Whatever you do, work at it with all your heart, as working for the Lord, not for men.

2010: Jeremiah 29:11 – For I know the plans I have for you, declares the Lord, plans to prosper you and not to harm you, plans to give you hope and a future.

2011: Psalm 3:8 – Let all the earth fear the Lord; let all the people of the world revere him.

Chapter 33
Mountain Lake
Achievers

In traveling to Mennonite settlements in many locations, various Canadian provinces, Mexico, Paraguay, Omsk, Siberia, Mennonite churches in Germany, and Mennonite churches in the United States, I am very grateful to my Savior Jesus Christ that I had the distinct privilege of having been born and raised by a Mennonite family in a Mennonite church in a Mennonite community that has a vibrant Christian history.

I received several pamphlets that revealed statistics of the many achievers that the greater Mountain Lake, Minnesota community has produced. After reading these "eye openers" and other historical documents concerning Mountain Lake and also several University of Minnesota graduate thesis papers, I had a heartfelt concern that a book that elucidated the history of hundreds of male and female achievers that had their roots in Mountain Lake should be written and published.

| W. J. Toews* | F. W. Hiebert | I. I. Bargen | H. J. Fast | Rev. J. J. Balzer |
| F. Balzer | A. Penner | S. Balzer | H. Friesen | G. Fast |

Prominent pioneers of Mountain Lake, MN.

When Carol and I traveled to the Midwest for my Aunt Emma Teichroew's 100th birthday celebration, it was my privilege to invite twelve interested Lakers to talk about this idea. There appeared to be significant interest, but no one wanted to head it up locally. The following year we had another meeting with even less interest. So I am hoping that the data included here will stimulate a thesis or article by someone else!

In this chapter I will cite statistics that record what a fruitful place Mountain Lake has always been as far as Christian workers are concerned. Putting these statistics together with my observations of Mennonite settlements worldwide leads me to appreciate even now what the Mennonite faith means.

The Great Revival of 1920 in Mountain Lake, Minnesota

(Credit: J. A. Schmidt)

Reverend J. A. Schmidt, the first pastor of the Alliance Church in Mountain Lake, wrote a pamphlet about the Great Revival of 1920 in Mountain Lake, Minnesota.

After 5 years of prayers for a revival, God answered these prayers in a mighty way. I quote Rev. Schmidt:

"Then in July 1920, God met them in an unexpected outpouring of the Holy Spirit. They expected God to work, but not quite in such a community-shaking revival. Two reasons may be given to account for this revival: first, the Mennonites are a God-fearing people and many, perhaps most of them, had family worship in their homes and were faithful in their attendance in Sunday school and church. Second, the undenominational prayer group had been praying for almost five years for revival."

A tent was erected in the city park and was filled to overflowing every night for two weeks. After hearing a message on the Spirit-filled life, (again I quote): "The altar was filled with Christians seeking to be filled with the Holy Spirit."

God did not disappoint them either. Included among those filled with the Spirit was the editor of the two local papers (one a German weekly). It changed the editor, his editorials and also the content of the paper. Schmidt worked in this printing office later and saw stacks of electrotypes of the American Tobacco Company, worth many hundreds of dollars in advertising space, which the editor refused to run. People from out of state wrote to ask what had happened to him.

Mr. W. J. Toews, the editor, translated Dr. Simpson's "Gospel of Healing" into the German language and ran it serially in the weekly German paper.

A conservative estimate is that 350 people were saved during the two weeks of meetings. The revival marked these young people. There was a spiritual wholesomeness and vigor about them that was unique. They were bold to witness for the Lord, especially in high school.

All churches were closed for the next two Sunday nights and cooperated in a measure by furnishing special singing for the tent meetings.

Only three local churches made conversion a condition of church membership. But ALL the local Mennonite Churches received these converts into membership without the customary Catechetical instruction. Thus was recognized a genuine work of the Holy Spirit in the hearts of the converts. All Mennonite churches had an additional baptismal service and reception of new members and one church had two additional baptismal services with reception of new members that summer.

Mountain Lake has always been a fruitful place as far as Christian workers are concerned. From 1870, when the town was settled by the Mennonites, till 1920, 100 men and women entered the ministry, an average of two a year. But in the next 40 years, from 1920-1960, there were 250 who entered the ministry, an average of 6½ a year. This is not an estimate, as we have the names of all who entered the ministry from the community. The first 25 years of the Alliance Church in Mountain Lake, 40 young people entered the ministry.

- J. A. Schmidt

The Call of God for Service in the Church

(Credit: Loyal Martin)

At least thirty-five missionaries and fifty-five pastors or pastor's wives have been sent out or called to service from the Mountain Lake and Carson (Delft), Minnesota Mennonite Brethren Churches over their 100+ year history. Why so many workers from these two churches? The response to this query comes from an analysis of the self-perceptions and reflections of current church members and of some of the workers who were drawn into service through these two churches.

Many Mennonite settlers came to southwestern Minnesota in the 1870's. By 1880 three hundred and fifty families had arrived in the Mountain Lake community. Six Mennonite Brethren families organized a church on 11 June 1877; the day of their first baptism. Heinrich Voth, a young school teacher from Russia, was one of those baptized. A year later he was called to lead the group and in 1885 was ordained by Elder Abraham Schellenberg.

The first meeting house was built north of Bingham Lake in 1886. Four years later a second building was constructed five miles south of Mountain Lake to accommodate those who had settled in that area. For many years the groups considered themselves one congregation with two meeting houses. The southern group eventually moved to the town of Mountain Lake, a small railway town, and the groups eventually established separate organizational structures. Not until the 1940's did the Bingham Lake group move into the villages of Delft, but it claimed the name of the township, Carson.

These congregations provided some of the first Mennonite Brethren missionaries for India (N. N. Hieberts, J. N. C. Hieberts, John A. Wiebes and John H. Voths) and for Africa (Heinrick Enns, Frank A. Janzens, Aaron Janzens and Martha Hiebert). An unofficial count lists missionaries and pastors from these churches by recent decades: 1970's-4: 1960's-11; 1950's-7. One person from the Carson Church lists 29 persons, ages 23-65, from that church who have given short terms of service to Mennonite Central Committee, Mennonite Brethren Christian Service and other agencies. Such short- term ministries have been in vogue only in the last decades. As this is written, one retired couple from the church has just returned from five months in Italy, where they engaged in construction work.

The above example is only part of the overall fruitfulness of other Mennonite communities as well, such as Coaldale, Alberta, Canada, Corn, Oklahoma, or Morden, Manitoba, Canada, and others.

Survey

External investigation would produce valuable information on the social dimensions of productive communities and churches. One such study will be suggested later in this paper. This current study, however, deals in the self-perceptions of current members and workers from the churches.

The writer pastored the Carson Church from 1961-68 and has interviewed selected older members of these churches. A survey was administered by the pastors in the spring of 1981. At the same time five missionaries and seven pastors from these churches responded to a questionnaire.

Among other things, church members were asked "How do you account for the large number of workers...from your church?" "What is your church doing this year to encourage persons to enter Christian service?" "What have you done personally to encourage someone to enter Christian service in the last year?" Workers from these churches were asked, "How did you come to a decision to enter vocational Christian service?"

Both current members and workers from the churches cited a general emphasis on mission, spearheaded by pastoral leadership, as the key element in recruiting workers from these churches. The joint quarterly meetings at which missionaries, mission board members or the local pastors spoke about missions are frequently mentioned. Testimonies of new recruits, reports from short term workers and, whenever possible, one of their own number home on furlough are featured at these meetings. Missionary support and special projects are actively promoted in the churches. Ladies' missionary societies' projects and vacation Bible school and youth group offerings are often designated for specific missions projects. "Those who went into full time Christian service were considered as having a very special position and were treated as such." One person said, "Whenever our own workers come home the church really comes alive."

There always seemed to be an expectation that there would be the "called ones', one missionary writes. "It was never a question of 'if God would call someone' but 'whom God would call'," a pastor says. "I can remember my primary Sunday School Teacher saying, 'now when some of you are missionaries you will need to know this verse.'"

Some, however, expressed concern. One person says that these churches sometimes stressed foreign missions to the exclusion of home missions or local evangelism. Another feels that a reaction has arisen resulting in a call to build the local program to the neglect of cross-cultural missions.

A second influence in recruiting workers is affirmation by individuals and the influence of the family. Some survey responses seem to merge the influence of significant adults, whether family or non-family. "Shoulder-tapping" and periodic encouragement by one or two persons to consider the ministry formed a recurring theme in the creation of a sense of call, as described by most of the workers from these churches. One pastor writes, "...one man played an important role in my life. On several occasions this man stopped to visit me...he would affirm that it was his conviction that God had called me into His service." It is not surprising that this farmer-salesman's son became a pastor and another son, who has been in short-term service, continues today as an active local church worker. A missionary wife writes, "In our family I feel there were expectations, even occasionally expressed, that they wouldn't be surprised if I became a missionary or pastor's wife. I knew that if we made such a decision we would have their full support." "Older brethren would talk to you in private about this – on the farm, at the grain elevator..." says one pastor.

One member points to Elder Heinrich Voth, an early leader of both churches, and Rev. A.J. Wiebe, a long-standing pastor of the Carson church, as models in giving assignments to young people who showed promise of leadership or service. The writer's experience with several of the Wiebe family indicates they carried on their father's search for new talent and willing workers. They also gave great personal energies to coach singers, Sunday School teachers and aspiring public speakers. Small wonder, then, that A.J. Wiebe's children include a pastor and a missionary and that seven of his grandchildren are ministers or missionaries.

The Mountain Lake Church has been funding a summer internship program for the last four years. Some earnings for a church endowment fund are designated to support the program, which has included local workers and a seminarian from another church in the district.

One missionary writes that her parents invited the pastor and deacons to their house once a year, implying that full-time Christian service was an item discussed in those visits.

"Our home always had a large number of missionaries and special speakers...this consistent exposure impressed on me the value of working full-time for the Lord. My home, especially my mother, held Christian service as one of the best things we could do – if the Lord called," says one pastor. Another pastor explains, "the ministry was never something you did if you failed in other careers; it was a first choice."

Prayer for workers was cited third in frequency by the survey respondents. One mother organized a weekly prayer meeting early in the life of these churches and saw several of her own children as well as numerous others enter missionary work. Others speak of naming persons in prayer meetings, persons whom they were asking God to call. One pastor says, "My home church took seriously that command of our Lord to 'pray out laborers.' This concern permeated the church and provided a healthy setting in which God could work." Coupling this prayer with specific support such as providing a tuition and book scholarship, encouraged several pastors while in preparation. One pastor mentions that when a Central District minister's scholarship "dried up", the Carson Church paid his tuition at Tabor College for two years.

The general ethos characterizing the churches is cited by several persons. "I have always felt that for all the energies we young people possessed back in the Carson days – some of which was directed positively, some negatively - we were made to feel a part of the worshipping community. Contrary to stories others tell of their early church experience, I felt affirmed, supported and loved. I believe that was significant in the decision I made."

Another pastor writes, "...they weren't dogmatic about doctrine but living theology was important." "I was always proud when our pastor was involved in community events. I felt we had the best one in town. That, coupled with a good music program in the church, made me glad genuinely to be a part of the church. This all helped to build an image of church work."

Schools get the credit for producing workers in the minds of four church members. Two cite a post-high school Bible school conducted in the early 1900's and again in the 30's and 40's. Another credit is the Christian Day School in Mountain Lake. One person has compiled the names of 29 persons who had entered Christian service work of some kind and indicates that 21 had attended Tabor College, 6 volunteered services as adults but encouraged their children or others to attend Tabor. "Only two were non-Tabor (people)...To me the above says that there is a greater chance that people will enter Christian service of some sort if they are prepared adequately for Christian living while receiving academic training. Tabor offers such training.

Table I

Question #4 – The sources of vocational decisions are sometimes divided into three categories. Please rate these according to percentage of importance to you *when* you *entered* Christian service.

  a. 54% Divine leading (an inner sense of God's call; however communicated to you).

  b. 15% Natural leading (a sense that you had personal skills, gifts and abilities that could be used well in Christian service).

  c. 29% Social leading (encouragement by family, friends, important leaders around you).

  d. 2% Other.

Question #5 – Please indicate the importance of things done by or through your local church to encourage/discourage your decision to enter vocational Christian service. Please indicate by percentages so that the total equals 100.

  a. 37% Appeals by pastors, missionaries or other speakers at public meetings.

  b. 19% Personal encouragement of your pastor.

  c. 19% Personal encouragement of other church workers such as your Sunday school teacher, youth sponsor, deacon.

  d. 17% Personal encouragement of family members.

  e. 6% Encouragement of the church as a body. For example, action of call by the church as a body or a church council, small group.

  f. 2% Other.

Conclusions

One general conclusion one can make from these survey responses is that a church reaps what it sows; stress Christian service and missionaries and ministers are produced. These churches stressed missions and the importance of vocational service for the Lord. They programmed for it, prayed for workers, involved themselves in the process of training them and valued the results. So people responded. The experience of other churches would bear this out. The Zoar M.B. Church of Inman, Kansas set a goal to pray out at least one worker in a twelve-month period in the early 70's. The church offered to pay seminary tuition for anyone who came forward. The Lord took such commitment seriously and so did two couples. Both are now in the pastorate in the same district.

Another study seems to bear out this general conclusion. Harold Loewen surveyed 116 persons in three Southern District churches to determine if they had sensed a call to service and, if so, how they had responded, based on several variables of encouragement (Table III).

(Table A4 – Harold Loewen Study)

NATURE OF THE CALL	ENTERED SERVICE	DID NOT ENTER SERVICE
Called by God and the Church	15	0
Not called by God nor the Church	0	43
Called by God, not the Church	6	7
Called by Church, not by God	0	1
Uncertain of God's call, Church called	1	2
Uncertain of God's call, No call by Church	0	9

The results of this study show that when a person senses a call of God upon his life and the church affirms that call, the probability of a positive response is very high (100% in his study). But when a person perceives an inner call of God, but it is not affirmed by the church, the likelihood of a positive response is cut in half.

Now that may be as it should be. A person may think he has a call of God but misreads the signs. When his/her inner perceptions are not born out by gifts and abilities to fulfill such ambitions nor affirmed by others who observe him/her, there may be reason to reevaluate the clarity of the perceived call.

Further Study Needed

Mennonite Brethren Churches were not alone in sending out workers from the Mountain Lake community.

More research is needed into the social phenomena of people leaving "worker producing" communities. Cynics might say that in Coaldale or Corn, Mountain Lake or Morden, people will do what is socially acceptable in the peer group. Can it be that some communities produced more young adults than could be absorbed on the farms and in the local businesses? One socially approved way to leave the community was to prepare for mission work or the ministry. But nursing and teaching as occupational choices need to be compared with mission work and the ministry.

Perhaps "full- time" Christian service is only one of numerous acceptable occupations and sending out is merely a sociological phenomenon of certain communities.

The writer would conclude with many others that the call to vocational Christian service has a deeply spiritual dimension. It is rooted in the life and character of a church and the spiritual commitment of its people. Other factors need to be investigated and considered but they will be, at best, peripheral to the spiritual center from which the call to service originates.

- Loyal Martin

THE MOUNTAIN LAKE ACHIEVERS STORY ONLY BARELY TOUCHES ON THE subject of the countless men and women Mountain Lake has produced. It is my profound desire that capable interested historians and writers of Mountain Lake will want to explore, research and delve into this important facet of Mountain Lake's history since its settlement in the 1870's until now.

I wish that I knew *all* who should be included, but if I were to attempt to name all of the *many* achievers from Mountain Lake, it would require another book!

I remember a number of the pastors in my home church, the First Mennonite. There was David Harder, I.J. Dick, L.R. Amstutz and after we left in 1952 at least three or four (maybe more) served. Alvin Kleinsasser and Harold Thiessen served as did Bruno Penner, who was raised in Mountain Lake. Some time after we moved to California, the congregation decided to build a substantial brick and masonry sanctuary. It was an impressive structure and my uncle George D. Rempel, a church member and a local masonry general contractor, created a very impressive building.

When the high school provided released-time religious instruction, I shall always remember Erland Waltner of the Bethel Church and his insightful teaching. The other Pastor that taught our classes who also could really "open" the word of God was B.J. Braun of the Carson-Delft Church. Mountain Lake area has really been very blessed by the many capable men of the Word who served the community.

Of the many successful individual Lakers who set an example of "making a name for Mountain Lake", there have been at least three college presidents. David Brandt was President of Tabor College and later, I believe, George Fox College. James Harder is or has been President of Bluffton College. (I knew his parents at First Mennonite Church). D. Merrill Ewert was President of Fresno Pacific University in Fresno, California for approximately ten years, and the school grew from somewhere over 2,000 students to well over 3,000 students. I believe it is the largest Mennonite University in the world.

Dr. Ewert's youngest uncle, Adam Ewert, was in my high school graduating class of 1945. Adam went on to earn his doctorate and taught parasitology at a prestigious medical school in Texas prior to his retirement. He has a very impressive resumé.

Another graduate who put Mountain Lake on the map was Robert Fast, who, as a civil engineer, completed his career as a city manager of a southern California municipality.

Ruth Schmidt, daughter of J.A. Schmidt, graduated summa cum laude from Augsburg College in 1952, received an MA in Spanish in 1955, and a PhD in 1962. Her teaching career began in Minnesota in 1952, and from 1982 until 1994 she served as Agnes Scott College's first female president.

Velma Teichroew, my double cousin with a masters degree, made her mark as a girls' physical education teacher and sports leader in a large Minnesota twin cities high school. She was cited by professional organizations for meritorious achievement in her chosen profession.

Robert Regier was professor of art at Bethel College in North Newton, Kansas until his retirement. He established a distinguished career at Bethel College and continues to use his vast experience and talent in the field of creative art.

Many other Lakers exceled in the arts.

Allan Eitzen was a prodigious artist and illustrator of children's books, and also co-author of children's books.

Ken Hiebert wrote a book "Graphic Design Sources" and taught at the University of the Arts at Philadelphia, PA, and received an honorary doctorate at this university.

Warren Kliewer wrote a number of plays and he also was an acclaimed actor.

Mary Balzer Buskirk became an expert crafter of weaving art and wrote a book "The Fabric Experience".

Harold Buller was at one time the European director of MCC. H. A. Fast of Bethel College was also a director of MCC for some time.

J. Winfield Fretz wrote a paper on the amazing cooperative organizations that developed quite early in the settlement of Mountain Lake. He says this community very likely had more successful cooperative ventures than any other Mennonite settlement. Several of these successfully continue to function.

In 1938 Ferdinand P. Schultz, then a teaching assistant at the University of Minnesota, wrote and published a Master's thesis, "A History of the Settlement of German Mennonites from Russia at Mountain Lake, Minnesota".

Another cousin, Esther Fast (her mother and my mother were sisters) has a son, Loren, who earned his PhD and directs the study of Genetics at Providence Hospital in Rhode Island and teaches several classes in medical research at Brown University. He and his wife are the parents of two sons who have both earned a PhD degree. Andy is a specialist in computer data mining. Jonathan is working in a research project to replace bleach with hydrogen peroxide.

Robert Jungas's resumé includes responsibilities at the Chemistry Department at Harvard University. Helmut and Siegfried Penner obtained degrees in advanced chemistry from MIT. Helmut worked at Fisk University and Siegfried as a chemist in a firm in Kansas. Their younger brother Bruno, a friend of mine, retired as a senior pastor, having served a lifetime in ministry.

Two of my good friends have made a tremendous difference in the world through their successful careers, have enhanced my life and countless other lives, and are still "achieving" to this day. Calvin Redekop, PhD, retired sociology professor of Eastern Mennonite University of Harrisonburg, Virginia has written many books and most are seminal works on unique subjects.

In 1951 Dr. Redekop was sent to Europe to help develop efforts to help rehabilitate the countries recovering from the devastation of World War II. He was the founder of the PAX Program that utilized men and women who volunteered for various assistance efforts in Europe and South America. He met with U.S. officials who administered alternate service. PAX men volunteered to work with Harry Harder in Paraguay to build the Trans Chaco Highway that reduced the time to ship cattle from the Mennonite settlements from weeks to less than one day. It is considered one of the most important economic contributions to the Mennonites in the Chaco.

Dr. Redekop's 1954 University of Minnesota Master Thesis on "The Cultured Assimilation of the Mennonites at Mountain Lake" is a 162 page insightful work.

Edgar Stoesz, with whom I rode to school on Shetland ponies in the mid 1930's, and who headed up a South American tour that I took to Paraguay and four other countries, completed a distinguished 37-year career with MCC. He has traveled to more than seventy countries. His guidance and lectures of Paraguay are priceless. He has written numerous books, several elucidate on the Mennonite experience in Paraguay.

Chapter 34
Favorite Quotations

PITHY QUOTES AND SUCCINCT SAYINGS AND STATEMENTS ON VARIOUS SUBJECTS have always intrigued me. I have collected a number of these quotes and following are a few of my favorite sayings that have all added serious meaning to my life.

Menno Simons said, "True evangelical faith cannot lie dormant; it clothes the naked, it feeds the hungry, it comforts the sorrowful, it shelters the destitute, it serves those that harm it, it binds up that which is wounded, it has become all things to all men."

Merrill Unger describing an enthusiasm for the scripture said, "A contagious enthusiasm among Christians for the word of God and a return to faith and obedience to its precepts will do more to point the way out of the present world distress and despair than all the plans and strivings of men."

John Haggai said, "Marriage is the supreme human relationship." He also said, "The ordinary citizens, thank God, still adhere to absolutes. A lie is an abomination. A vow is sacred. An injustice cannot be excused. It is they who have saved the republic from creeping degradation while their 'betters' were 'derelict.'"

Charles Swindoll said, "The longer I live, the more I realize the impact of attitude on life. Attitude, to me, is more important than facts. It is more important than the past, than education, than money, than circumstances, than failures, than successes, than what other people think or say or do. It is more important than appearance, giftedness, or skill. It will make or break a company...a church...a home.

The remarkable thing is we have a choice every day regarding the attitude we will embrace for that day. We cannot change our past...we cannot change the fact that people will act in a certain way. We cannot change the inevitable. The only thing we can do is play on the one string we have, and that is our attitude…

I am convinced that life is 10% what happens to me and 90% how I react to it. And so it is with you…We are in charge of our attitudes." (My daughter gave me a greeting card with this quotation on the front.)

Gleb Yakonin said, "Religion is like salt which protects humanity from decomposition and disintegration. Any attempt to banish it from social life invariably leads to a degradation of society."

P.T. Forsyth has made the observation, "Unless there is within us that which is above us, we shall soon yield to that which is about us."

Jim Elliot said, "He is no fool who gives what he cannot keep to gain what he cannot lose."

The ultimate purpose of prayer is not to get what you want but to learn to want what God gives.

What matters is not faith and works; it is not faith or works; it is faith that works. Faith by itself, if it does not have works, is dead - James 2:17.

Ruth Bell Graham's associate said, "It is more difficult to live the Christian life under freedom than under repression."

Martha Washington said, "I have learned that the greater part of our misery or unhappiness is determined not by our circumstances but by our disposition."

We need to have helpful suggestions to move conversation to get people to think about Jesus.

A mission statement: Helping people get from where they are to where they should be.

Another mission statement: "God expects the church in each generation to get out on the open seas of human needs; to head for the battlefield; to get off the sidelines and get into the game."

Helen Keller wrote, "Character cannot be developed in ease and quiet. Only through experience of trial and suffering can the soul be strengthened, ambition inspired and success achieved." She also said, "The best and most beautiful in the world cannot be seen or even touched. They must be felt with the heart."

Thomas Edison said, "Opportunity is missed by most people because it is dressed in overalls and looks like work."

J.B. Toews, an iconic amazing leader of the Mennonite Brethren denomination, who was born and reared and educated in Ukraine in the Molotschna Colony, said, "From the Russian Mennonite past we take the fire, not the ash."

He also said, "A church that forgets the past cannot understand the present and lacks direction for the future."

Adolf Reimer of South Russia said in 1920 before he died, "Lord Jesus, how is your gospel so simple, and your grace so marvelous." He was an outstanding Mennonite Brethren evangelist.

Harold John Ochenga said, "I don't believe God has ever used anyone in a powerful way who has not first suffered."

Aleksandr I. Solzhenitsyn said, "A people needs defeat just as an individual needs suffering and misfortune; they compel the deepening of the inner life and generate a spiritual upsurge."

Hemingway said, "The world breaks everyone but afterward many are strong at broken places."

C.S. Lewis said, "Pain is God's megaphone."

Oswald Chambers said, "The cross of Jesus is the supreme evidence of the love of God."

"No one may truly know Christ except one follows him in life." Hans Denck.

Suffering can teach what we can't learn in any other way.

George Washington Carver said, "How far you go in life depends on you being tender with the young, compassionate with the aged, sympathetic with the striving, and tolerant of the weak and strong. Because someday in life you will have been all of these."

Lorna Dupong said, "Manners are the oil that keeps the friction out of society."

"The spiritual banquet God has prepared for us in his word is a cause of great joy." David Mc Casland.

Mark Twain said the two most important days in your life are the day you were born and the day you figure out why.

God calls us to get in the game, not to keep score.

Mark Twain also said it was not the parts of the Bible that he did not understand that bothered him the most, but the parts he did understand.

Theodore Roosevelt once observed, "A thorough knowledge of the Bible is worth more than a college education."

Gandhi said, "Action expresses priorities."

Chapter 35
The Wonder of the Word

Some years ago a significant article that really spoke to me appeared in the Christian Leader. I have unfortunately forgotten the author, but I copied the outline in my Bible years ago.

The Bible is a love letter from God. God reveals himself through Christ and puts before us the inescapable question whether we will love him with our heart, soul, strength and mind.

Carol's grandfather, William Aaron Siebert, reading his Bible.

The Bible is utterly relevant; the Bible demonstrates a viable basis for life upon earth – that love has to be learned. "The word of God is living and active, sharper than any double-edged sword." (Hebrews 4:12), "Thy word is a lamp to my feet and a light to my path." (Psalm 119:105). (This verse Psalm 119:105 was placed above the altar of the First Mennonite Church, my home church in Mountain Lake, Minnesota.) "Let the word of Christ dwell in you richly." (Colossians 3:16): "Now that you have purified yourselves by obeying the truth so that you have sincere love for your brothers, love one another deeply from the heart."

God has been at work throughout history to bring humankind to salvation. We must have a consensus on steps of obedience that need to be taken in response to truths learned. We must take very seriously the ministry of the Holy Spirit. (I Corinthians 2:9-16, Acts 1:8, Ephesians 3:16). We need to evaluate what we have done and its effects on others.

We should celebrate victories and encourage when there has been failure. We must comfort and support others when they have suffered because of their obedience (John 15:10, 11); "If you obey my commands you will remain in my love just as I have obeyed my Father's command and remain in His love." All shall bow before Jesus Christ, God.

The book of James tells us that "a person is justified by what he does and not by faith alone." (James 2:24).

(James 2:14-18): "What good is it, my brothers, if any man claims to have faith but has no deeds? Can such faith save him? Suppose a brother or sister is without clothes and daily food. If one of you says to him 'Go, I wish you well; keep warm and well fed;' but does nothing about his physical needs, what good is it? In the same way faith by itself, if it is not accompanied by action, is dead. But someone will say 'You have faith, I have deeds.' Show me your faith without deeds and I will show you my faith by what I do." (James 2:26): "As the body without the spirit is dead, so faith without deeds is dead."

(Ecclesiastes 3:1): "There is a time for everything and a season for every activity under heaven." (Ecclesiastes 3:11-13): "He has made everything beautiful in its time. He has also set eternity in the hearts of men; yet they cannot fathom what God has done from beginning to end. I know that there is nothing better for men than to be happy and do good while they live. That every man may eat and drink, and find satisfaction in all his toil – this is the gift of God."

(Joshua 4:23, 24): "For the Lord your God dried up the Jordan before you until you had crossed over. He did this so that all the peoples of the earth might know that the hand of the Lord is powerful and so that you might always fear the Lord your God."

(Proverbs 1:7): "The fear of the Lord is the beginning of knowledge."

(Proverbs 3:5,6): "Trust in the Lord with all your heart and lean not on your own understanding; in all your ways acknowledge him and he will make your paths straight."

A number of years ago Ken Kudo, a missionary we supported, called from Sao Paulo, Brazil and in the course of our conversation he quoted Proverbs 27:17; "As iron sharpens iron so one man sharpens another." I consider this my machinist and iron worker's verse. It is one of my many favorite Proverbs verses.

(Philippians 4:4-7): "Rejoice in the Lord always. I will say it again: Rejoice! Let your gentleness be evident to all. The Lord is near. Do not be anxious about anything, but in everything, by prayer and petition, with thanksgiving, present your requests to God. And the peace of God, which transcends all understanding, will guard your hearts and your minds in Christ Jesus." (Verse 9): "Whatever you have learned or received or heard from me, or seen in me - put it into practice. And the God of peace will be with you." (Verse 19): "And my God will meet all your needs according to his glorious riches in Christ Jesus."

When Werner Kroeker was the senior Pastor of Lincoln Glen Church in San Jose in the 1980s he led a Wednesday morning Bible study at breakfast. His wife Elsie Ann, who is a gourmet chef, provided a very delicious breakfast that she prepared with the best ingredients available. On one occasion Werner taught us a lesson from II Peter 1:1-11. I will quote 1:10; (making one's calling and election sure) "His divine power has given us everything we need for life and godliness through our knowledge of him who called us by his own glory and goodness. Through these he has given us his very great and precious promises, so that through them you may participate in the divine nature and escape the corruption in the world by evil desires. For this reason, make every effort to add to your faith goodness; and to goodness, knowledge; and to knowledge, self-control; and to self-control, perseverance; and to perseverance, godliness; and to godliness, brotherly kindness; and to brotherly kindness, love. For if you possess these qualities in increasing measure, they will keep you from being ineffective and unproductive in your knowledge of our Lord Jesus Christ. But if any one does not have them he is nearsighted and blind, and has forgotten that he has been cleansed from his past sins.

Therefore, my brothers, be all the more eager to make your calling and election sure. For if you do these things, you will never fall, and you will receive a rich welcome into the eternal kingdom of our Lord and Savior Jesus Christ." (II Peter 1:3-11).

Carol and I both love the Bible. In adding more verses I noticed she wrote Psalm 92 verses one and two on a "Things I Gotta Do Today reminder." The verses are "It is a good thing to give thanks unto the Lord, and to sing praises unto thy name, O most High; to show forth thy loving-kindness in the morning, and thy faithfulness every night." (Scofield Bible).

(Deuteronomy 15:7,8): "If there is a poor man among your brothers in any of the towns of the land that the Lord your God is giving you, do not be hardhearted or tight-fisted toward your poor brother. Rather be open-handed and freely lend him whatever he needs."

More scripture verses: (I Corinthians 13:8) "Love never fails."

(Psalm 19:1): "The heavens declare the glory of God; the skies proclaim the work of his hands."

(I Thessalonians 5:16): "Be joyful always; pray continually; give thanks in all circumstances, for this is God's will for you in Christ Jesus."

(Isaiah 45:5): I am the Lord and there is no other; apart from me there is no God."

God clearly tells us in Ephesians 2:8, 9: "For it is by grace you have been saved, through faith – and this not from yourselves, it is the gift of God – not by works, so that no one can boast."

When Carol kept a journal about our seeking an adoption of an infant, she entered this verse: (Psalm 37:4): "Delight yourself in the Lord and he will give you the desires of your heart." And God *did* fulfill the desire of our heart!

Carol loves these words of Psalm 145:1-4: "I will extol thee, my God, O king, and I will bless thy name forever and ever. Every day will I bless thee, and I will praise thy name forever and ever. Great is the Lord, and greatly to be praised; and his greatness is unsearchable. One generation shall praise thy works to another, and shall declare thy mighty acts." (Scofield Bible)

The following verse is for you, dear readers (Ephesians 3:20, 21): "Now unto him who is able to do *exceedingly abundantly* above all that we ask or think, according to the power that worketh in us, unto him be glory in the church by Christ Jesus throughout all ages, world without end. Amen." (Scofield Bible)

Chapter 36
Epilogue

MY LIFE HAD BEEN SINGULARLY BLESSED SINCE I HAVE MENNONITE HERITAGE. Although my father was not of Mennonite heritage he was virtually a Mennonite because I believe he attended the First Mennonite Church of Mountain Lake, Minnesota all his life. He attended country school with predominately Mennonite pupils and most of the farm families were Mennonite. He spoke German and Holland-Dutch at home and learned Plautdietsch from his peers at school, in the neighborhood, at church; and when he met my mother Kate Teichroew this large clan all spoke Plautdietsch, and of course my family was fluent in English.

Christ and Kate Voshage (Harold's parents) in 1960, Reedley, CA.

I have a large appreciation for the Mennonite faith and practice. It was part of my growing up in Mountain Lake. I was baptized into it. I chose to volunteer in many programs and travel where the faith is strong.

There are many reasons why I wanted to write about the Mennonite world I've observed. This has cemented and really affirmed my deep appreciation for the Mennonite theology, faith and practice. In retrospect growing up in Mountain Lake, Minnesota, in travels to South America, particularly Paraguay, the Mennonite colonies in Mexico, the thriving Mennonite colonies in Siberia, observing Canadian Mennonite settlements in La Crete and High Level, the thriving settlements in Abbotsford, Calgary, Kelowna, Saskatoon, Winnipeg and Steinbeck, Winkler, and St Catherines all enlarged my appreciation of my Mennonite heritage.

The U.S. Mennonite communities I have seen include New Holland and Akron, Pennsylvania; Harrisonburg, Virginia; Sarasota, Florida; Pandora, Kidron and Archbold, in Northern and Western Ohio; also North Newton, Garden City, Meade, Wichita, Hillsboro, Henderson, Kansas; Ogalalla, Nebraska; and Freeman and Marion, So. Dakota. In California the Fresno area has thousands of Mennonites, Fresno Pacific University (the largest Mennonite University in the world), Reedley, Dinuba and Bakersfield. The North American Mennonite presence is extensive with many Mennonite churches.

Another reason of my affinity for the Mennonite faith is how the Mennonite Brethren plant churches. Working in Dresden, Germany on a church plant under the leadership of Lawrence and Selma Warkentin a month in 1995 and visiting this church several times, becoming good friends with families there, and observing the Warkentin's children (Paul and Ina who pastor a 400 person congregation in Bielefeld) has been very rewarding. Working on the development of Lithuania Christian College University in Klaipeda, Lithuania for two months in 1994 and having had the privilege of visiting the University at its 20th anniversary and again on a tour last year has really impressed upon me the vision of Mennonite Brethren leaders.

Harold with Selma & Lawrence Warkentin at his Saratoga home.

The opportunities I have had to volunteer on various construction projects initiated by Mennonite agencies has shown me the enthusiasm and professionalism and energy of the leadership for service to the church and to a world in need.

The title for this chapter could be *A Grateful Husband.* It goes without saying this book would not have been completed without the incredible organization and editing skills that Carol has. From the very first inception of my idea she made sense of the development of the book. Her critical skills in writing, organizing, editing, composition and developing subject matter and titling and properly sequencing chapters made it all pull together.

Harold and Carol Voshage.

Tonight after relaxing just before our bedtime, I sat on the couch opposite her and told her I wanted to look at her and tell her how much I appreciate and love her after our 62+ years of marriage, I needed to savor her beauty and compliment her on our great years of marriage. I cannot find adequate superlatives to describe my feelings toward Carol, the Love of my Life. I simply cannot thank her adequately for her unwavering support and love for me ever since the September day we met at my Uncle Abe Teichroew's farm in 1950. If only more marital relationships were this successful, divorce and separation would be unheard of.

She has initiated and encouraged a number of my volunteer adventures. Without her support and actual initial promotion for me to participate (Papua New Guinea and Echo Ranch Bible Camp in Alaska) it is debatable if I would have left my comfort zone, particularly to New Guinea.

In concluding the epilogue, again I am reminded of the heritage my great-grand-mother Goossen left me. She was the personification of the Godly beliefs and lives that these dear family members gave me as a heavenly legacy.

Returning to a previous paragraph where I was talking to Carol across the coffee table, I am again reminded of what a great life our marriage and my life in particular has been.

The hard times that I (we) experienced, in retrospect actually produced benefits that introduced us to families who have become lifetime brothers and sisters in the Lord. This is tangible evidence of God's gracious leading, direction and will for my life.

Although it might have been mentioned previously, in closing the final chapter, I feel it is essential to reiterate that the Mennonite faith is quite unique. I strongly believe there are not many religious organizations that are dedicated to not only leading people to a saving knowledge of Jesus Christ, but also to help people earn a living, help families after disasters, assist in relocating and reestablishing, as people begin a new life, both physically and spiritually.

In closing, I owe much gratitude to my family's Mennonite heritage, my home community of Mountain Lake, Minnesota and its many Mennonite churches, and the continuing influence and direction that God has wielded in my life to this time.

I thank God for both the good times and bad, because He used all to teach me, heal me, and cause me to grow. From the time in September of 1941 when I accepted Christ as my Lord and Saviour at a revival meeting in Mountain Lake, my life was changed and God became my Pilot through life.

It is my desire that readers of this book would accept Christ as their Saviour, if they are not already born-again believers. For as God teaches us in Romans 10:9: "That if you confess with your mouth, 'Jesus is Lord', and believe in your heart that God raised him from the dead, you will be saved."

May God be glorified through this memoir of a grateful Mennonite!

Acknowledgements

THESE CLOSING PAGES NEED TO BE PREFACED BY CITING MY WIFE, CAROL, AS the catalyst in actually providing me with the organizational methods that made sense of this entire endeavor. Frankly, without her input, this book would only have been an aspiration – nothing more!

My gratitude is endless to Janet Gossen, who has fabulous command of the computer. I would have been lost but for her expertise in typing, organizing chapters, and graciously retyping after Carol's editing. She was always cheerfully willing to rearrange, retitle, or to remind me of a needless repetition! Her computer knowledge has many times saved the day!

She and her sister, Dr. Evelyn Gossen Neufeld, are also cousins of mine – my Grandmother Teichroew was a Goossen. Thanks to Evelyn for letting Janet utilize her computer and her printer for this undertaking, and her further editing.

I thank both Voshage and Teichroew relatives who had in the past collected geneology of the families.

Special thanks to my Teichroew cousin, Esther Penner Fast, who wrote the chapter on "Hog Butchering". Her memories of those exciting events bring it clearly to mind.

My appreciation to Vernette Teichroew Regier, whose books on the "Cousins" gave me much information about the Voshage and Teichroew families.

Thanks to Lila Penner Neufeld for sharing an historical picture I needed

Although my name (Voshage) was not a Mennonite name, my extended family on *both* sides was *very* Mennonite! I cherished each cousin, especially because I was an only child. I felt that Alton and Melroy Penner were my "brothers", and my "sisters" were double-cousins Velma Teichroew, Vernette Teichroew Regier and Elaine Teichroew Unruh.

Delbert and Anna Franz offered a helpful list of changes needed, plus additional information.

Professionals who have graciously obtained documents on Mennonite history from Fresno Pacific University are: Dr. Paul Toews, Professor of history and Director of the Center for Mennonite Brethren Studies; Kevin Enns-Rempel, Archivist and Librarian at Fresno Pacific University; and Dr. Peter J. Klassen, author and historian. The paragraph on Nestor Makhno is from a lecture by Dr. Toews.

Much gratitude to Loyal Martin, whose article that I cited was published in "Direction" magazine in the October 1981 issue, and is now in the archives of the Center for Mennonite Brethren Studies at the Fresno Pacific University Library. Thanks to Noe Hernandez, who located it there.

Edgar Stoesz has generously contributed information on MCC, as has Kevin King regarding MDS, and Wally Krocker on MEDA. Victor Goering has shared with me about CPS Camp life.

I have received much helpful advice from authors Edgar Stoesz and Cal Redekop, as well as from Edmund Janzen. I also learned much about memoir writing from the books of Katie Funk Wiebe, along with considerable input from Norma Jost Voth.

Thanks to Paul Warkentin and Burkhard Seebaum in Germany for their information about Voshage families and their village of Vahlbruch in that country.

Many thanks to those who have engendered much pleasure for me in past years as I traveled and toured; tour guides Nick Lerescu, Walter and Marina Unger, Edgar Stoesz, Wilmer Martin, David Friesen, Dave Worth, Dr. Peter J. Klassen, Dr. Paul Toews, Alan Peters, and many more who shared their knowledge; and my long-time travel agent who made it easy – Susan Reimer Stewart.

May I also express gratefulness to my family and friends (Walt and Fran Griggs – he helped constantly with my computer woes!) and Manor table-mates (Keith and Kunio) who both had to put up with constant references to the progress of "the book"! Thank you all for putting up with me!

Our next-door neighbors and friends, Atlee and Twyla Stroup, have been constant "encouragers". Atlee is a retired professor and Twyla was a teacher; they each were very supportive.

I have enjoyed my association with my publisher, Friesen Press, and their representative: Debbie Anderson has been very helpful. She introduced me later to Erin McCullough, Author Account Manager. Christoph Koniczek was the final Author Account Manager who patiently assisted us in the final proofing and complicated submission of the finished manuscript. My thanks to each of these.

We were privileged to obtain the service of Steven Ollenburger, a graphic design artist, who scanned the pictures as well as blended the two photos into the cover design.

Above all else, I am forever grateful to God, my heavenly father, who I feel planted this idea in my mind to express my appreciation of my heritage, and gave me strength to complete the task. May God bless each one who helped to make this memoir possible.

Harold A. Voshage
July 2, 2013

Endorsements

HAROLD IS A FRIEND OF MDS. AND MDS IS FORTUNATE TO HAVE MANY VOLUN-
teers like Harold who have compassion coursing through their veins. Working on
over ten MDS disaster projects in California e.g. wildfires, earthquakes, Harold,
like many other volunteers, was the hands and feet of Jesus. His devotion to God
is evident, as you will read in these pages. May you too be inspired to serve the
Creator of the Universe!

Kevin King,
Executive Director,
Mennonite Disaster Service.

This memoir relates the bumps and starts of a Minnesota farm boy become
California business owner. It is the story of a mostly Mennonite ethnic acclimating
to the wider world. From the country to the suburbs. From Plautdietsch to Silicon
Valley. It's also a story of deep immersion in the Mennonite circles that envelop him,
especially within the evangelical Mennonite Brethren branch of the faith to which
he becomes committed. Voshage relates the hours of depression he encountered
along the way. But most remarkable are the countries charitable works and trips he
takes globally—part of a quest as an abiding Mennonite to stay connected with the
history, faith, and family that birthed him.

Alan Teichroew
Archivist
Library of Congress

An enthusiastic follower of Jesus Christ as he treks along the Path of Life sharing the
Joy of the Lord with friends and acquaintances. Here's his story. Enjoy!

Paul E. (Gene) Dunmire
Retired Banker

We congratulate Harold for his determination to record fascinating and personal
dimensions of his journey that began in Minnesota and reached into the larger
world, which he explored with great passion. In drawing us into this journey our

own lives become illuminated and enriched through the remarkable detail that he recalls and shares.

Your double cousins:
Velma Teichroew
Vernette Teichroew Regier (Bob Regier)
Elaine Teichroew Unruh (Lee Unruh)

Harold's contemporaries and persons of historical interest will thrive on interesting anecdotes from an earlier era. These include an excellent description of butchering hogs, serving in Civilian Public Service and almost innumerable service experiences, while building a prosperous business. I found myself re-living my youth at points since, as he acknowledges, we grew up as neighbors and classmates.

Thank you, Harold for harvesting this interesting story from your prodigious memory.

Edgar Stoesz
Author
Akron, PA

Dear Harold, Wow, what a story; what a life; what a wife, who encouraged you to do so many exciting things; what a testimony. This book will be an inspiration to those who read it. The young will understand that many things are possible even when adversities enter our lives. Early retirees will note that there still is a big exciting, challenging world out there. And, the elderly will be reminded that God is still always with us. I'm impressed – and a little envious. Most of us at our age are reduced to doing the daily crossword puzzle to stimulate our minds and walk around the block to keep our bodies working. You still write, travel and do many exciting things.

With Best Regards, Your High School Classmate,
Adam Ewert

"Grateful" is an adjective. Voshage turned it into a verb. His gratefuness was expressed by a host of volunteer activities with various benevolent agencies. This is the true meaning of being grateful.

Paul Toews
Professor Emeritus
Fresno Pacific University

Printed in Canada